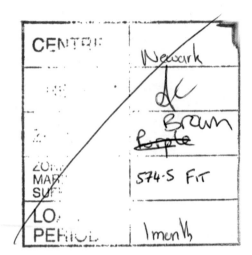

CENTR…	Newark
…	dc
…	Brown
…	~~people~~
ZON… MAR… SU…	574·S FiT
LO… PERIOD	1 month

WILDLIFE FOR MAN

WILDLIFE FOR MAN

How and why we should
conserve our species

Richard Fitter

*This book was written in fulfilment
of the IUCN/SSC source-book contract
for UNEP*

Illustrated by
Norman Arlott, Kim Franklin,
Sally Hughes and Charles Stitt

Collins
Grafton Street, London

William Collins Sons and Co Ltd
London · Glasgow · Sydney · Auckland
Toronto · Johannesburg

This book is the result of collaboration between the United Nations Environment Programme (UNEP) and the Species Survival Commission of IUCN. UNEP was founded in 1972 and has a secretariat based in Nairobi, Kenya. It comprises four components: a governing council for environmental programmes, a small secretariat to act as the focus for environmental action and coordination within the UN system, a voluntary environment fund to finance the programmes, and an environmental coordination board, consisting of members of all relevant UN bodies. UNEP aims to coordinate the work of, promote policy initiatives with, and provide environmental information to these other members of the UN family.

First published in Great Britain 1986

© Richard Fitter and the International Union for Conservation of Nature and Natural Resources 1986

Filmset by Clark Constable, Edinburgh and London

Colour reproduction by Alpha Reprographics, Harefield, Middlesex

Printed and bound in Great Britain by Butler & Tanner Ltd, Frome, Somerset

Contents

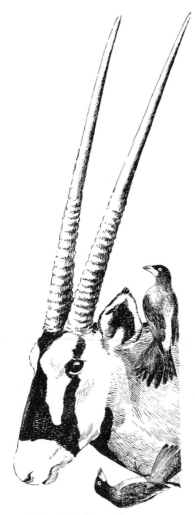

Yellow-billed oxpeckers on oryx

Chairman's Introduction

This book is about species conservation. It began life as one of the source-books planned by IUCN to supplement its World Conservation Strategy launched in 1980, and provides more facts than could be included in that severely condensed document. It presents the facts about plant and animal species, and how man can and *should* manage and use them as both actual and potential resources.

It is a book that has evolved, and has a complicated history. IUCN originally planned six source-books for the Strategy, and in 1979 gave its Species Survival Commission the task of compiling the one on species conservation. Editor and authors were commissioned to write a series of chapters, mainly based on systematic groups: plants, invertebrates, fishes, reptiles and amphibians, birds and mammals. By 1982, however, much still remained to be done, and the editor wished to resign, so the SSC asked the Chairman of its Steering Committee, Richard Fitter, to take over. The SSC is extremely grateful to the authors of these original chapters: Kai Curry-Lindahl, F. Wayne King, Gren Lucas, Robert Miller, Bob Pyle, Hugh Synge and Sue Wells. We must also thank the three members of the SSC who have read the whole book at various stages of its preparation: Archie Carr III, F. Wayne King and Harry Messel.

Richard Fitter, as one of the world's leading natural history writers and a long-time SSC member, of course approached the task directly and pragmatically, and, while making use of some of the original material, changed the plan, organising the book under general headings instead of systematic groups, so that eventually he included only a small proportion of the original material. The overall responsibility for the book has remained throughout with the Steering Committee of the SSC.

The book is not a history of the SSC as such, but reflects the development of the SSC's, and therefore IUCN's, ever changing and evolving thinking and policy development on species conservation. This evolution in conservation thinking, planning and action, led by the SSC and the 'invisible college' of its specialist groups, often calls for the quiet, behind-the-scenes, diplomatic approach. At other times it needs the full pressure that publicity at all levels can bring to bear, another skill to be found within the IUCN/WWF family. Richard Fitter has assembled here a great mass of evidence to support his own and the SSC's unswerving conviction that the world will come to understand that the future of mankind lies in using and managing species, both plants and animals, wild and domesticated, as flag-bearers for ecosystems, not just in crude life-support terms, but in the quality of life as well. This too is the basic conviction of the World Conservation Strategy, just as it was of those great creators of the modern wildlife conservation movement, Pieter van Tienhoven, Hal Coolidge and Sir Peter Scott, two of them my predecessors as SSC Chairman, and of all those other dedicated men and women who have freely given their energy, skills, time and wealth to create IUCN and its Species Survival Commission.

Our wildlife must be cared for, and integrated into all our planning at the beginning of the process, not as an afterthought. The World Conservation Strategy lays out the realities simply and clearly. We ignore them at our peril.

Gren Lucas
Chairman, IUCN Species Survival Commission,
January 1986

Cacao tree

Prefatory Note

To emphasise the importance of individual species to mankind, many more scientific names, which stand out on the page, are given in Chapter 1 than elsewhere. This will underline the fact that such vitally important plants and animals for human welfare as wheat, conifers, cattle and honeybees, are species, just like orchids, roses, giant pandas and butterflies. Further to emphasise the great number and diversity of species throughout the world, examples are given wherever possible, both throughout the major geographical regions of the world, and over the whole range of plants and animals, lower as well as higher plants, invertebrates as well as vertebrates, lower vertebrates as well as mammals and birds.

The Past and Present of Genetic Resources

Part I

African elephant

Cacao tree

Wildlife as a Genetic Resource

1

Every day of our lives, every man, woman and child in the world depends on living plants and animals for vital parts of their welfare. It is not just a matter of convenience, or of personal whim, that animals and plants should continue to exist. It is, in every sense of the phrase, a matter of life and death.

Plants and animals, both wild and domesticated, are the living units of the ecosystems in which all human beings live. They contribute to human welfare in three main ways:

1. They provide the material basis of human life: food, clothing and fuel, for nutrition, for warmth and artificial light, and for the maintenance of health and general well-being.

2. They provide the knowledge that is essential for not only maintaining this material basis, but avoiding a widespread regression to more primitive conditions. Unless we preserve representative samples of the genetic resources constituted by all animals and plants, not just those with a present known value, but also those whose value to mankind has not yet been fully worked out, our quality of life will deteriorate. We still do not know enough about even such basic domesticated species as cattle and bread wheat, let alone their wild relatives, to derive the maximum human benefit from them.

3. They make a significant contribution to man's enjoyment of his environment, both in his mundane day-to-day recreational pleasures and in his wonderment at the mysteries of the universe. All major religions agree in one way or another that 'man shall not live by bread alone', and more and more people everywhere now agree with William Wordsworth, whose 'heart with pleasure fills, and dances with the daffodils' rather than Peter Bell, to whom 'a primrose by a river's brim, a yellow primrose was to him, and it was nothing more'.

We can divide animal and plant species into three groups, according to their impact on human welfare:

1. Species which are actively exploited for some aspect of human welfare, e.g. fish stocks in the oceans, a most important food; fruit-flies *Drosophila*, invaluable for genetic research; and the spring flowers of the alpine meadows, which have uplifted the hearts of many generations of Europeans.

2. Species which are known to hold the potential of such exploitation, but for one reason or another, including scarcity, are not yet exploited, e.g. the African eland *Taurotragus oryx*, a potential new domesticated ungulate; various rare species of ebony on some of the southern oceanic islands, notably *Diospyros reticulata* on Mauritius, whose genes are needed to

Eland

maintain or enhance the genetic diversity of the important commercial ebony *D. ebenum*; and the newly discovered maize relative *Zea diploperennis* in Mexico, for a similar genetic service to the common maize or sweetcorn *Z.mays*.

3. All other species, whose potential for contributing to human welfare has not yet been realised or not recognised sufficiently. We cannot, in our present state of knowledge, say that any species is either positively useless or wholly harmful to human welfare. Even the smallpox virus, now reduced to a very few cultures in a very few laboratories, may, if current research succeeds, be hybridised for use in vaccines against other diseases, such as rabies and hepatitis.

The World Conservation Strategy has proposed three specific objectives of living resource conservation. They are:
  (i) the preservation of genetic diversity,
 (ii) the maintenance of essential ecological processes and life-support systems, and
(iii) ensuring the sustainable utilisation of species and ecosystems.
  In practical terms these are:
  (i) the maintenance of viable stocks of all animal and plant species;
 (ii) the maintenance of pure air and water and fertile soil;
(iii) the preservation of enough stocks of animals and plants, both domesticated and wild, to permit them to be cropped, harvested, or otherwise used or enjoyed indefinitely.

All three aims are plain common sense, yet the present social and institutional arrangements of the world lead to the widespread disregard of all three by both governments and individuals.

Genetic diversity is defined in the World Conservation Strategy as 'the range of genetic material found in the world's organisms', but this definition has two distinct aspects. One is the enormous range of gene pools (i.e. all the genes in an interbreeding population) represented by the millions of animal and plant species still extant today; these are in a very real sense the genetic resource potential needed for both the present and the future welfare of mankind. The second aspect is the variability of the genes within each individual species; this has enabled man to breed many widely differing varieties of, for instance, roses, apples, pigeons and dogs.

Economics used to be called 'the science of *ceteris paribus*' because so many of its statements were prefaced by the proviso 'other things being equal'. Thus economists often seem to assume that natural resources are infinitely replaceable. Nowadays, of course, even pure air and water cannot be taken for granted as free goods; they have to be paid for, collectively, like everything else. Yet economists still appear to believe that fresh supplies of natural resources, both renewable and unrenewable, will always be available so long as the price is pitched high enough. Somehow they have to be persuaded to change their assumptions, to accord with the reality of a world in which natural genetic resources, for instance of fish and timber, are being used up at a rate that will ensure a major human disaster within a generation and a half at the most, i.e., by the late twenties of the next century. In fifteen years' time there will be some 6 billion people in the world, an increase of 50 per cent since 1975. Even now many people, just to survive from day to day, are forced to overgraze rangelands and cut down essential shelter trees, thus destroying the very resources needed to free them from poverty. By the beginning of the next century even larger numbers will be forced to do so, unless remedial action is taken very soon.

One view of modern civilisation is that it is overwhelmingly based on comparatively recent technological advances. Homes in developed countries are stocked with refrigerators, TV sets, stereos, videos, washing machines, telephones, and so on. People travel in motor cars, aeroplanes, and still widely in that great nineteenth-century feat of technology, the railway train. Immense factories, filled with computers and machine tools, produce all these, and also great quantities of military hardware, using mineral resources such as coal, iron, copper and silicon. So many people in positions of authority and influence believe in the primacy of this technological world view, that the reality that human welfare is still fundamentally based on genetic resources is more and more widely ignored. As a result, genetic resources themselves are treated just like the supposedly inexhaustible mineral resources. Challenged on this point, economists usually say that in the past more resources have always been forthcoming when prices have risen, or technology has improved. Coal can be mined deeper down, or oil-rigs can go further out to sea in deeper waters. All available evidence suggests that this is no longer true for mineral resources - we shall perhaps know definitely around the year 2035. It is still true in the short term for domesticated or cultivated genetic resources - witness the disastrous success of the European Common Agricultural Policy, with its wine lakes and butter mountains. But it certainly is not, and indeed cannot, be true for wild genetic resources. Raising the price of these quickly exhausts them, as shown by the devastating effect of uncontrolled competition on such common-property resources as whale and fur-seal stocks during the past 150 years. Indeed, virtually the whole history of large-scale commercial exploitation of wild genetic resources is one of the reduction of thriving populations to commercial, and often nearly to actual extinction.

The use of wild populations of animals and plants is the oldest form of land use known to man, and is still practised throughout the world by both rich and poor nations, as the Zimbabwe Minister of National Resources recently told the International Crocodile Symposium at Victoria Falls. Human society depends on genetic resources for virtually all its food, nearly half its medicines, much of its clothing, and in some regions virtually all its fuel and building materials, as well as, of course, an important part of its mental and spiritual welfare. Non-renewable mineral resources can supply fuel, building materials and some artificial fabrics, but cannot possibly supply all these other human needs, at any rate within the foreseeable future. Our future thus depends almost entirely on our capacity to conserve the goose that lays the golden eggs by maintaining genetic resources as renewable resources. The assumption that genetic resources can be mined like coal and gravel leads us straight down the Gadarene slope to human extinction; for how else are we to interpret policies which will more or less halve both the available fertile arable land and the tropical forests in the world by the end of the century, and halve it again by the year 2020, while human population increases by more than 50 per cent in the same period?

Genetic resources are no more nor less than stocks or populations of plants and animals, both wild and cultivated or domesticated. The recent tendency to confine the term to a limited number of commercially important crop species and their wild relatives, is not only unscientific but devalues it for all other uses. These stocks are composed of perhaps as many as 30 million species, each a separate gene pool with its own genetic diversity. Since ecosystems are composed of mixed populations of plants and animals, associated together in an infinitely complex web, species are in fact the component elements or building blocks of ecosystems. Species and ecosystems are thus two sides of the same coin. The founders of ecology realised this, and called one aspect of their new science autecology - the study of individual species - and the other synecology - the study of communities of animals and plants. The study of ecosystems has taken synecology to its logical conclusion, but this does not mean that autecology has become unimportant. The science of ecology still consists of both aspects, inextricably intertwined.

The genetic resources of the world have many uses, but may conveniently be discussed under twelve headings:

1. Food, drink and nutrition
2. Clothing and fabrics
3. Building and manufacturing
4. Fuel and energy
5. Human health
6. Ornamentation
7. Scientific research and the safeguarding of knowledge
8. Biological control
9. Pets and gardens
10. Recreational hunting and field sports
11. The enjoyment of wildlife
12. Wildlife as a social symbol

1. Food and Drink

Bread wheat

Emmer

Any human meal depends almost entirely on genetic resources. Only a very few ingredients, such as table salt, have not come from an animal or plant. A typical western meal might draw on nearly a dozen plant and two or three animal families: beef (Bovidae), plaice (Pleuronectidae) or eggs (Phasianidae) for the main dish; potatoes (Solanaceae) and cabbage (Cruciferae) or peas (Leguminosae) for cooked vegetables; lettuce (Compositae), cucumber (Cucurbitaceae) and tomatoes (Solanaceae) for salad; wheat (Gramineae) for bread; apples (Rosaceae), oranges (Rutaceae) and bananas (Musaceae) for dessert; and, to drink, beer from barley (Gramineae), wine from grapes (Vitaceae), or Coca-Cola, still flavoured with the West African cola nuts *Cola vera* and *C. acuminata* (Sterculiaceae).

A typical eastern meal might draw on a similar range of families: chicken (Phasianidae), wheat and rice (Gramineae) and lentils and peas (Leguminosae), with peppers (Piperaceae, Solanaceae) and curry-leaf (Rutaceae) for flavouring; and for dessert, mangoes (Anacardiaceae) and guavas (Myrtaceae); all washed down with a drink made from one of a wide range of fermented grains or fruits, such as *Sorghum, Panicum* or other grasses (Gramineae), as well as nowadays the ubiquitous Coca-Cola.

All these foodstuffs derive from genetic resources, that is to say from wild, domesticated or cultivated animal and plant species, and will only be available to mankind as long as their stocks are maintained, with an adequate genetic diversity, in an environment in which they can thrive. They are all components of ecosystems, some of them artificial, such as cornfields or orchards, and if their stocks are to be maintained, these ecosystems must be conserved and usually also carefully managed. Altogether man has learnt to use at least 3000 plant species for food, but has cultivated only 150 to the extent that they are traded at all widely. Today the great majority of people are actually fed by only about fifteen plant species, but at least another 75,000 edible plants are not being seriously exploited.

Most foods derive from cultivated plants or domesticated animals, and from two families in particular, the grasses (Gramineae) and the Bovidae, to which cattle, sheep and goats belong. Grains such as wheat, barley, rye, oats, rice and corn (maize) are all the seeds of grasses, and more than half our sugar (not to mention molasses and rum) comes from grasses of the genus *Saccharum*. Fermented grain from grass species produces a wide range of beers and other alcoholic drinks, including whisky, whose malt is barley that has been steeped in water to start it germinating and is then kiln-dried. Grasses are also grazed by cattle, sheep and goats, to produce meat, milk, cheese, hides, wool and other products. When it is either cold or dry, domestic livestock are also largely fed on barley, oats, rice and other grains. So for human welfare the Gramineae are perhaps the most important single family of all.

Vegetables and salads come from a wide range of plant families, such as the Cruciferae (cabbages and their derivatives, turnips, radishes, water-cress), Leguminosae (peas, beans, lentils, groundnuts and other pulses) and Umbelliferae (carrots, celery, parsnips, angelica). So do fruits, most notably the Rosaceae (apples, pears, plums, cherries), the Rutaceae (oranges, lemons, limes and other citrus fruits) and the numerous families that yield such tropical fruits as bananas, guavas, mangoes, pineapples and papayas.

Among mammal food sources, besides the Bovidae, the closely related Suidae yield pork, ham, bacon and lard. Poultry and eggs come mainly from the Phasianidae (domestic fowl) and Anatidae (ducks, geese). We also eat fish from many families, notably the Salmonidae (salmon, trout), Gadidae (cod, haddock) and Clupeidae (herring). The two honeybees, *Apis mellifera* and *A.indica*, prime sources of honey, are among the remarkably few domesticated invertebrates, but are domesticated only in the sense that they can be induced to nest in artificial hives, where they are more easily exploited.

Rainbow trout

An immense range of plants provide vegetable oils for both culinary and industrial purposes. Fixed or fatty oils used in cooking come not only from the well-known olive *Olea europaea*, but also from sunflower *Helianthus annuus*; oil-seed palm *Elaeis guineensis*, whose burgeoning cultivation destroys much of the remaining wild habitat in lowland South-East Asia; oil-seed rape *Brassica napus* var. *oleifera*, which produces colza oil and

Oil-seed palm

colours bright yellow so many of the fields of western Europe; and more than fifty other plants. Palm oil is a good example of a vegetable product with many uses: as a food in West Africa, as an ingredient of margarine, as fuel, and in the manufacture of soap, candles and even tinplate. Essential and volatile oils used for flavouring, perfumery and medicinal purposes come from an even wider range: camphor from *Cinnamomum camphora*, cloves from *Eugenia caryophyllus*, lavender from *Lavandula officinalis* and many others. Oil, for both cooking and lighting, has also been produced from many mammals, notably seals and whales, and even from birds, such as penguins and the South American oil-bird *Steatornis caripensis*.

Those who claim that because almost all these species are domesticated or cultivated, we can safely neglect the wild species, must be reminded both of the continuing vital role of wild plants and animals in the diet of people in much of the tropical world, and of the need for constant infusions of wild genes to maintain the genetic diversity of cultivated species. To those who are city-based, the part played by bushmeat, fish, wild fruit, berries and herbs in the nutrition of villagers and tribesmen throughout the under-developed world may seem of small importance. But not so long ago 81 per cent of the diet of the ordinary African came from 79 species of wild plants, the balance of 19 per cent being made up by bushmeat from wild animals, while more recently 614 out of 740 tribes surveyed depended largely on wild animals and wild plants for their food. Moreover, in the sea, wild genetic resources of fish are of substantial importance, and whale stocks too would still be a significant food and oil resource, if they had not been so mismanaged, by international consensus.

A great many wild fruits and vegetables provide both sustenance and essential trace elements and vitamins in the human diet; in many parts of the world they are still staple foods. Thus in Indonesia tribal peoples have used at least 4000 plant species for food, though fewer than 400 have been cultivated at all widely. Similarly, in Papua New Guinea only 43 out of 251 tree species with edible fruits are cultivated. Palms and seaweeds are the two most important groups of plants still harvested from the wild for food. Sago is still produced from wild palms in South-East Asia, Papua New Guinea and Venezuela; elsewhere wild palms, and in Brazil hearts of palm (which entails the destruction of the tree), yield edible oils and salads. Seaweeds are eaten, raw or cooked, both in many developing countries, and in Japan, Wales and other developed countries. Koreans in particular eat large amounts of kelp, mostly dried.

In Africa the leaves of the baobab *Adansonia digitata* are cooked and eaten; and around Lake Chad waterleaf *Talinum triangulare* (Portu-lacaceae), an alkaline waterweed with a high protein and vitamin B12 content, is eaten as a green vegetable. Some wild plants yield salt for human consumption: a *Polygonum* is used by the Fulanis in northern Cameroon, and the Tougas of the Zambia-Zimbabwe border use five different species. In droughts bush plants are the only source of water for the Bushmen of the Central Kalahari Desert and the Basarwas of Botswana.

Similar examples can be found in Asia and Latin America. In northern India villagers go to the forests every spring to collect morels *Morchella esculenta*, fungi which fetch a high price in local markets. In Iran and Afghanistan about 60,000 tons of pistachio nuts from wild *Pistachia vera* trees are harvested and exported each year. Brazil is appropriately the major producer of Brazil nuts *Bertholletia excelsa*, harvested from natural forests in the Amazon basin. The Sori Indians, at the northern end of the Gulf of California in Mexico, harvest the seed-heads of eel-grass *Zostera* from the delta of the Colorado River, and grind them into a flour to make tortillas.

Oil-bird

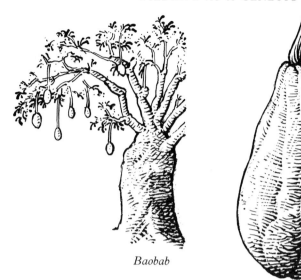

Baobab

Even in highly industrialised Britain, such wild fruits as bilberries *Vaccinium myrtillus* on the Yorkshire and Scottish moors (in Scotland they are called blaeberries), watercress *Nasturtium* and mushrooms *Agaricus bisporus* add important variety to rural diets, and every September countless town and country dwellers go out along the country hedgerows to pick blackberries from the wild bramble *Rubus fruticosus*. In North America the annual harvest of blueberries *Vaccinium* spp. parallels that of bilberries in Britain, and most of the hazelnuts on the American market come from the native hazel *Corylus americana*, often gathered wild. In continental Europe many species of edible fungi are gathered and sold in local markets; one of the best known is the underground truffle *Tuber* spp., harvested with the aid of specially trained dogs. In Japan the aquatic fern *Ceratopteris pterioides* is cultivated as a spring vegetable.

The two major invertebrate groups that contribute to human diet are the crustaceans and the molluscs. Shrimps are almost certainly the world's most valuable wild animals; the total annual value of the exports of fresh and frozen shrimps from India, Indonesia, Mexico and other developing countries is one billion US dollars. Indeed for Panama, Pakistan, Madagascar and some other countries shrimps are the main source of foreign exchange. Penaeid shrimps, often harvested from aquaculture ponds, are especially important in Costa Rica and Ecuador. Krill *Euphausia superba*, a shrimp-like crustacean of the southern oceans, is also now widely exploited. Of the score of marine invertebrates fished for human consumption in Australian waters, most are crustaceans - saltwater crayfish *Jasus lalandei*, lobsters, crabs and prawns, similar to those fished in European, North American and Far Eastern waters, but of different species. The Japanese also eat the branchiopod crustacean *Lingula*. In many northern countries freshwater crayfishes *Astacus* spp. are regarded as delicacies.

The marine molluscs eaten in Australia include the opisthobranchs known as *bêche-de-mer* or sea slugs; abalones *Notihaliotis ruber*, closely related to both the abalones *Haliotis rufescens* fished off California, and the ormers *H. tuberculata* taken at low tide in the Mediterranean and as far north as Jersey and Guernsey off northern France; and the famous Sydney rock oyster *Saxostrea commercialis*, a relative of the oyster *Ostrea edulis*, whose succulence is said to have been one of the attractions of Britannia to the Romans. Squids, octopuses and other cephalopod molluscs are fished and eaten in almost all the warmer parts of the world, notably in Japan, where the favourite is the surume ika *Todarodes pacificus*.

One of the best known culinary land molluscs is the Roman snail *Helix pomatia*, which is responsible for the old-fashioned stereotype of Frenchmen as snail-eaters. Various species of giant snail *Achatina* are widely eaten in Africa. The main contribution of wild terrestrial arthropods to human diet comes from honey gathered from wild bees, but in some parts of the world termites, and the large fat grubs of moths or beetles, are also regarded as delicacies. From one colony of *Macrotermes* termites in Uganda four sackfuls a year were harvested, and the nutritive value of termites was demonstrated when lightly roasted wingless termites, from the market at Léopoldville, Zaire, proved to be 44 per cent fat and 36 per cent protein. Another vital invertebrate contribution to human food supplies is pollination.

Fishes, both marine and freshwater, are human food throughout the world, and have rarely if ever attracted taboos, as some mammal meat has done. Monastic fishponds, especially for carp *Cyprinus carpio* in ancient China and medieval Europe, set a trend that was largely forgotten in the west during the great rush of the industrial and agricultural revolutions. Only comparatively recently have fish farms, mainly for salmonids, again become significant factors in the fish supplies of developed countries, though aquaculture has always been important in China. In Benin, West Africa, fish are caught from shallow lagoons that are managed so as to maximise the growth of the algae and other plants on which they feed. Marine fish farms are found in some coastal estuaries and deltas in the Philippines, especially for the milkfish *Chanos chanos*, as well as in some shallow Scottish lochs.

For the main bulk of our fish supplies, however, we still rely on wild fish, which are increasingly overfished both in fresh water and in the sea. There are major lake fisheries in the great African lakes, Victoria, Chad and Nyasa, with various species of *Tilapia* as their mainstay. In both Africa and Asia the major river systems and their flood plains, such as the Mekong in South-East Asia and the Congo in Central Africa, provide vital additions to local protein supplies. In general the most important freshwater food fishes belong to the carp (Cyprinidae) and catfish (Siluridae and Ictaluridae) families, but the Salmonidae and the eel *Anguilla anguilla* are also important. Nevertheless, most of our fish protein supply comes from the sea, and all maritime nations, including some, like Poland, with only a tiny coastline, have sea-fishing fleets. The most important marine fish families in the northern hemisphere are the cod (Gadidae), herring (Clupeidae), and mackerel and tunny (Scombridae) families, together with the flatfish (Pleuronectidae and Soleidae). Sea fishing actually forms the basis of the economies of some maritime countries, notably Iceland and Peru.

Marine turtles are much the most important human food source among reptiles and amphibians. Their flesh sustained many a crew of mariners in the tropical oceans during the heroic age of sail; together with their eggs it is still an important, if overexploited, source of protein for coastal populations in the warmer parts of the world. The seven South American *Podocnemis* river turtles have long been important sources of meat and eggs for local people, but these too have been overexploited, leading to high prices so that now many fewer people can enjoy them. Snakes and lizards are important items of diet in China and elsewhere in Asia and the Pacific, as well as in Latin America. The fancy the French and Swiss have for the

Common guillemot or murre

flesh of the edible frog *Rana esculenta* is only one of numerous instances where amphibians also provide a small but tasty supply of protein.

Birds, of course, provide eggs and meat almost everywhere, though in the developed world wild eggs have been almost completely replaced by eggs from the domestic fowl *Gallus gallus*. Colonial nesters, such as gulls, auks and penguins, are the most important sources of wild eggs: for instance, in Iceland, where guillemot *Uria aalge*, razorbill *Alca torda* and kittiwake *Rissa tridactyla* eggs are still collected annually from the steep cliffs of Grimsey Island; in the Falklands, where the eggs of four species of penguin have been taken for food ever since men reached the islands; in Irian Jaya, where the eggs of the magpie goose *Anseranas semipalmata* are a much-prized source of food; and in Sulawesi, where the eggs of the maleo fowl *Macroephalon maleo* are dug from the warm sand in which they are laid. Bird meat too is eaten almost everywhere; not only Kentucky Fried Chicken or Norfolk Turkeys, but wild pheasants, guinea-fowl and other game-birds, ducks, geese, pigeons and even parrots and songbirds. In the Cocachito region of Brazil, wild birds contribute 2.6 per cent of the protein needs of the community, and in Guyana sandpipers, plovers and other shore-birds are an important food source for the coastal villagers. In coastal areas, many seabirds are still harvested: puffins *Fratercula arctica* from Bjarnarey Island off southern Iceland; young gannets *Sula bassana* annually from the Hebridean island of Sula Sgeir, following an ancient tradition of the men of Ness, for whom salted *gugas* were once a staple diet; and boobies and frigate birds, collected twice a year from North Keeling Island by the Cocos (Keeling) islanders in the Indian Ocean. Some regions, such as Mediterranean Europe, have a tradition of taking thrushes, warblers and other small songbirds for the pot, and the ortolan *Emberiza hortulana* has been considered a special delicacy since Roman times. In Cyprus alone up to ten million birds are shot, netted or limed annually for this purpose. This habit has irked the citizens of northern Europe, who now enjoy small birds by watching them instead of eating them, though their ancestors too used to kill and eat them.

The larger mammals have, of course, always made a major input to human protein supplies. Deer, antelopes and other Bovidae have been the most important, but villagers whose crops have been ravaged by elephants or hippos, or who have no other protein available, naturally have no hesitation in eating them when they are able to kill them. In North America both the white-tailed deer *Odocoileus virginianus* and the mule or blacktail deer *O.hemionus* make a significant contribution to protein supplies, and in Central Europe and New Zealand venison from the red deer *Cervus elaphus* (sometimes now farmed or ranched) is regularly sold in the shops. In Sweden the 150,000 elk *Alces alces* shot by sportsmen each year represent more than a quarter of the national consumption of meat. In Africa the total contribution of wild animals, mainly mammals, to the diet is as high as 80 per cent in Ghana, 70 per cent in Zaire, 60-70 per cent in Liberia and 60 per cent in Botswana. In the Leonardo da Vinci region of Amazonian Brazil wild animals supply about one-fifth of the total protein intake.

A wide range of small mammals are also eaten; rabbits, hares and many large rodents, such as grasscutters *Cricetomys* in West Africa and capybaras *Hydrochoerus hydrochaeris* and viscachas *Lagidium viscaccia* in northern South America, not to mention pangolins, hyraxes and even monkeys and apes. In Botswana, hunters kill some 2.2 million spring hares *Pedetes capensis* a year, and so provide as much meat as 20,000 cattle would produce. In Liberia bushmeat, sold in markets throughout the country, is usually quartered antelope (especially duikers) or monkey, wood-smoked until it is dry enough to keep for two weeks. In Morocco, squirrels and

Mistle thrush

Rock hyrax

porcupines are eaten, and the Seychelles and Guam are two of the many oceanic islands where the giant fruit bats *Pteropus*, called flying foxes, are an especial delicacy. Indeed few mammals cannot be eaten at all: the Inuit (Eskimos) eat sealmeat, and dugongs *Dugong dugon* caught in tropical fishermen's nets are widely relished. Yet remarkably few attempts have so far been made to domesticate or ranch these excellent sources of food.

2. Clothing and Fabrics

Until comparatively recently, virtually the whole of mankind's needs for clothing, footwear, bedding and furnishings relied on genetic natural resources in the form of domesticated or cultivated stock: for instance, wool from sheep and in South America from llamas *Lama glama* and alpacas *L.pacos*; leather mainly from cattle, sheep and goats; cotton from *Gossypium* spp. (Malvaceae); linen from flax *Linum usitatissimum*; and silk from the cocoons of the moth *Bombyx morio*. Many furs also come from the farming of such species as the mink *Mustela vison* and the silver fox, a colour morph of the North American red fox *Vulpes fulva*. Indeed in North America today some 60 per cent of the fur trade is based on farmed mink.

However, skins and furs from wild animals are still of great importance to mankind today. The skins and hides of the larger mammals and reptiles that are killed for food, notably antelopes and deer, have always been an additional source of leather. Antelope hides from several North African gazelles are widely sold in Europe under the name of African gazelle or African deerskin. Pigskin gloves are often made from South American peccaries, and the skins of the giant neotropical rodent, the capybara, are also made into gloves under the trade name *carpincho*. The Fuegians of southernmost Patagonia even clad themselves in penguin skins, while the flippers of sea turtles are used by fishermen in Kutch, North-west India, to make crude shoes for walking on coral reefs. Until early this century, the bark of the oak *Quercus robur* was used in Europe to tan leather, and in Central America mangrove bark is still so used.

Furs from otters *Lutra*, martens *Martes*, other Mustelidae and beavers *Castor*, which are large rodents, are still widely obtained from wild-trapped animals, especially in Canada and the USSR. The USSR is the largest single producer of wild mink, the largest overall producer being Scandinavian. Until the recent controversy surrounding the annual harvest of harp and hooded seals *Phoca groenlandica* and *Cystophora cristata* off the east coast of Canada, sealskins too have been a significant part of the world fur trade. However, the decline of furs as articles of clothing, or rather their elevation into luxury garments, reflects the overexploitation of the wild populations, as witness especially the fur seals and the vicuña *Vicugna vicugua* discussed on pp. 180 and 181.

Feathers from a great many bird species, not least the domestic fowl, are widely used to stuff pillows and other furnishings, as is horsehair from domesticated horses. In particular, the down from the nests of eiders *Somateria mollissima* is gathered, especially in Iceland, and used to stuff bedding, though eider down has been superseded by cheaper materials for most eiderdowns. An important invertebrate-based fabric is silk, which was being produced in China before 1300 BC from domesticated silk-worms, the larvae of the moth *Bombyx morio*, which are fed on cultivated white mulberries *Morus alba*.

In the developed world today all natural materials, even cotton and wool, are rapidly joining silk as luxury items, since clothing, footwear and fabrics are being increasingly made from mineral sources. Outside the small luxury market even furs are now often artificial, simulating the skins of leopard

Capybaras

Vicuña

Panthera pardus and other wild animals. In undeveloped areas, however, and especially in rural communities, fabrics and leather from natural and sometimes wild sources will continue to be used for clothing and footwear for some time to come. Properly managed farmed or ranched stocks, e.g. of crocodiles in the tropics, and of fur-bearers such as mink and silver fox in many northern areas, will also make their contribution, but as a cash crop, i.e. a crop that is sold for cash rather than used to feed or clothe the local community.

3. Building, Manufacturing

Ever since man first discovered the cutting qualities of flints and other sharp stones, and learned to fashion axes and fell trees and shrubs, timber of one kind or another has been used for constructing human dwellings, boats, carts, furniture and innumerable other artefacts. Thus, early in the present century, oak was used throughout much of Europe and North America for railway wagons, colliery tubs, canal barges and lock gates, wheel spikes and coffins; and on farms for gates, fences, cow stalls, hay racks and feeding troughs. Throughout the world today substantial amounts of locally cut timber, including mangroves, are still used, not only to build houses, but also for a wide range of other purposes from boat building to furniture, pit props and water pipes.

Papyrus

In the developed world and except for specialised uses such as roofing, timber is now giving way to other materials, though as pulpwood it is still the basis of the substantial paper and newsprint industry. In the developing world natural building materials, not just timber but also rattans, bamboos and other stout grasses, continue to be of vital importance. In China and Japan bamboo, formerly used only for house-building and firewood, now goes into a wide range of products, from plywood and plastics to furniture and other durables, not to mention its use as food and medicine. In many parts of the tropics, canes and grasses are cut for local use as building materials. In the developed world the use of thatch for roofing has become a luxury, but in Iraq whole houses are still made from the reed *Phragmites australis*, a tall grass which is also still harvested for thatching both around the Neusiedlersee in Austria, and in parts of England. Various sedges, especially *Cyperus papyrus* and *Scirpus* spp, are widely used in Africa for thatch and matting, as are screw-pines *Pandanus* on islands throughout the Pacific.

Rattan comes from the stems of spiny climbing palms belonging to the major group of scaly-fruited palms, the Lepidocaryoideae, and is much used for furniture manufacture in the tropics. However, much of the furniture marketed as rattan is actually made of cheaper and more easily obtainable materials, such as bamboo, willow, the reed or buri *Arundo donax*, or the petioles of the palm *Corypha utan*. Villagers also have many uses for rattan from cordage, binding and thatch to medicine, tinder and toys. Rattan is the second most valuable forest product in South-east Asia after timber; yet there is virtually no policy for conserving either product for sustainable use, though in central Kalimantan two rattan species have been cultivated on a large scale for many years. In Colombia, lianas (woody vines) are similarly used to make 'mimbre' furniture.

European equivalents of the rattan are the osier *Salix viminalis*, still grown and harvested in special osier beds, the long whippy twigs being woven into basketware, and the bulrush *Scirpus lacustris*.

Rubber from *Hevea brasiliensis* (Euphorbiaceae) is a good example of a wild plant which created a whole industry in the nineteenth century, largely thanks to the ingenuity of Sir Joseph Hooker, Director of the Royal Botanic

Gardens, Kew, who helped it on its way from Brazil to Ceylon and Malaya. Natural rubber is still in great demand, especially for specialised uses, such as in electronics and for radial and aircraft tyres. It is still being planted in Malaysia and on a small scale some is still tapped from wild rubber trees in Amazonian Brazil. Recently, however, it has been challenged by mineral substitutes created from petroleum.

A great many other plants have been used to produce rubber-like substances, among them *Ficus elastica*, which yielded the original india-rubber, and species of dandelion *Taraxacum*, golden-rod *Solidago*, milk-weed *Asclepias*, and spurge *Euphorbia*. Guayule *Parthenium argentatum*, a daisy-like plant from the deserts of Mexico and Arizona, has been used to produce both rubber and plastics, especially in wartime. All these plants are still available to us as natural genetic resources, and their use consumes much less energy than artificial rubber.

Vegetable oils are not only sources of food, but together with animal fats they are widely used industrially. Thus Carnauba wax, an important leather polish, comes from the palm *Copernicia cerifera*, and linseed oil from flax *Linum usitatissimum*. The jojoba bush *Simmondsia chinensis* from Mexico and Arizona has recently been found to have similar properties to sperm oil from the endangered sperm whale *Physeter catodon*, and may well in future form a base for cosmetics, since it appears not to cause allergies even to the most sensitive skins. Many resins are also used in industry, for instance from the maritime pine *Pinus pinaster* of southern Europe. Other resins come from various species of Burseraceae, frankincense from *Boswellia* and myrrh from *Commiphora*; both grow in southern Arabia.

The large brown seaweeds, variously called kelp, tangle or oarweed, have been widely used as an agricultural fertiliser. In the Outer Hebrides, off western Scotland, the so-called lazy-beds, compounded of seaweed and peat, have been built up over the centuries into highly fertile patches of farmland. A local alginate factory sent its products to the moon, as fireproofing for the astronauts' notepads. Agar agar, a carbohydrate obtained from seaweeds, is enormously important to the pharmaceutical industry, so the extensive kelp beds in the Falkland Islands were surveyed in 1947, and a pilot plant for the production of alginates was set up in 1970. Regrettably financial difficulties prevented the hoped-for annual harvesting of 360,000 tons of kelp, which would have yielded 30,000 tons of dried milled kelp, so the plant closed down.

Guano, the nutrient-rich droppings of seabirds, is another important natural resource used for agricultural fertiliser. The most famous guano islands, said at one time to represent the largest concentration of birds in the world, are off the coast of Peru. In 1910 the industry exported some 400,000 tons of guano a year, but many of the original deposits, accumulated over some thousands of years, have now been mined out. The three principal birds which have built up the Peruvian guano deposits at their nesting colonies are the guanay cormorant *Phalacrocorax bougainvillei*, the Peruvian booby *Sula variegata* and the brown pelican *Pelecanus occidentalis*. Some 5000 tons of guano are also collected each year from the offshore South African colonies of the jackass penguin *Spheniscus demersus*.

Guanay cormorants

4. Fuel and Energy

The discovery of fire, before hand-axes were invented, opened up immense scope for using natural materials for human welfare. Timber and faggots have been used for fuel for many millennia, and over much of the world are still the only fuel available for cooking and heating. More than 1500 million people, nearly three-quarters of the population of developing countries, cook and heat their homes with wood every day. Wood and charcoal, believed to be the most ancient manufactured product, provide at least four-fifths of all energy used in Asian villages: in Nepal they supply 87 per cent of it. In Niamey, the capital of Niger, 90 per cent of the people cook with wood or charcoal. Charcoal can be produced from timber coppiced on a rotation, and so helps to conserve the resource.

Another natural fuel is cow dung, which has, however, the disadvantage of gradually removing phosphorus and other important minerals from the soil and releasing them into the atmosphere. In countries where fertilisers are widely used, it may not matter if the dung and urine of livestock does not fertilise the fields they graze, but in India and other eastern countries the burning of cow dung as a fuel has substantially impoverished soil fertility. Taken together, the stripping of trees and shrubs from the land for timber and firewood and the burning of cow dung as fuel, especially when coupled with overgrazing and overuse of water supplies, are a precise recipe for the disastrous desertification that has overtaken so many parts of the Third World.

Electricity, gas and mineral oils have almost everywhere superseded animal and vegetable fats for burning in lamps, even in regions like the Arctic, where the supply of animal fats could still supply small settlements. However, colza oil from rape *Brassica napus* var. *oleifera*, is still used in lamps and also has various industrial uses. As with building materials, this whole field of lighting, heating and cooking is one where higher living standards have led to transfer from renewable genetic-based to non-renewable mineral resources.

The domestication of animals and plants was encouraged and accelerated because tamed animals, notably oxen and horses, proved so useful for augmenting human energy in the process of cultivating the emerging crop plants. Until the nineteenth century, the extra power derived from the muscular effort of horses, oxen, buffaloes, elephants, camels, llamas, reindeer, and in some places even smaller animals, such as large dogs, was one of the most important uses of genetic resources for human welfare. The invention of the oxcart was one of the seminal events in human history, and in India, for instance, beasts of burden still produce more energy than electricity power stations. Over much of the Third World buffaloes are still vitally important, especially as they also provide milk and, ultimately, meat as well. In hilly areas elephants are both more manoeuvrable than machines and less harmful to the environment. In Burma some 4000 trained elephants *Elephas maximus* still extract about half the country's timber each year, and work elephants can still be seen on the roads of Sri Lanka.

Although in developed countries tractors and other vehicles have taken over, and have even replaced camels over most of Arabia, oil supplies will not last for ever. Moreover if, in consequence, oil prices eventually rise again, animal power will continue to be needed, at least in the tropics, for many years to come. Hence the gene pools of the domestic and wild stocks combined will continue to be of vital importance. In due course, petroleum itself may well be replaced by biologically based fuels that make direct or indirect use of photosynthesis. Much research has already been done on ways of converting vegetable biomass to alcohol and other fuels, and no doubt before long it will become economically feasible to grow and harvest such prolific plants as cattails *Typha latifolia* and water hyacinth *Eichhornia crassipes* for this purpose. We may also be able to exploit the plants, such as the caper spurge *Euphorbia lathyris* and other members of the Euphorbiaceae, which actually produce oil-like hydrocarbons. This brings us back to the importance of keeping all our options in the natural world open in case we make new discoveries.

Oil-seed rape

5. Human Health

The drugs we use to maintain human health are still predominantly derived from plant and animal species. Although current pharmaceutical research is busy synthesising the substances produced by animals and plants, we are still nowhere near being able to dispense with either wild or cultivated genetic resources in medicine today. Each year more than two-fifths of prescriptions in the United States contain a drug based on a higher plant (25 per cent), bacteria (13 per cent) or animal (3 per cent) as the active ingredient. Moreover, the value of medicines derived from higher plants alone is of the order of $8-10 billion a year. Yet the drugs we have are the result of investigating only a tiny fraction of the world's species, a further indication of how rash we are to allow animals and plants to become extinct before we know their potential. The fact that some 70 per cent of all plants known to have anti-cancer properties grow in moist tropical forests, one of the most threatened of all habitats, shows how serious the situation is.

The three main applications of genetic resources for medical drugs are:
(1) as direct curative or therapeutic agents;
(2) as materials for starting the synthesis of drugs;
(3) as models for drug synthesis.

1. Direct curative or therapeutic agents include digitoxin from foxgloves *Digitalis*, atropine from deadly nightshade *Atropa belladonna* and morphine from the opium poppy *Papaver somniferum*, all three still the leading drugs in their respective fields. Other plant alkaloids of medical value include caffeine, cocaine, colchicine, ephedrine, ipepac, nicotine, quinine and reserpine. Some families, notably the Solanaceae, which yields hyoscyamine (from henbane *Hyoscyamus niger*) and lycoscyamine as well as atropine, are especially valuable drug sources. In Australia, for instance, a large output of narcotic alkaloids, including both hyoscyamine and lycoscyamine, is based on native plants of the genus *Duboisia* that belong to this family. Perhaps the most famous of all therapeutic organisms is the mould *Penicillium notatum*, whose derivative penicillin started the antibiotic revolution in modern medicine. Some plants, such as the North American ginseng *Panaxia quinquefolia*, which is exported in some quantity to the Far East, are more highly valued in oriental than in western medicine.

2. Materials for starting the synthesis of drugs include diosgenin, derived from Mexican and Guatemalan yams *Dioscorea* and used for synthesising most oral contraceptives.

3. Models for drug synthesis include the well-known cocaine, extracted from the neotropical coca shrub *Erythroxylum coca*, which led to the development of modern local anaesthetics.

The genus *Catharanthus* (Apocynaceae) provides a striking example of the actual and potential medical value of plants. The well-known Madagascar periwinkle *C.roseus* is an attractive tropical garden plant that has yielded no fewer than seventy alkaloids, some of them of actual clinical value for treating cancer. One of these, vincristine, has largely eliminated both Hodgkin's disease and acute leukaemia. A closely related species, *C.coriaceus*, is critically threatened by loss of habitat, largely due to brush fires in its very few deciduous forest sites in Madagascar. It may well be even more valuable for the treatment of cancer than its common relative; if it is allowed to become extinct, we shall never know. Another member of this family, the Queensland tree *Alstonia constricta*, is a source of reserpine, used to treat mental illness.

Ironically some drugs of the highest importance in medicine have recently acquired a bad name due to their widespread misuse for non-

Madagascar periwinkle

medical purposes. Besides heroin, derived from the opium poppy and formerly consumed as opium, there is marijuana from hemp *Cannabis sativa*, which not long ago was a standard constituent of birdseed mixtures; in the Middle Ages it was widely grown to provide fibre for ropes. Another such drug is the hallucogen psilocybin, derived from a genus of mushrooms *Psilocybe*, which grow commonly in the European countryside. Two other drugs, alcohol from a wide range of vegetable sources, and tobacco from *Nicotiana tabacum* (Solanaceae again) can be equally or even more harmful if used in excess, but their use is sanctioned by widespread social custom, as indeed is the use of heroin and marijuana in some countries. The use of all these natural substances can thus be regarded as enhancing human welfare in some respects, while detracting from it in others when abused.

Animals are also important sources of drugs; some quite obscure animals produce some most valuable drugs. Every marine phylum, for instance, yields substances with some kind of anti-cancer activity; such drugs have been derived from sharks, sting rays, corals, sea anemones, molluscs, segmented and proboscis worms, sponges, sea squirts, sea cucumbers and horseshoe crabs. Sharks' livers contain lipids that enhance human resistance to cancer, and the horseshoe crab *Limulus* not only has a serum that

Horseshoe crab

isolates tumour cells and white blood cells from the whole blood of cancer patients, but is also the source of substances used to detect bacterial toxins in human body fluids. Invertebrates are proving to yield increasing numbers of antibiotic agents, blood coagulants and anti-coagulants, and neuromuscular as well as anti-cancer compounds. Ara-C, effective against herpes, encephalitis and various cancers, is synthesised from a Caribbean sponge; other sponges provide broad-spectrum antibiotics. Prostaglandins, used in tranquillisers and drugs to suppress hypertension, can be derived from black or gorgonian corals (Antipatharia); other corals have yielded substances that may prove to control bacilli and tumours. Tunicates produce compounds toxic to leukaemia cells, and female *Boniella*, members of the small and obscure phylum Echiuroidea, yield a substance that is effective against mouth cancers.

One of the most famous of all invertebrates used in medicine is the now seriously endangered medicinal leech *Hirudo medicinalis*. Only 150 years ago leeches were used to bleed patients as a medical cure-all, with as great enthusiasm (and as great ignorance of its side-effects) as many pills which are used today. During the nineteenth century one billion leeches were imported into France alone. The anti-coagulant properties of the medicinal leech are now known to be of the highest medical and scientific value; indeed we suffer today from the reckless way in which the medical profession once squandered the leech resource on a therapy now known to have been of dubious, if not negative value.

The medical uses of many products from the higher vertebrates are today considered by western medicine to verge on superstition, but are still highly regarded by medical authorities in much of Asia. Thus rhino horn is used in

Black or gorgonian coral (Antipatharia)

Chital or axis deer

Giant salamander

Musk deer

some eastern countries as an aphrodisiac and in others to treat fevers. Repeated scientific tests by western medical researchers have so far failed to validate this eastern faith in it. Nevertheless the continued demand for rhino horn from India, China and South-east Asia, coupled with the demand for rhino horn to make dagger handles in Yemen, has made the Rhinocerotidae perhaps the most endangered family of large animals in the world. There is also a tremendous demand for bear gall-bladders in Japan, and in Indonesia tears collected on swabs from the eyes of young dugongs are still sold as an aphrodisiac. Many other mammals and lower vertebrates are also used in oriental medicine, but since western medical authorities are so sceptical of their value, it is not easy to assess their importance to human welfare. Yet even if they proved only to be placebos, they would presumably have some value by giving confidence and helping the patients' natural defences to effect the cure.

One of the more controversial oriental medical substances is *pantui*, the non-ossified growing antlers of certain deer, which have been used medically in China for hundreds of years. Both wild and farmed deer of several species, including red deer or elk *Cervus elaphus* and chital *C. axis*, are now used to produce *pantui*, for instance in China, the USSR and New Zealand. The USSR now has 70,000 farmed or ranched red deer and 50,000 chital. This industry, where the antler velvet is taken from young antlers that are amputated painlessly, is not be confused with the less benign industry that kills the animal and supplies the international market with antlers still attached to the skull, for use as a macabre decoration.

Many smaller vertebrates, some of them now seriously depleted, also supply the demands of oriental medicine. Both the giant salamander *Andrias japonicus* of Japan and the tiger snake *Notechis scutatus* of Australia are nearly extinct for this reason; the tiger snake's venom is also highly regarded in biochemical research. The scarcity in China of the terrapin *Chinemys reevesii*, traditionally used there for a wide variety of ailments, has led to other terrapins and tortoises being imported in large numbers from all over south-east Asia. Western medicine uses the South African clawed toad *Xenopus laevis* both for pregnancy tests and in teaching biology.

An enormous reservoir of knowledge of plant and animal drugs still resides in those cultures dismissively described in their own countries as 'tribals' and in Europe as gipsies; this is steadily being lost as the tribals and gipsies gravitate to the cities and are lost in their slums. Thus when the Kurichean tribals of North Kerala in southern India have urinary disorders they rely on the seeds of a wild banana to cure them, and the Murai girls of Madhya Pradesh, also in India, freely indulge in pre-marital sex, secure in the knowledge of a combination of naturally occurring drugs that will prevent pregnancy.

One of the more recondite uses of wildlife are the towers of silence, Parsee burial places in such Indian cities as Bombay and Bangalore, where corpses, instead of being buried, are exposed to be stripped of flesh by vultures.

6. Ornamentation

On the borderline between the material and aesthetic or spiritual aspects of human welfare lies ornamentation, which is directed towards the maintenance of the individual's self-confidence and standing among his or her fellows. To many people, furs, feathers and other luxury clothing, together with refinements and adornments, such as perfumes and jewellery, are essential to their being satisfied with their appearance, and they will go to great lengths to maintain their self-respect through ornamentation, often at the expense of basic material needs. So these needs cannot be dismissed as unjustified, superfluous or trivial.

The contribution of animals and plants to this aspect of human welfare is extensive and varied. Since the dawn of history they have yielded dyes, to paint the human skin or colour the drabness of fabrics. In the Near East and the Mediterranean basin the famous Tyrian purple was distilled from the dog-whelk relative *Murex brandaris*, and Iron Age Europe used a blue dye derived from woad *Isatis tinctoria* (Cruciferae). Indigo comes from species of *Indigofera*, members of the great pea and bean family (Leguminosae) native to India and Sumatra. It was a staple of the East Indies trade until the invention of chemical aniline dyes. Cochineal, the scarlet dye which is now synthesised chemically, was formerly made from dried females of an insect, *Dactylopis coccus*, which feeds on cacti; in the Canary Islands the cochineal insect was 'grazed' on the thornless cactus *Nopalia cochinilifera*. Various sponges (Porifera) have for many centuries been gathered in the Mediterranean and Caribbean and used for human toilet, providing one of the classic cases of overexploitation of the resource.

Monal pheasant

Musk is a thick oily substance secreted by the prepucial gland of male musk deer *Moschus moschiferus* in the Himalayas. When removed and dried to a powder, it is much used in oriental medicine and in the perfume industry. Perfumes also come from other animals, such as the sperm whale, and from many plants, among them lavender *Lavandula spicata* (Labiatae) and the damask rose *Rosa damascena*, whose dried petals distil an aromatic oil known as attar or otto of roses.

Luxury leathers and furs come from many mammals and reptiles, some, such as the beaver *Castor canadensis* and marten *Martes americana*, being still harvested as a wild sustainable resource. Others, such as the leopard *Panthera pardus* and other spotted cats, have been kept off the international market largely for fear of overexploitation. Mammal leathers and fibres have almost all, at one time, been used as clothing by peasant and tribal communities, and only in the past hundred years or so have many of them become luxury items. However, in Inca times in Peru, the wool of the vicuña was already reserved for the rich, with the death penalty for anybody who wore it without the express permission of the Inca himself. The common people had to be satisfied with clothes made of wool from the guanaco *Lama guanicoe*. Most reptile leathers are luxury items, whether used for shoes or belts or handbags, and whether deriving from crocodilians, lizards, snakes or marine turtles.

Walrus

Feathers and bird skins too are, and perhaps to some extent always have been, luxury items, except in such special cases as the Fuegian use of bird skins mentioned on p.ooo. Bird plumes are still important in some tribal ceremonies and customs, as in Papua New Guinea, where young men pay for their brides with bird-of-paradise feathers. When not in use, these feathers are carefully protected in specially carved long wooden boxes, and are passed on as family heirlooms. In northern India, professional poachers in Himachal Pradesh sell the crest feathers of monal pheasants *Lophophorus impeyanus* to decorate hats. In Argentina a recent proposal to exploit one of the vast colonies of Magellan penguins *Spheniscus magellanicus* to make skin purses and gloves, at a rate of exploitation that would soon lead to the extinction of the resource, seems unlikely to succeed.

Elephants and other large-toothed mammals, such as hippos *Hippopotamus* and walruses *Odobenus* have for thousands of years been providing ivory to adorn the human domestic environment with ornaments and personal trinkets. Within the past fifteen years or so elephant ivory has

Hippopotamus

become one of the most valuable commodities in international trade, the consequences of which are discussed on p. 165.

The hawksbill turtle *Eretmochelys imbricata*, widespread in the tropical oceans, is now seriously depleted as a result of the demand for its shell to manufacture ornaments. In Japan a highly skilled artisan community on Kyushu used to carve a great range of ornaments and useful articles from tortoiseshell, mainly from this species. Japanese women wore exquisite ornaments, such as chrysanthemums beautifully carved with every petal separate, in their wigs during wedding ceremonies; today these are extreme luxury items. The modern Japanese tortoiseshell trade consists mainly of hairclips, rings, combs and small items of jewellery, using also the green *Chelonia mydas* and ridley *Lepidochelys olivacea* turtles.

Corals are only one of many natural substances to be used for jewellery, and the black corals (Antipatharia) in particular have been seriously overexploited. A great many molluscs and sea-urchins are also collected, sometimes alive, and sold as ornaments and curios, mainly to tourists. In shell shops in Florida sand dollars, which are clypeasteroid echinoderms, either collected locally or imported from Mexico, are second only to the pink queen conch *Strombus gigas* as the most popular items sold there. In the Everglades National Park Florida tree snails *Liguus* are so sought-after that they may be collected only from October to March, with a bag limit of ten snails of each colour form. Sabellid or fan-worms, which are polychaetes with a fan of brightly coloured tentacles, are now collected in large numbers to decorate marine aquaria.

Quite a number of molluscs yield pearls; these are intrusive foreign bodies which the animal renders harmless by covering with nacre (mother-of-pearl) from its shell. Other molluscs are fished for the mother-of-pearl itself, which is much valued in ornamentation. Pearl oysters *Pinctada* are widely fished in the tropics, and the freshwater mussel *Margaritifer margaritifer* is still collected for pearls in the Scottish River Spey. Before the age of plastic there was a big demand for mother-of-pearl to make buttons, and thousands of tons of mussels were dredged annually from the Mississippi for this purpose.

Flowers are an almost universal form of personal adornment as well as of homes and public places, as gifts and garlands for the living and in wreaths for the dead. Bunches of such colourful wild flowers as snakeshead fritillary *Fritillaria meleagris* and wild gladiolus *Gladiolus illyricus* were to be seen in markets in southern England until quite recently, and many people in Britain still go out in spring to pick bunches of primroses *Primula vulgaris* and bluebells *Hyacinthoides non-scripta*. In developed countries flower decoration using cultivated flowers is a considerable industry, which also provides one of the few commercial uses of mosses and lichens. The lichen *Cladonia stellaris* is exported from Scandinavia in considerable quantities - 2397 tonnes in one recent year - for use in wreaths, floral decorations and architects' models. Moss was being gathered in southern England as late as the 1950s, for sale to local florists.

Snakeshead fritillary

7. Scientific Research and the Safeguarding of Knowledge

Scientific research has produced the high standard of living of the developed world. If the rest of the world is to raise itself to anywhere near the standards of the average west, or even east, European country, scientific research will have to be more closely directed to making use of the genetic resources which are the chief material asset of many less developed countries. Scientific research relates to genetic resources in three main ways:

1. Basic research, especially genetic research;

2. The use of animals and plants for testing in the production of drugs and other products, and for surgical techniques and prostheses; and

3. The use of genes from wild stocks or old cultivated or domesticated stocks, both to strengthen the gene pools of animals and plants of economic and social importance, and for recombinant DNA research and the biosynthesis of new products.

Two groups of animals are outstandingly important for basic scientific research: the primates, because of their similarity to man, and the fruit-flies *Drosophila*, more particularly *D. melanogaster*, used in genetic research because of their short life-cycle and the large chromosomes in the salivary glands of their larvae. However, *Drosophila* is now being superseded by several micro-organisms for genetic research. A white form of the common rat *Rattus norvegicus* is also very widely used by biologists.

Nine-banded armadillo

The use of primates in biomedical research and testing has made a significant contribution to advances in human health and disease control. They are important and often essential for research into malaria, cardio-vascular diseases, cancers and hepatitis, and also for the production and testing of drugs and vaccines. World-wide, some 30 primate species are currently being used, notably the Asian rhesus monkey *Macaca mulatta*, the African green or vervet monkey *Cercopithecus aethiops*, the South American squirrel monkey *Saimiri sciurus* and owl monkey *Aotus trivirgatus*, and the now endangered chimpanzee *Pan troglodytes*. Another endangered primate, the cotton-top marmoset *Saguinus oedipus* from Colombia, is of especial importance in hepatitis research. A great many baboons *Papio*, as well as rhesus and other macaques, are used in the testing of polio and other vaccines.

The nine-banded armadillo *Dasypus novemcinctus*, as the only animal other than man known to contract leprosy, is being used in the search for its cure. The American opossum *Didelphis marsupialis* is considered ideal for studies of animal anatomy, the nature of some tumours and embryogenesis. The African clawed toad is used in human pregnancy tests. In another field, the discovery that the hairs of the polar bear *Thalarctos maritimus* absorb heat unusually well is aiding the design and production of materials for better cold-weather clothing and for solar energy collectors.

Bread wheat

Emmer

Species of special value in genetic research include the giant tortoises *Geochelone elephantopus* and ground finches (Geospizinae) of the Galapagos Islands; the variation of each species from island to island helped to give Charles Darwin his seminal ideas on natural selection. The endemic *Partula* snails on Moorea in the Society Islands in the Pacific show a similar high ratio of speciation. Two European Lepidoptera are also key species in genetic research: the peppered moth *Biston betularia*, whose industrial melanism is one of the best recent demonstrations of the mechanism of evolution; and the scarlet tiger moth *Panaxia dominula*, whose population at a fen near Oxford is a classic instance of balanced polymorphism.

As the World Conservation Strategy points out, the genetic material needed to achieve continued improvements in yields, nutritional quality, flavour, pest and disease resistance and adaptation to different soils and climates, is found both in the domesticated and cultivated varieties of the species that serve the needs of mankind, and in their wild relatives. This is quite apart from the unknown potential of the enormous number of species whose use to mankind has never been investigated. Man has come a long way since the first farmers in the Middle East started out with the primitive wheats einkorn *Triticum monococcum* and emmer *T.dicoccum*. Nowadays the average lifetime of cultivars of our modern bread wheat *T.aestivum* in Europe and North America is estimated at no more than 5-15 years, and the figure for other cereals is similar. New strains of pests and diseases constantly appear; climates change; soils lose their fertility; and many other factors, even the whims of tidy-minded bureaucrats and the quirks of consumer demand, help to make current varieties obsolete or no longer viable.

Unless there is a wide gene pool to fall back on, crops may suddenly fail, as the potato *Solanum tuberosum* did in Ireland in the 1840s due to the fungus *Phytophthora infestans*, and the grape-vine *Vitis vinifera* in Europe in the 1860s, when the grape louse *Phylloxera vastatrix* attacked its roots. The European wine industry was then saved only because North American vines, notably the fox grape *V.labrusca* and the summer grape *V.aestivalis*, were resistant to the louse and so provided rootstocks on to which *V.vinifera* could be grafted. The more recent epidemics which have virtually destroyed the large chestnut *Castanea dentata* populations of eastern North America, and the elms *Ulmus* of England and the eastern United States, and which today threaten the coconut palms *Cocos nucifera* of the Caribbean, also show how easily disease can almost eliminate plants that are valuable to man, whether materially or aesthetically; and how vital it is to conserve disease-resistant strains. Since we do not know what fresh epidemics may develop, we need to preserve the maximum potential for resistance, by maintaining as many stocks as possible, both domesticated and wild.

As the Prescott-Allens have shown (many of the examples given here were cited by them), intensive selection for high performance and uniformity has very dangerously narrowed the genetic base of much modern food production. Three-quarters of the wheat crop of the Canadian prairies is produced by only four varieties, one of which (Neepawa) is sown on more than half the prairie wheatlands. Only three parents have been used to breed most of the wheat now being planted in India. Almost three-quarters of the potato crop of the United States also depends on only four varieties, and the US pea crop relies on just two cultivars. The European Commission actually suppresses the growing or sale of all but a few favoured potato varieties. Almost all the coffee trees in Brazil originate from a single plant of *Coffea arabica*, and the whole soybean industry in the United States is based on six plants of *Glycine max* from one locality in Asia.

The recent introduction of high-yielding seeds and modern agricultural techniques in developing countries has been called the Green Revolution. Though it is so valuable and progressive a development in many ways, it has nevertheless not only greatly increased the energy input needed for food production, but has had a striking effect on the genetic diversity of rice *Oryza sativa* in particular. The wide range of disease-resistant traditional varieties that peasant farmers have bred and used for thousands of years were replaced almost overnight by a few high-yielding varieties chosen by scientists. Only eleven parents were used to breed the cultivars developed by the International Rice Research Institute in the Philippines, which are now planted throughout eastern Asia from India to Korea. Ironically, desperate attempts are now being made to breed back into the world's main crops, by means of multiline varieties, the genetic diversity unwittingly abandoned when scientists and administrators failed to realise the full import of their actions in promoting the Green Revolution.

Already many wild relatives and domesticated varieties of important crop plants have been allowed to become extinct, and many more are in danger of becoming so. On Socotra, off the Horn of Africa, only four

Coffee

ancient trees of the endemic pomegranate *Punica protopunica* were surviving when a botanist last visited the island in 1967, and if it had not already been propagated in botanic gardens, its potential to improve the cultivated pomegranate *P. granatum*, which has few other wild relatives, would have been lost. Wild stocks of the Monterey pine *Pinus radiata*, an important timber tree, are now down to five small populations in its native California; these should clearly be preserved to safeguard its genetic diversity.

Resistance to pests and diseases is the virtue most sought by plant breeders, and many wild species have brought this faculty to the rescue of their cultivated relatives. Wild prickly lettuce *Lactuca serriola*, a wayside weed in Europe and North America, has been bred into some butterhead varieties of the cultivated lettuce *L.sativa* to give them resistance to downy mildew. Wild *Saccharum spontaneum* has injected resistance to five diseases into cultivars of sugarcane *S.officinarum*. The Scottish Plant Breeding Station has used four neotropical species of *Solanum* to breed resistance to viruses and blight into the potato. The Californian avocado industry has been anxiously searching for a strain with a blight-resistant rootstock that would be genetically compatible with its cultivated tree *Persea americana*; this may well be the caoba *P.theobromifolia*, a close relative, whose only surviving stock is in Ecuador in a small reserve of less than one square kilometre, which contains the only remaining patch of lowland wet forest on the western slope of the Andes. The cacao (cocoa) industry, based mainly on *Theobroma cacao* (Sterculiaceae), has greatly benefited from wild and semi-wild material. The London cocoa trade financed an expedition to search for wild species and varieties in Amazonian Ecuador, and some of its collections are now held in the large greenhouse at Kew where the Royal Botanic Gardens grows several hundred cocoa clones. Both resistance to the three main cocoa diseases, and increased yields, have resulted from this research. It has also been claimed that if wild species had not been used to stiffen the resistance of the tomato *Lycopersicon esculentum* to its many diseases, especially verticillium and fusarium, it could not now be grown commercially. A tomato relative from the Galapagos can grow in salt water, which opens the possibility of growing tomatoes in saline soil.

Cross-breeding with wild relatives has increased yields and improved quality in a great many other crops, including sunflowers *Helianthus*, sugarcane and potatoes. The 'Irish' potatoes were strengthened by *Solanum demissum* from Mexico, one of the plants used also to stiffen resistance to disease. The East Malling Research Station in Kent claims to have rescued the British cherry industry with its new rootstock Malling Colt, by using *Prunus pseudocerasus* from northern China, which enables the trees to produce more fruit rather than more wood. Examples of quality being improved by cross-breeding with wild relatives include more protein-rich cassava, more easily processed potatoes, sweeter and tastier pineapples, stronger cotton fibres, more pungent mustard from a Nepalese *Brassica* and bitterer beer from American varieties of the hop *Humulus lupulus*. Plant breeding can also enable crops to extend their range by adapting to different environments. Grape-vines crossed with *Vitis amurensis* from the Siberian Far East, and with *V.caribaea* from Venezuela and the Caribbean, can grow in both cooler and warmer climates; crosses with wild *Lupinus angustifolius* from southern Europe have enabled Australian lupin growers to extend into drier areas with shorter growing seasons. Frost resistance has been bred into potatoes from their neotropical relative *Solanum acaule*, and drought resistance into cassava *Manihot esculenta* from one of its wild relatives. A new tool was placed in the hands of growers of corn/sweetcorn/maize *Zea mays* by the recent discovery of a

Cacao tree

Cassava

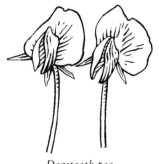

Dogstooth pea

perennial relative of this annual crop, *Z.diploperennis* in ten scattered areas over a remote mountainous part of Mexico. Because it thrives in wetter areas, breeding with this species may expand the cultivation range of corn by as much as a tenth. It may also become possible to grow corn as a perennial crop, rather than as an annual one as at present, and save a large input of expensive energy every year. On the other side of the world a chance find of a hitherto unknown species of *Citrus*, whose lemon-yellow fruit was picked up on a path in an upland rainforest in West Malaysia, may help citrus growers to breed a strain that is more tolerant of wet conditions.

In some parts of India, many thousands of people are being poisoned every year because the widely used dogstooth pea *Lathyrus sativus* in their diet contains the neurotoxin ODAP (oxalyldiaminopropionic acid); eaten in quantity, it induces an irreversible paralysis of the legs, or even death. However, elsewhere in India, the varieties of the pea that are grown and eaten contain much less ODAP, and so are much less poisonous. The genes of these varieties are therefore urgently needed to make all the pea crops grown in India safe to eat. This is yet another instance of the vital importance of maintaining the diversity of animal and plant species, of actual or potential value to mankind.

Similar problems and potential benefits arise from cross-breeding domestic animal breeds with their wild relatives. Two examples of rare domestic breeds that have proved to be of great value are Wensleydale (Yorkshire) sheep, which have been used to produce a heat-tolerant breed, yielding good-quality wool in the subtropics, and the Cornish hen, once bred only by specialist poultry fanciers, but now, because of its ability to grow and yield meat quickly, effectively the basis of the broiler industry.

The cow is arguably the most important economic animal in the world, producing meat, milk and hides. Yet some 115 out of 145 indigenous cattle breeds in Europe and the Mediterranean are threatened with extinction, without anybody having worked out how useful each of their gene pools might be to future animal breeders. The original *Bos taurus* inhabited temperate forests of the western Palaearctic, and to adapt it for the tropics much cross-breeding and selection has been needed, including perhaps even the creation of a new species, the zebu *B.indicus*, which is not known ever to have been wild. The world can therefore ill afford to lose any of the currently endangered other species of wild cattle, such as the banteng *B.sondaicus* and seladang *B.gaurus* of South-east Asia; or the almost extinct kouprey *B.sauveli*, believed to survive in very small numbers on the borders of Cambodia and Thailand, which has never yet bred in captivity. Interest has been expressed in the possibility of crossing banteng with the native Balinese cattle, now believed to be domesticated banteng, because they are twice as large and appear to offer a great potential for raising milk and meat yields. The kouprey might well prove to be resistant to many of the cattle diseases prevalent in South-east Asia, but the ravages of hunting and war make it doubtful whether it will ever be possible to establish a captive breeding colony.

Domesticated buffaloes *Bubalus bubalis* are as important as cattle in many parts of the tropics and subtropics, and sometimes even more so. There are estimated to be some 130 million throughout the world, including the swamp buffalo, a work animal used also for meat but not for milk; and the river buffalo, which provides some 70 per cent of the milk used in India. Yet the wild buffalo (as distinct from the numerous feral stocks, for instance in Australia and Sri Lanka, whose genes are obviously important for breeding domestic buffaloes) is seriously threatened, both by habitat destruction and because it is not a good neighbour to peasant cultivators. But it may be the

Zebu

peasants who suffer in the long run if the genes of the wild buffalo stocks are not preserved.

Both animals and plants are often used as indicators to monitor environmental pollution, especially by heavy metals, not only in research but also in practice. In West Germany, for instance, the municipal authorities use goldfish *Carassius auratus* to monitor the levels of cadmium, mercury and zinc in the water. Two mosses, *Pleurozium schreberi* and *Hylocomium splendens*, were used to demonstrate that contamination by lead was nine times, by cadmium twice and by zinc 1.5 times higher in the Roztocze National Park in Poland, which is near the Lublin coalfield, than in northern Finland. Both lichens and the moss *Hypnum cupressiforme* have also been used to measure differences in the industrial heavy-metal pollution found in the environment. Lichens have also proved valuable indicators for measuring industrial pollution generally, as well as radioactive fallout. Only one lichen, *Lecanora conizaeoides*, can tolerate the high degree of atmospheric pollution that exists in a city such as Belfast, in Northern Ireland, but where smoke exceeds 20-25 mg per 100 m³ and sulphur dioxide registers more than 3 parts per million, even this hardy species is unlikely to be found. The first leafy lichens encountered on a walk out of Belfast are species of *Parmelia*, notably *P. saxatilis*, indicating that smoke contamination has fallen below 5 mg per 100 m³ and sulphur dioxide to less than 1.5 parts per million.

The water hyacinth *Eichhornia crassipes*, a serious pest in the tropics because it chokes so many waterways, has recently been found to be a first-class pollution filter. It absorbs directly from the water, as nutrients, not only nitrates, phosphates and potassium, but also toxic wastes such as pesticides and heavy metals. Both Disney World in Florida and the city of San Diego in California cleanse their water by harvesting water hyacinth.

Water hyacinth

8. Biological Control

Some species are particularly important because they can control other species whose populations have grown to the point of becoming pests. Pest species are often aliens, as with rats in many parts of the world, but they may well be natives, as with vole plagues in Europe. All predators have a potential value for controlling animal pests, likewise herbivores for plant weed species, and parasites, bacteria and other causes of animal and plant diseases. But unless the introduced agent of control attacks the target pest species only, it is likely to harm other beneficial species. The best form of biological control therefore consists of introducing sufficient numbers of one or more predators, parasites or diseases that prey only on the pest or weed, often in conjunction with other methods of control; this is called integrated control.

The first known example of biological control was the domestication of the cat *Felis catus* in ancient Egypt, partly to keep down the rats and mice that even then were ravaging the stores of corn. Before cats became widespread in ancient Greece and Rome, polecats *Mustela putorius*, (presumably the ancestors of European ferrets *M. furo*) were used, but according to Petronius they were blamed for the disappearance of pet birds as well.

Polecat

Biological control can be a chancy business unless it is properly researched, as its history in Jamaica shows. As long ago as 1762 the ant *Formica rufa* was brought there to prey on young rats; it did so for a time, but then itself became a pest. In 1844 a second futile attempt at rat control was made with the giant toad *Bufo marinus*. Finally in 1872 the common Indian mongoose *Herpestes edwardsi* was used, although mongooses are diurnal and rats nocturnal in their habits. At first successful against the rats, the mongooses soon disastrously turned to more congenial diurnal prey, not only domestic fowls and ground-nesting native birds, but also the endemic snakes and lizards, one of which, the yellow snake *Epicrates subflavus*, was already preying on the rats.

The first modern, genuinely successful, biological control project came in 1890 with the use of a ladybird beetle to control the cottony cushion scale which was devastating the citrus orchards of California. This was followed by the well known success of the neotropical moth *Cactoblastis cactorum* against the introduced prickly pear *Opuntia inermis*, which was spreading through Queensland at the rate of 10 million acres a year.

Biological control, both by encouraging existing predators and by importing alien predators or diseases to deal with alien pests, is now a well established tool of pest control, although many chemists, naturally preferring chemical methods, still regard it as of minor importance. Thus manatees *Trichechus manatus* are being used to control waterweeds in reservoirs in Brazil, Guyana and other parts of South America. Special bat towers have been built in Texas and elsewhere with the joint object of controlling malarial mosquitoes and selling the resultant bat guano. Many estate managers in West Malaysia are erecting nest-boxes to encourage the numerous barn owls *Tyto alba* that have arrived to feed on the Malayan wood rats *Rattus tiomanicus*, ricefield rats *R. argentiventer* and little Polynesian rats *R. exulans* that eat the oil-palm nuts *Elaeis guineensis*. In India and Bangladesh people protect snakes, especially the rat snake *Ptyas mucosus*, because they kill rats, and China protects frogs because they eat so many insects.

Indian scientists have recently supplied parasites both to Papua New Guinea, to control stem-boring caterpillars, and to Oman to control gall-midges, native to India and now spreading in the tropics, which attack mango *Mangifera indica* leaves to an extent that affects photosynthesis. In recent years many other pests have been controlled or partly controlled by imported predators: coconut leaf-mining beetles *Promecotheca* by eulophid wasps; the widespread tropical weed *Lantana* in Uganda and elsewhere by the lace-bug *Teleonemis scrupulosa*; the tropical aquatic fern *Salvinia* in Sri Lanka and Papua New Guinea by a still unnamed Australian weevil; noctuid moths *Mythimna* on New Zealand pastures; the European geometrid winter moth *Opheroptera brumata* on broad-leaved trees in Canada; and waterweeds in Florida and Africa. The United States alone has controlled 120 insect pests by importing 223 of their natural enemies.

However, we still suffer from many of the old errors, due to experimenting without any real knowledge of the ecology of the introduced species. The amateur introduction of the myxoma virus into France in the early 1950s, to reduce the numbers of the rabbit *Oryctolagus cuniculus*, was a classic error, for the virus quickly got out of control. In Hawaii too, no fewer than seventeen insects and molluscs have been introduced to control the giant African snail *Achatina fulica*, itself misguidedly introduced in 1936 and now a crop pest. Eight beetles, two predaceous two-winged flies and seven snails have not only failed to extirpate the giant snail, but many of them now prey so heavily on the endemic Hawaiian snails of the families Amastridae, Endodontidae and Zonitidae that several species are threatened with extinction.

Mango

9. Pets and Gardens

The ancient and deep-rooted desire for the companionship of animals has recently been shown to be a vital factor in maintaining the mental health and general wellbeing of lonely old people. Indeed, the whole array of domesticated animals may well owe their origin to some Cro-Magnon or Neanderthal child or old person adopting an orphaned wolf cub. The great variety of animal species kept as pets in the modern world comprises not only innumerable mammals, birds and fishes, but even reptiles and amphibians – lizards and axolotls *Siredon* – and invertebrates, like the stick insects *Carausius morosus*, which are relatives of the grasshoppers and locusts.

Captive-bred pets – dogs, cats, rabbits, guinea-pigs *Cavia porcellus*, budgerigars *Melopsittacus undulatus* and goldfish *Carassius auratus* – add greatly to human happiness and are no threat to wild stocks. Yet, as is shown, the wild stocks are threatened by the capture and export to western countries of huge numbers of wild tropical fish of many species; land tortoises *Testudo graeca* and *T.hermanni* from the Mediterranean basin; and parrots, parakeets and lovebirds, especially from Australia.

Pet animals and birds are also widely popular in the Third World. As long ago as 1772, the French navigator de Bougainville found numerous tamed pigeons in Samoa, and today in south-eastern Brazil almost every human habitation, even in the towns, has several, up to a dozen or more, small birds in cages. Seed-eaters of the genus *Sporophila* are particularly popular, and those most often seen in cages are the ones least often still seen in the wild. In Bali too, few households are without at least one caged bird.

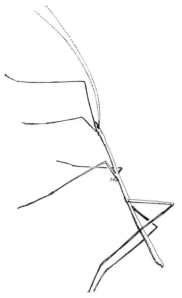

Stick insect Carausius morosus

Indoor and garden plants are the plant equivalents of pets. The great array of ornamental shrubs, bulbs and other house and garden plants bring enormous pleasure to a very large number of people, not only in temperate climates but also in the tropics. Ironically, what is believed to be the world's commonest house plant, the African violet *Saintpaulia ionantha* is a very rare species from the Usambara Mountains in Tanzania, which have many endemic animal and plant species. In Sabah and Sarawak, *Phalaenopsis* orchids adorn a great many balconies, the favourite being *P.amabilis*. Many garden shrubs and other plants now seen in European and North American gardens originated from seeds and cuttings brought back from China, Burma and the Himalayas by pioneer plant hunters, such as Armand David, Reginald Farrer and George Forrest, witness the names *Viburnum davidii*, *Rhododendron farrerae* and *Primula forrestii*.

Pet animals and garden plants both contribute greatly to human pleasure and wellbeing, especially in societies which have overcome the basic problems of food, shelter and clothing; many more wild plants could still be brought into cultivation to embellish our gardens, though we should probably be satisfied with those animals we already use as pets.

African violet

10. Recreational Hunting and Field Sports

Hunting evolved as an economic necessity and an essential part of the human life-style long before agriculture was invented. Later it became a pleasurable activity and a sport, and so in most societies still continues well after the economic need for it has disappeared. Today some people, mainly tribal, hunt wild mammals and birds, and many more hunt fish, as a primary part of their economy, either for food or to sell. Much more widespread is the combination of hunting both for the economic value of the prey and as a form of recreation or virility symbol. Shooting and liming birds around the Mediterranean, and the Inuit hunt for the bowhead whale *Balaena mysticetus* are notable examples.

Only in the more highly developed countries, mainly in Europe and North America, have shooting and fishing become almost entirely a recreation, or sometimes a means of asserting a masculine identity, often with an elaborate social ritual. This is often when hunting becomes controversial. From the dawn of history rulers and nobles have regarded the hunting of certain animals as their special privilege. In Europe it was the red deer and in India the tiger *Panthera tigris*. But the people have always hunted too, often risking severe penalties if they were caught. However much those who prefer to watch their wildlife undisturbed, and who go into the country primarily for its quietness, may dislike the idea, hunting wild animals still gives a very substantial amount of pleasure world-wide.

As it happens, sportsmen were among the first to promote the idea of species conservation, and the game reserve long preceded the wildlife sanctuary. The British founders, in 1903, of what later became the Fauna and Flora Preservation Society were almost all keen sportsmen, and were nicknamed 'the penitent butchers' for their pains. In the United States, wildlife conservation today is largely underpinned by the sale of hunting and fishing licences, and by taxes on the sale of sporting arms and ammunition and fishing tackle.

Almost any large mammal or bird can be the hunter's quarry, but in temperate countries deer (Cervidae), gamebirds such as pheasants, partridges, quail and francolins (Phasianidae), and wildfowl (ducks and geese, Anatidae) are among the most favoured. Most countries have their special favourites: the elk (moose) *Alces alces* in Sweden, the white-tailed deer *Odocoileus virginianus* in the United States, the fox *Vulpes vulpes* in England and the turtle dove *Streptopelia turtur* in south-west France.

Falconry is a specialised form of hunting using a bird of prey as the actual killer, notably the gyr *Falco rusticolus*, lanner *F.biarmicus* and peregrine falcons *F.peregrinus*, together with the goshawk *Accipiter gentilis*. The quarry may be hares, gamebirds, herons or, especially in the Middle East, houbara bustards *Chlamydotis undulata*. The impact of falconry on both predator and quarry species is discussed on p. 84.

Angling is an almost universal sport, though one which in many countries is hard to separate from subsistence or commercial fishing. Members of the salmon family Salmonidae, notably the Atlantic salmon *Salmo salar* and the brown trout *S.trutta*, are among a very large number of species that are fished for both purposes, sometimes by the same people, and as a result the brown trout has been widely introduced into the rivers of the temperate parts of the southern hemisphere. One of the social distinctions referred to is that between fishing for salmonids and so-called coarse fishing; this is often for members of the carp family Cyprinidae, such as the roach *Rutilus rutilus* in Europe or the North American Centrarchidae, such as the two black basses *Micropterus salmoides* and *M. dolomiei*. Angling has probably brought more human satisfaction than any other sport connected with wildlife. Marine fish are also caught for pleasure, including flatfish, such as the dab *Limanda limanda*, and bass *Morone labrax* inshore, and various species of tunny *Thunnus* and even small sharks in the open sea. Bait for anglers can also be quite a significant minor economic interest. Ontario alone exported some 500 million earthworms, worth \$17.5 million, to the United States in one recent year.

11. The Enjoyment of Wildlife

Throughout the world, many millions of people greatly enjoy the natural environment created by wild animals and plants. There is a tendency to treat the environment as somehow distinct from its component animals and

Lanner falcon

plants, and indeed some environments, such as ice caps, deserts and lava flows are effectively devoid of wildlife, but few people go to such places for recreation or mental refreshment. For most people, the attraction of visiting a wilderness area, spending a day in the countryside, or strolling in a town park, lies in the diversity of wildlife that these areas have to offer. Hedgeless farmed landscapes with only wheatfields in sight, or hillsides planted with conifers, may have their own grandeur, but for the full enjoyment of wildlife there must be some contrasting elements. Well-kept parks and gardens satisfy some people, but others feel the need for wilderness even if they are rarely able to go there.

Alongside this general enjoyment of nature is the specific enjoyment of animals and plants. In the developed world today probably more people enjoy watching and observing wild animals and plants than ever before, as witness the innumerable natural history and bird protection societies. Two of these alone, the National Audubon Society in the United States, and the Royal Society for the Protection of Birds in Britain, have a combined membership of more than three-quarters of a million. The larger mammals, birds, butterflies, trees and wild flowers are the groups most widely enjoyed, but many naturalists and nature lovers have more specialised tastes, such as bats, snakes and fungi. What is more, a great many people feel strongly that the great whales should be preserved, not because they ever expect to see one themselves, but just for the satisfaction of knowing that these great creatures still roam the oceans undisturbed.

A growing number of people are fortunate enough either to live nearby, or to be able to travel to see for themselves some of the great wildlife spectacles of the world: the floral display of an Alpine or Rocky Mountain meadow in June; the miraculously colourful coral gardens of tropical atolls such as the Maldive Islands; the massed curtains of hibernating monarch butterflies draping the trees in Mexico and California; the pink ribbon of millions of flamingoes lining the shores of Lake Nakuru in Kenya; the countless Magellan penguins assembled by their nesting holes in the vast rookery at Punta Tombo, Argentina; the day-long passage of migrating broad-winged hawks and other birds of prey past Hawk Mountain in the Appalachians; and the majestic spectacle of the annual wildebeest migration across the Serengeti and Mara plains in East Africa. These are all sights that those who can afford it will cross oceans and continents to see. They thus enter the realm of economics more positively than the simpler delights of rambling round Walden Pond in Massachusetts or Selborne village in southern England. These spectacles are the basis of an important slice of the international tourist industry; in countries such as Kenya, Zimbabwe and Rwanda they play a major part in earning foreign exchange and justifying to finance ministers the cost of maintaining national parks and wildlife refuges.

The many people who cannot travel to see wildlife can visit zoos, other collections of captive animals, botanic gardens and parks designed purely for pleasure; these all provide both enjoyment and a better understanding of the natural world.

It was the great Anglo-Irish orator Edmund Burke who complained that the age of sophists, economists and calculators had arrived, and the great Welsh orator Aneurin Bevan who castigated one of his colleagues as 'a desiccated calculating machine'. Their cries have to be constantly repeated when we try to persuade modern politicians and churchmen that the aesthetic and spiritual values of wildlife are at least as important as the material ones. Christianity has always been hampered in relation to wildlife by its limited interpretation of the divine injunction to 'replenish the earth, and subdue it : and have dominion over the fish of the sea, and over the fowl

Broad-winged hawks

Banyan

of the air, and over every living thing that moveth over the face of the earth'. This has been a factor in making the Christian churches relatively unresponsive to the conservation ethic, for their fundamentalists, including a recent US Secretary of the Interior, regard this text as a divine injunction to exploit, or even overexploit, wildlife for the benefit of mankind. Less extreme churchmen may think otherwise, but few do much to encourage a more enlightened way of carrying out this divine stewardship.

Even Buddhism, which does have an enlightened attitude towards wildlife, has not been very successful in restraining its devotees from killing wild animals. Yet throughout Asia often the only surviving groves of trees or other patches of natural vegetation surround temples or shrines. One of the most famous of such sacred groves is the Sarnath deer park on the Ganges near Benares, India, where Gautama Buddha preached some 2500 years ago. In Bali any giant tree growing near a spring, a well, a lake or a waterfall is holy, and nobody may harm it or contaminate the water. Since ancient times these trees have often been either peepul or bo trees *Ficus religiosa* or banyans *F.benghalensis*, relatives of the economically valuable fig *F.carica*; both are still among the most venerated trees in the world.

It was an Indian holy man who told a ruler of Sri Lanka in the third century BC: 'The birds of the air and the beasts have as equal a right to live and move about in any part of this land as thou. The land belongs to the people and all living things; thou art only its guardian'. As a result Sri Lanka's first wildlife sanctuary was established. Even today, strong local sentiment protects peacocks and rhesus monkeys in most parts of India, and orang-utans among the Iban in parts of Sarawak; in Brunei monkeys, pigs and many other animals are effectively protected because the people are mostly devout Muslims. In Ghana too, at least one village protects a troop of colobus monkeys for religious reasons, while in Cameroon a local taboo prevents any hunting on Mount Kupe. In Madagascar a traditional taboo of the Sakalar people against eating land tortoises has protected the now extremely rare angonoka *Geochelone yniphora*. The potential for the religious leaders of the world to promote a more rational attitude towards human exploitation of wildlife is clearly there. But few have yet felt impelled to do so, and even fewer politicians.

12. Wildlife as a Social Symbol

In some societies wildlife fulfils a much more basic need than just providing enjoyment and mental refreshment. It often symbolises people's fundamental beliefs about both their place in society and their value judgments on the environment. In many indigenous cultures throughout the world, animals are central to the totem system. Thus in Zimbabwe every Shona or Ndebele child is born into its father's totem, which will vitally influence the child's own character and future; he or she will make a special effort to emulate the qualities in which the totem animal is held to excel. Among the Shonas the members of the Shimba totem praise and emulate the strength and authority of the lion; those in the Nzou totem admire the size, wonder and majestic tusks of the elephant; and in the Shato totem they admire and understand the patience and craftiness of the python.

A pale reflection of the totem system occurs even in fully developed countries, in such national symbols as the British lion, the American eagle and the French cock, not to mention the double-headed eagle of the Hapsburg Empire. The bald eagle's official classification as an endangered bird has greatly helped the movement to save endangered species in the United States, where most of the individual states also have their own state symbols – mammals, birds, plants, and even reptiles and insects. Thus

Hawaii has the nene goose *Branta sandvicensis* as its state bird, California the desert tortoise *Gopherus agassizi* as its state reptile, and North Dakota the pasque flower *Pulsatilla patens* as its state plant. Trinidad and Tobago has recently adopted the threatened scarlet ibis *Eudocimus ruber* as its national symbol. Another notable Third World national symbol is Guatemala's quetzal *Pharomachrus mocinno*, the most gorgeous of the trogons, a brilliant green bird with an immensely long tail. Alas, the bird's notoriety seems to result in its more frequent capture as a pet, rather than affording it protection. The quetzal has been a special bird for centuries; in the days of Montezuma, the great sixteenth century Mexican king, the use of its plumes was restricted to royalty and nobility.

Conservationists have so far hardly begun to exploit the possibilities inherent in the widespread survival of totems, and the more recent creation of national symbols. Animals and plants are also widely used as symbols of human qualities in speech and literature, through such similes as 'busy as a bee' or 'prickly as a cactus', and in poetic images such as Blake's 'Tyger, tyger, burning bright'. The part they play in human cultural activities, notably literature and the visual arts, is immense. Moreover, as Francis Klingender pointed out, 'animals were the first subject to challenge the artistic faculties of men', as shown by cave art all over the world. Wildlife is thus deeply embedded in all our present cultures, western as well as oriental, Marxist (consider their invective against capitalist hyaenas) as well as tribal. All of them would be greatly impoverished by the disappearance from the wild of the species or groups of animals and plants so familiar to us through these figures of speech.

Nene or Hawaiian goose

2 The Diversity of Life: Genes, Species and Ecosystems

There is considerable dispute as to the origin of life on earth, but none as to its diversity. Whether life arose from a primeval soup, dust from outer space, or a combination of the two, its subsequent split into the five kingdoms of bacteria, unicellular organisms, fungi, plants and animals (though there is some doubt about the exact boundary between them) and their massive radiations into millions of species have produced an enormous diversity of living forms.

The templates of life are genes, made of deoxyribonucleic acid (DNA), which pass the essential characteristics of life from one generation to another. Gene, genus (*plural*, genera), genesis and generation all derive from the ancient Greek *genos*, meaning descent. Genetics is the study of heredity, and genetic resources are natural renewable resources, i.e. wildlife, both animals and plants, as distinct from such non-renewable mineral resources as iron ore, coal and petroleum.

Evolution is the process of gradual change by which the original genes which started life on earth produced the multifarious present-day forms of life. Through cumulative changes in successive generations, variations produced in the genes by mutation and other mechanisms have combined with selective adaptation to produce life forms as diverse as a mushroom and a coast redwood, a grasshopper and a giraffe.

Genes represent sections of the famous DNA double helix and are transmitted on chromosomes, twisted threads of protein and DNA found in the nucleus of cells. When a cell divides, so do the chromosomes, copying faithfully the genetic code in each gene. In sexual reproduction the division halves the genetic information, and fusion of the sex cells is needed to restore the full complement. All living organisms are built of cells, though those of bacteria are less organised; the most primitive (protozoa and planktonic algae) are one-celled.

From bacteria and protozoans onwards, we are dealing with individuals grouped into species, and just as genes are the micro-units with which biologists deal, so species and their various subdivisions and aggregations are the macro-units. Indeed in one sense species are the vehicles that genes use to perpetuate themselves. Laymen use the terms 'species', 'race', 'variety' and 'kind' more or less interchangeably. To biologists, however, the first three have precise meanings while the fourth is just a literary word.

The scientific definition of a species is a group of individual animals or plants which potentially can interbreed only with each other. This is a definition that frays slightly at the edges, but taxonomists nowadays tend to reclassify any interbreeding species as subspecies, as they have recently done with the North American woodpeckers *Colaptes auratus*, *C.cafer* and

Silver-washed fritillary

C.chrysoides, the yellow-shafted, red-shafted and golden flickers, all now regarded as subspecies of *C.auratus*. A subspecies, also called a race, is a subdivision or population of a species with distinct common characteristics, usually separated geographically from other populations. Subspecies sometimes interbreed along their boundaries, as with the flickers and also the Eurasian carrion and hooded crows *Corvus corone corone* and *C.corone cornix*, whose interbreeding zone crosses Scotland.

A variety, in its strict biological meaning, is a distinct form of a plant species, often due to a single gene change, such as the var. *quinquevulnera* of the Eurasian small-flowered catchfly *Silene gallica*, which has a large deep crimson spot at the base of each white or pale pink petal. Albino variants also occasionally turn up in many red, pink, blue or purple-flowered species, one of the most familiar in Europe being that of ling heather *Calluna vulgaris*, the 'lucky white heather' of the superstitious. In animals these simple variations are called morphs or colour phases, as in the bridled form of the guillemot or common murre *Uria aalge*, which has a narrow white eye-ring and a line back from the eye, and the silver-grey variety *valezina* of the Eurasian silver-washed fritillary butterfly *Argynnis paphia*.

Taxonomists group species into higher categories which have little real validity outside the classifications invented by the taxonomists themselves, from the great eighteenth-century Swedish naturalist Linnaeus onwards. Thus the catchfly just mentioned is in the same genus or group of species as the red and white campions *Silene dioica* and *S. pratensis*, and the carrion crow is likewise congeneric with the raven *Corvus corax*. Genera are then grouped into families, the catchflies and campions, for instance, along with the pinks *Dianthus* and the chickweeds *Stellaria*, in the Caryophyllaceae; the crows and ravens go in the Corvidae, together with the magpies *Pica* and the various genera of jays, such as the North American *Cyanocitta* and the Eurasian *Garrulus*. Animal families usually end in -idae, but plant ones in -aceae, the grasses Gramineae being one exception. The higher groupings – orders, classes and phyla in the animal kingdom, classes and divisions in the four other kingdoms – are more artificial constructs still.

Most macroscopic species are so distinct from each other that they can be distinguished by the naked eye, though vertebrates and higher plants are generally easier to tell apart than invertebrates and lower plants. Even among the vertebrates and higher plants, however, some species groups and pairs are not so easily separated. In Africa the *Cisticola* warblers and in North America both the *Empidonax* flycatchers and the parulid wood warblers in their fall plumages are notorious in this respect. There are also some species of the Holarctic sedges *Carex* which experts will not name until they have examined the ripe fruit with a lens. Tribal people, on the other hand, have often distinguished visually similar species long before the scientists appeared. When Michael Graham was studying the fishes of Lake Victoria in East Africa in the 1920s, he discovered a new species of cichlid fish, later named *Tilapia grahami*, which was well known to local fishermen but had been overlooked by western biologists. In New Guinea too, Ernst Mayr found that the local hunters had names for all but one of the 137 species of birds in the Arfak Mountains.

1. Speciation

The evolutionary process by which species are formed is called speciation. New species may be formed when, over a long period of time, any population of animals or plants is divided into two or more geographically or ecologically separated groups, and are unable to hybridise at their interfaces.

Small-flowered catchfly

Azure-winged magpie

Such separations may occur when ice ages, or other long-term climatic changes, drive populations to the opposite sides of a land mass. This must have happened both to the two meadowlarks in North America, which did speciate as the eastern *Sturnella magna* and the western *S.neglecta*, and to the azure-winged magpie *Cyanopica cyanus* in Eurasia, which however has remained the same species in south-west Europe as in the Far East. Separations may also occur when natural or man-made forces eliminate intervening habitat, as with the mountain forests of tropical Africa, making what was a continuum into a series of 'islands'. The labiate *Coleus elongatus*, confined to a single rocky outcrop in Sri Lanka, is a plant species believed to have arisen as a result of this process.

This island effect also occurs when the original stock colonises an existing island, as an ancestral brent goose *Branta bernicla* did in Hawaii, to become the nene *B. sandvicensis*, and an ancestral tortoise in the Galapagos to become *Geochelone elephantopus*. The later development of a distinct subspecies of tortoise on each major island of the archipelago illustrates the process of speciation clearly (as it did first to Darwin), such geographical subspecies being one important step towards the formation of new species. The tortoises from the various islands can still interbreed if brought together, but do not get the opportunity unless man intervenes. The Galapagos mockingbirds actually have speciated on three islands: those on Floreana, Española and San Cristobal are each regarded as a species distinct from *Nesomimus parvulus*, which occupies the remaining islands.

Giant tortoise

On a smaller scale, aquatic organisms may speciate when water levels change, cutting off parts of lakes or rivers, or when cave systems become separated into distinct sections, inaccessible from each other. Thus several species and subspecies of seal have developed after their parent stocks were isolated in landlocked lakes and inland seas: the Baikal seal *Phoca sibirica* in Lake Baikal in Siberia, the Caspian seal *P.caspica* in the Caspian Sea, and the Saimaa seal in Lake Saimaa in southern Finland. The Saimaa seal illustrates the process particularly clearly, for it is the subspecies *saimensis* of the ringed seal *P.hispida*, which breeds nearby in the Baltic Sea, from which Lake Saimaa was cut off comparatively recently in geological terms.

The genes of most species normally carry a considerable reservoir of potential variation, as has recently been proved in Sweden with the Atlantic salmon and the brown trout. The salmon has become subdivided, over the past 10,000 to 15,000 years, into numerous genetically distinct populations, both within and between major drainage areas. Similarly with the trout, twin lakes at Lake Bunnerssjörna each contain two such subpopulations with apparently complete reproductive isolation. The genetic divergence within each of these population pairs was very small, but it was there, an example of evolution beginning within a single lake. Evolution has actually occurred in many other lakes worldwide, such as Lake Tanganyika and other African lakes, with their many distinct species of the cichlid fishes *Tilapia*.

So it is not surprising to find that widely distributed species vary considerably in different parts of their continuous range. Thus the Eurasian great tit *Parus major* has seventeen races, including the very distinctive Indian grey tit *P.m. stupae*, and the Holarctic herring gull has ten. These existing differences will, of course, intensify if parts of the population are isolated, say by a drying up of the steppes or a southward advance of the tundra, since mutation, recombination of genes, inbreeding and the whole process of natural selection will continuously work towards adapting any isolated stock to its changing environment.

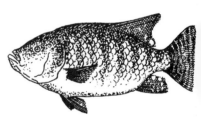

Tilapia

New plant species may also arise when the chromosomes of a hitherto infertile hybrid are doubled. This is what happened after the introduced North American cord grass *Spartina alternifolia* hybridised with the native *S. maritima* in southern England. The resulting new species, *S. anglica*, has since colonised much of the coastline of Britain and adjacent Europe. Likewise the common European hemp-nettle *Galeopsis tetrahit* appears to be a cross between two other *Galeopsis* species, after a similar happening.

Though it may take thousands of years for stocks to develop to the point of becoming new species through being unable to interbreed with their parent stocks, morphological changes not involving a genetic barrier can sweep through wild populations in a remarkably short time. Thus in the past hundred years or so industrial melanism has completely altered the balance between normal and melanic forms in a number of insect species in smoke-polluted areas. The peppered moth *Biston betularia* in northern England provides a remarkable example. Not only did its melanic form

Flying lizard

Rhododendron hirsutum

virtually replace the normal one because against soot-covered backgrounds the moth was camouflaged against its predators, but now that smoke pollution is being controlled, the normal form is increasing again. Another rapid change has been the evolution of a sandy-coloured form of the house mouse to match the background of its new habitat, the sand dunes of North Bull Island, close to Dublin, Ireland.

Closely related species may be prevented from interbreeding by various behavioural isolating mechanisms. Courtship rituals and displays are among the most important. Male Asian flying lizards *Draco* and neotropical anole lizards *Anolis* attract mates by extending a brightly coloured throat fan and bobbing their heads. The exact timing of the throat-fan displays and head bobs is specific to each species and attracts the females of that species only. Similar devices apply to the courtship rituals of dabbling ducks and of many of the centrarchid fishes of North America and cichlid fishes of Africa and South America. Yet in captivity, deprived of the choice of a mate, they will all freely interbreed within their own genus or family. Likewise, male moths are attracted only by the pheromones (airborne scented chemicals) produced by females of their own species.

Closely related species that inhabit the same geographic area may also be prevented from hybridising by different breeding seasons. In north-eastern North America, for instance, the wood frog *Rana sylvatica* breeds in the early spring, while the green frog *R. clamitans* does so a month later. Closely related plants may likewise avoid hybridising by flowering at different times, or perhaps more often by having different soil or other ecological preferences in the same region. One of the species pair may be a calcicole, growing in basic or calcareous soil, and the other a calcifuge that requires acid soil: in Europe, for instance, the two alpine rhododendrons *Rhododendron hirsutum* (calcicole) and *R. ferrugineum* (calcifuge) and the two common spotted orchids *Dactylorhiza fuchsii* (calcicole) and *D. maculata* (calcifuge). Habitat also separates several congeneric species of crocodile: the estuarine and Siamese crocodiles *Crocodylus porosus* and *C. siamensis* and the American and Cuban crocodiles *C. acutus* and *C. rhombifer* are two species pairs that interbreed in captivity, but not in the wild because the first of each pair inhabits estuarine or coastal waters, while the second lives in fresh water.

Even when all these difficulties are overcome, there are still genetic barriers. Either ova cannot be fertilised, or births are aborted, or young when born are sickly, or the offspring is healthy but sterile. Quite closely related species can be genetically incompatible in this way. Goats and sheep, belonging to the different genera *Capra* and *Ovis*, can mate, but the resulting embryo invariably dies before birth. A stage further is reached by some species of tobacco, which can hybridise, but their offspring develop tumours and die before they are old enough to flower or fruit. Finally the mule, the hybrid between the horse *Equus caballus* and the ass *E. asinus*, is quite healthy but also completely sterile. If these behavioural and genetic barriers had not evolved, species could not have perpetuated themselves. Life would have been a mishmash of more or less similar forms.

Indeed 'a mishmash of more or less similar forms' is just what man has achieved in many areas by moving stocks of animals and plants around. The US Forest Service, for instance, has reported that 'the indiscriminate stocking' of 'virtually every habitable water' throughout the western United States with untold millions of rainbow trout *Salmo gairdnerii* and cutthroat trout *S. clarkii* and their subsequent interbreeding with the native trout species has led to 'the almost complete elimination of pure native trout stocks'. Much the same has happened in Europe with widespread translocation of different stocks of the brown trout, even in such apparently remote and unspoiled regions as the Scottish Highlands, where the Vikings seem to have led the way. This story can be repeated for most, if not all, the major game animals in Europe, such as red deer, grey partridge and ring-necked pheasant.

2. The Total Number of Species

By extrapolating from habitats in which the numbers of species are well documented to others where numbers are poorly known, and taking into account the rate at which new species are being discovered, Tom Lovejoy of WWF-USA has estimated that there are between 3 and 10 million species of animals and plants in the world today, including, of course, all deep-sea and other marine species. This may, however, prove to be a gross underestimate, since some quite recent research in the rainforests of Panama, Brazil and Peru, using non-persistent insecticide smoke in the canopy, suggests that there may be as many as 30 million arthropods alone.

Rainbow trout

So far only around a million and a half animal and plant species have actually been described by scientists, two-thirds of them in the temperate regions, where relatively fewer species exist. An additional 10,000 new species are being discovered and described each year; no fewer than 80 new flowering plants have been found in the state of Utah alone in the past fifteen years. At this rate it will take some 1000-1500 years to describe all the remaining species. However, man-made changes are likely to bring about the extinction of between 15 and 25 per cent of the world's species within the next 20 years. Most of these extinctions will occur in species-rich tropical ecosystems, especially rainforests and cloud forests, and will involve many species that may never be discovered at all. Indeed, a great many undiscovered species must already have become extinct, especially in the rainforests and their rivers, and on oceanic islands. A major genetic resource has thus been lost, and is continuing to be lost, even before we have a chance to assess its value, and this does not just include a myriad of insects and fungi, but freshwater fish of potential food value and higher plants that might yield life-saving drugs.

The vertebrates are the most completely known class of species, animal or plant, with an estimated total of almost 39,000, including approximately 4237 mammals, 8580 birds, 6054 reptiles, 2760 amphibians and 19,350 fishes. The fishes are the least known group and are believed to have the largest number of undescribed species awaiting discovery. The vertebrates of the Holarctic, the north temperate zone that covers Europe, the USSR, China, Japan and North America, are the best known to science, with China as a relative lacuna. There are very many more invertebrate species, with 1.4 million already described and many millions more undiscovered. More than half of all known invertebrates are insects, the largest class in the arthropod phylum.

The flowering plants, numbering some 280,000, are the best known class of plants; even so, a substantial number of species await discovery and scientific description, although of course many of these are well known to tribal people. Indeed, Professor R. E. Schultes, Chairman of the SSC Ethnobotany Group, believes there may be as many as half a million flowering plants in the world. About 160,000 flowering plant species grow in the tropics, half of them in Latin America, of which at least 10,000 are believed to be unknown to science. Numbers of bacteria, algae, fungi, lichens, mosses and ferns are very much greater.

Another way of looking at the importance of species in the biosphere is to calculate their biomass, the total weight of living organisms in any area. Thus the vast herds of wildebeest, zebra and other ungulates that migrate through the Serengeti Plains of Tanzania have been estimated to have a biomass of between 7 and 11 grams per square metre. Yet in the Malaysian rainforest the biomass of termites alone is between six and six times as great as that of all the mammals and birds; and the biomass of earthworms in an orchard in eastern England has been estimated at 287 g/m², or between 25 and 40 times as much as the Serengeti ungulates. So it is all too easy to underestimate the importance of invertebrates in ecosystems. Elephants should be contrasted, not with mice, but with termites and earthworms, which form the animal base of the ecosystem whose summit is the elephant. Of course there are plant and fungus bases and summits too, from mycorrhizal fungi to baobabs and redwoods.

3. Centres of Maximum Diversity and Endemism

Scattered about the world are regions and localities, sometimes quite extensive, that hold an exceptional diversity of species; this is usually due to the presence of a large number of endemics, i.e. species which are found nowhere else. The preservation of adequate samples of such habitats is of the utmost importance if their genetic resources are to be saved.

Tropical forests are the most extensive areas of maximum diversity. Although they occupy only 7 per cent of the land surface of the globe, they hold two-fifths of all known species, a greater range of animals and plants than any other terrestrial habitat. The lowland forests of eastern Brazil are a good example of both species diversity and multiple endemics. In addition to many primates, they hold 940 bird species; 214 are endemic, of which 80 per cent are birds of humid lowland forests. Yet these forests are among the most endangered habitats in the world. Losses in three states show what has happened: in Sao Paulo, forest cover had been reduced by 1979 from an original 85 per cent to 7 per cent; in Espirito Santo, one of the richest states in endemic forest species, an original forest area of 38,000 km² had fallen by 1973 to 3650 km²; in Seregipe, the original 40 per cent forest cover is now down to 0.1 per cent. Obviously, all the wildlife has been acutely affected. The habitat of the golden lion tamarin, a marmoset with a lion-like mane, has been reduced to two tiny fragments of forest in the state of Rio de Janeiro. Fewer than 100 individuals survive in the wild, mainly in the Poco d'Anta reserve; without protection here the tamarin would exist only in captivity.

Golden lion tamarin

Similar centres of endemism for forest birds exist in East Africa, in some of the isolated mountain ranges, notably the Usambara, Uluguru and Uzungwa Mountains in Tanzania, and in coastal forests, such as Arabuko-Sokoke in Kenya. The Usambaras, in particular, hold unusually high proportions of forest endemics in millipedes (Diplopoda), 84 per cent; lizards, 64 per cent; and Sphecidae (Hymenoptera), 37 per cent. In West Africa, Mount Nimba includes among its long list of endemics the otter shrew *Micropotamogale lamottei* and the toad *Nectophrynoides occidentalis*, the only tailless amphibian in the world that is completely viviparous. Madeira is noted for its endemic millipedes, with no fewer than 25 species of the genus *Cylindrouilus*.

The Cape Floristic Kingdom is the richest of the world's six major assemblages of plant species, yet it is confined to a short strip of coast in Cape Province, that occupies no more than 4 per cent of the land area of the Republic of South Africa. It is equivalent in rank to the Boreal Kingdom, which covers the whole of the Holarctic, i.e. all of Europe, northern Asia and North America. This Fynbos flora, with its wealth of heaths (Ericaceae) and proteas, has 1300 species per 10 km² compared with 395 and 420 for its nearest rivals, which are in the neotropics. Its 6000 species are concentrated in relict patches roughly the size of the Kruger National Park, and totalling 1.8 million hectares, which represent only 40 per cent of the original extent of the Fynbos. Some 70 per cent of the species are endemics, and 1244 are threatened in some way, 36 of them probably recently extinct, 96 endangered, 125 vulnerable, 336 critically rare and 544 probably in hazard. This is the greatest known concentration of threatened plants in any temperate region.

Islands and archipelagos provide many centres of endemism. This is partly because species may just get marooned, as have four laurels in the Canary Islands, *Laurus azorica, Apollonias barbusana, Ocotea foetens* and *Persea indica*, all relics of the now virtually extinct Mediterranean flora that occupied southern Europe in the Tertiary era, some 15-40 million years ago. Isolation and the absence of competition both also encourage evolutionary radiation. In Australia, for instance, the marsupials have radiated to fill most of the niches occupied by placental mammals in the rest of the world. Kangaroos fill the ungulates' herbivore niche; the thylacine, or so-called Tasmanian wolf, may still occupy the carnivorous predator niche of wolves and the larger cats; and the various marsupial mice fill the small rodent niche. Madagascar saw a similar radiation by primitive placental mammals: lemurs replace monkeys, and three endemic viverrids, the Malagasy civet *Fossa fossa*, the fanalouc *Eupleres goudotii* and the fossa *Cryptoprocta ferox* fill the carnivores' niches. Madagascar also has many endemic plants, and even an endemic family, the Didieriaceae, trees or shrubs adapted to semi-desert conditions, resembling in many ways both cacti and the tree euphorbias of the African savannas. Indeed, two-thirds of Madagascar's estimated 250,000 animal and plant species are endemic; most of them live in forests, and 90 per cent of the forests have now been destroyed.

Fossa

Archipelagos obviously offer greater opportunities for multiple endemism, because the relative isolation of each island allows further evolution of distinct forms. The most famous such island group is the Galapagos, which yielded Darwin's restatement of evolution theory. The mockingbirds and giant tortoises were mentioned on p. 43, and David Lack made the classic analysis of the ground-finches Geospizinae. This subfamily of seed-eaters has radiated and adapted so as to fill niches occupied elsewhere by grosbeaks and hawfinches with their very stout kernel-cracking bills; ordinary seed-eaters, such as finches or weaverbirds; insectivorous warblers, and treecreepers and small woodpeckers. Each group has a bill adapted to its own specialised way of food-seeking.

A similar radiation has occurred in another isolated archipelago, Hawaii, although here a great many of the endemic forms, including birds and flowering plants, have been exterminated, both by direct killing and by habitat destruction. The pomace flies *Drosophila* are a particularly striking example, with some 900 species occupying a very wide range of habitats, originating, it is believed, from only one or two ancestral species. This total includes some 200 pomace fly species believed to be still awaiting discovery, and of course there may be many more extinct endemics. In the Marquesas, a less isolated Pacific archipelago, continuing forest destruction by grazing livestock threatens two endemic bird species and seven subspecies; indeed two subspecies are probably already extinct.

In the western Pacific, where the ocean trench faunas all have a more or less common origin and so share the same genera, some 60 per cent of the species in individual trenches or trench systems are endemic. This is why species conservation needs to be taken into account in any future plans for exploiting the sea-bed.

4. Species in Ecosystems

Ecosystems encompass much more than what nineteenth-century natural-ists meant by habitat. An ecosystem comprises not only species and their habitat, but also the processes by which the two interact. Each animal and plant is an integral part of its own ecosystem, to which it has become adapted and without which (or something very like it) it cannot survive in the wild. The whole web of interactions, together with their physical background, comprises the ecosystem, which may be as large as the Gobi Desert or as small as a single thermal pool. Whole species can thus occupy tiny ecosystems, as the midge *Edwardsina tasmaniensis* in a single waterfall in Tasmania and the wolf spider *Adelocosa anops* in a few lava tubes in Hawaii.

Each ecosystem is influenced by three sets of factors:

1. *Climatic*, the long-term influence of the weather, especially temper-ature and rainfall.

2. *Edaphic*, the effects of the soil and other parts of the physical environment.

3. *Biotic*, the impact of living animals and plants, such as the grazing of vegetation by herbivores, or the shading out of grassland plants by trees and shrubs. A special biotic factor is the anthropogenic one, the influence of man, whether by direct killing of animals or felling of trees, or indirectly through drainage or grazing by livestock.

Darwin's food chain

Cats eat mice

An ecosystem runs on energy, which ultimately derives from the sun. In above-ground terrestrial ecosystems, such as forests, grasslands or salt-marshes, the green plants capture the energy of sunlight, using their chlorophyll or green colouring matter, while the herbivorous or grazing animals, such as insects, wild geese and antelopes, get the bulk of their energy from the plants. Carnivorous animals, however, obtain their energy second, third or even fourth hand, by feeding on the herbivores or smaller carnivores, often laced with some vegetable matter. The whole process is a food chain, with each link a plant, a herbivore or a carnivore.

Darwin's famous food chain showed how the frequency of clovers in a district might depend on the number of domestic cats. Cats eat field-mice, which destroy the nests and combs of bumblebees, which are the principal pollinators of clovers. An African food chain might run from the Nile crocodile which eats the barbel, a fish which preys on bream and carp, which in turn feed on the mosquitoes that carry malaria. Thus overhunting of crocodiles to make luxury goods could lead to increased malaria in African villages. The original cedars of Lebanon are suffering from a fungus disease *Lophodermium pinastri*, because they are being weakened by the defoliation produced by the numbers of insects, which thrive in the absence of birds, which are shot by man.

Once they are mature, animals and plants at the top of the food chain, such as the elephants and rhinos among herbivores, and the great cats among carnivores, are normally not vulnerable to predators, but mature forest trees, such as oak, sal *Shorea* or redwood, though not threatened as individuals, can still form part of a food chain with their foliage. Even species at the top of the chain, however, eventually die and become carrion or rotten wood; then they enter a different food chain by providing energy for numerous scavengers, from carrion beetles and crows to fungi and furniture beetles.

The feeding regimes of herbivores, carnivores, scavengers, saprophytes,

Bumblebees pollinate clover

parasites and some other groups thus provide a continuous flow of energy through each ecosystem. Much of this energy is lost on the way, either as heat during digestion or other metabolic processes, or by migration when animals or plant seeds pass into another ecosystem; but the whole ecosystem is continuously reinforced by fresh solar energy acquired by the green plants through photosynthesis.

Ecology, the science as distinct from the political catchword, studies this flow of energy through ecosystems, and the way in which all the numerous species, from protozoans and seaweeds and snails to sparrows and seals and oaks, fit into the infinitely complex web that every ecosystem constitutes. Wildlife conservation is in fact the maintenance of the energy flow through each ecosystem or habitat, whether alpine meadow, peat bog, gallery forest or tundra. Its prime aim is to maintain the variety of species, and so of genetic resources, and the web of their interrelationships. For each animal and plant specialises in converting energy at some stage of some food chain, even if it is a more or less omnivorous, like the European badger, the coatimundi or the Malayan sun bear.

Coatimundi

Left to themselves, ecosystems proceed over long periods of time towards a hypothetical climax. The tropical rainforests in the Equatorial belt, the tundra that rings the far north of the Holarctic, and the saltmarshes around the coasts of Europe and North America are all such climaxes. Over most of the developed parts of the world, however, the natural succession has been upset by man, and is deflected by agriculture, plantation forestry, or some other economic activity. Even much of the tropical rainforest is semi-natural or secondary, where the natural forces are repeatedly interrupted by fire or hurricanes. More recently widespread temporary cultivation, the 'slash and burn' or swidden technique, has frustrated the natural succession in the rainforest. Even the East African savannas, with their immense herds of antelopes, zebras and other ungulates, remain as grassland and do not become forests largely because of fire, which is sometimes natural but is more often due to the pyromania which is deeply embedded in the behaviour patterns of rural man. In this case the elephant also plays a part, periodically uprooting trees and thus restoring bush to savanna, as has happened especially in the Tsavo East National Park in Kenya in recent years.

Zebra

In the cultivated parts of the world man creates his own artificial, or at least semi-natural, ecosystems that replace the communities of wild plants and animals with cultivated crops and farm animals. These bring with them a group of well adapted wild plants and animals, which, because they compete with man's purposes, are stigmatised as weeds or pests. The distinguished ecologist Sir Frank Fraser Darling, however, pointed out that the destruction of natural or semi-natural habitat is not necessarily a bad thing, provided no species actually become extinct. Fresh and more complex ecosystems, which otherwise might never have existed, may be created as a result. The chalk grasslands of southern England, for instance, maintained for hundreds of years by sheep grazing, have a very rich community of flowering plants and their associated insects; likewise the Mediterranean *maquis*, end product of millennia of overgrazing and burning.

Any change in an ecosystem that either reduces or increases its genetic diversity, as when an old grass meadow is ploughed up, or grazing ceases and allows the meadow to develop into woodland, will affect the flow of energy. In either case some species inhabiting the ecosystem may be put at a disadvantage and others may benefit, sometimes greatly. In depleted ecosystems one or two species, their natural checks removed, may increase disproportionately, thus diverting more of the energy flow through themselves. A classic instance occurred when a group of moose walked across the ice one winter to the hitherto mooseless Isle Royale in Lake Superior, and subsequently increased to the point of grossly overbrowsing the range (see p. 137). The balance was restored when a pack of wolves also crossed the ice and began to prey on the moose.

As depleted species are often tied to a particular habitat or microhabitat, their stocks can usually only be built up again if the existing energy flow is at least maintained and preferably increased. This is *conservation*, a positive act directed towards rebuilding stocks, as distinct from *preservation*, which used to imply just putting a fence round an area and leaving it alone. A classic instance of the limitations of this kind of preservation occurred with the buttercup *Ranunculus ophioglossifolius*, found only in two small ponds in southern England. One pond was acquired and fenced in, to keep cattle out. After a few years, however, nearly all the surviving plants were actually outside the fence; in some years none at all were inside it. It turned out that the germination of the seeds depended on cattle hoofprints making bare places round the pond, although human footprints would also do. When the cattle were fenced out of the pond, the plant became endangered within its own reserve.

The basic pattern of animal and plant population dynamics is one of many young being born or hatched or many seeds germinating each season, but only a few surviving. If all young animals and plants were to survive, there would soon be no room on earth for each fresh annual increment. In a stable population, the very long-term and slow-moving mechanism of evolution selects only a small fraction of each generation to provide the breeding stock of the next. Whatever may be established in future about the mechanism of the great evolutionary radiations, such as those of the mammals and flowering plants, classic Darwinian evolution clearly works at the level of micro-evolution, from year to year. Thus, each winter, innumerable individual wild animals and plants die because they have proved biologically inefficient in some way or other, usually in finding enough to eat or evading predation. So the first rule of good conservation is to harvest or crop, at the end of each breeding season, no more than the number of individuals that would otherwise die or fail to germinate, thereby assuring enough parents to breed the next generation. This is what is meant by exploitation on a sustainable yield basis, and even this may mean depriving some natural predator of its prey, or herbivore or frugivore of its sustenance. Only if a stock is already expanding is it permissible to crop more than is needed, to correct the natural mortality and sustain a steady population. It was the erroneous belief that the Antarctic stocks of the minke whale were increasing that led the International Whaling Commission in the early 1980s to agree on what many whale scientists held to be excessive quotas, which later had to be severely cut back.

The maintenance of more or less stable ecosystems, what used to be called the balance of nature, thus depends very much on the maintenance of species diversity. Just how vulnerable and fragile this balance and diversity is, is discussed in Chapters 5 and 6, which deal with the two prime threats, overexploitation and habitat destruction.

Depletion, Endangerment and Extinction 3

Much ecological theory is based on the concept of an equilibrium community (climax), just as economics postulates an equilibrium to which economic forces tend. In both disciplines these equilibria, insofar as they exist, are not static, but dynamic. An oakwood, a pinewood and a dipterocarp forest are all such climaxes, but though they appear to be constant, they are in fact changing all the time. Even the most majestic redwood is inexorably bound for death, and on its fall the whole cycle begins again; another redwood rises in its place, so that the forest as a whole looks the same. Ecosystems, at all their stages, are made up of a multitude of animal and plant populations, each one either increasing, decreasing or in a fluctuating steady state, which is as near to being stable as a natural population ever gets.

It is against this background that the process of extinction, so conspicuous in this present age of rapid change, must be examined. Just as every individual living organism (except for some clonal plants, such as bracken and certain grasses) proceeds to an ultimate death, which may with long-lived trees such as the bristlecone pine *Pinus aristata* be some thousands of years later, so every distinct animal and plant population (whether the whole or only part of a species) waxes to a peak and ultimately wanes to extinction. This process too may be lengthy and, as with the coelacanth, the tuatara and cockroaches, may take tens or even hundreds of millions of years. The problem today is the recent great acceleration of the rate of extinction, almost entirely due to human activity.

The process of decline can have its ups and downs, as was shown by the striking terminal fluctuations of the isolated population of the now extinct heath hen at Martha's Vineyard, Massachusetts. An animal on its way to extinction can undergo a temporary, quite dramatic increase, if, as is the case with all grouse, cyclical fluctuations are normal. Therefore, one difficulty we face in managing genetic resources is to know when a downward trend is temporary, and when it is permanent and likely to end in extinction.

Since we do not know just how many species there are, we cannot calculate either the total current rate of extinction, or how much of it is due to human influence; we can only be sure that this proportion is substantial. Estimates, such as the loss of one-quarter of the world's animals and plants by the twenty-first century, or one million extinctions in Amazonia by the end of this century, representing nearly 40,000 species a year, or one species per minute worldwide at the present time, may all sound exaggerated, but the current rate of habitat destruction would have seemed equally extravagant if forecast by a naturalist in 1886, or even in 1936.

Bristlecone pine

51

Tom Lovejoy has made an estimate, for both animals and plants, based on the known rate of extinction for mammals and with a number of inevitably arbitrary assumptions. His main problem was how to take into account the undescribed species, believed to be 85 per cent of the total. Mammals are often large, so we know more about their extinctions within historic times than about those of any other group except birds. Lovejoy therefore assumed that for each mammal species known to become extinct, a further 50 animal or plant species would independently become extinct, and also that the factors responsible for each of these extinctions would carry off an additional ten species. Multiplying these two figures means that for each recorded mammal extinction, some 500 other animals and plants would also have become extinct. We have records of twelve mammal species becoming extinct in the period 1770-1870, when human influences may be assumed to have been less important than in 1870-1970, when there were 43 mammal extinctions. This gives us an average extinction rate of some 6000 species of all kinds per century during the past 500 years. Since even in the late eighteenth and early nineteenth centuries a great many species were being exterminated by man, Lovejoy thought it safer to give the current natural extinction rate of all species as between 1000 and 10,000 per century.

The number of bird extinctions for the earliest recorded period, 1670-1770, is ten, on which basis the total extinction rate would be 5000 per century. To get some idea of the influence of man on the rate of extinction, we can then take the mammal and bird figures for 1870-1970 (mammals 43, birds 41), which produce an extinction rate of 21,500 based on mammals or 20,500 based on birds. Though these calculations depend on quite arbitrary assumptions, they do at least suggest that for earlier centuries we are talking about tens of thousands, not hundreds of thousands of extinctions.

There are comparatively few undescribed mammal and bird species, except perhaps for bats and rodents, so we are on firmer ground in examining the rates of extinction of these two groups without using them to extrapolate the rates for all living things. The increasing impact of man on the rate of extinction appears from the following table, which shows the percentages of known extinctions as a proportion of all known species of both mammals and birds.

Century	Mammals	Birds
17th	0.19	0.01 (the dodo)
18th	0.21	0.23
19th	0.47	0.45
20th	0.54	0.22

The near coincidence between the mammal and bird figures for the eighteenth and nineteenth centuries is remarkable, but the bird extinction rates for the nineteenth and twentieth centuries are affected by the fact that as many as seven Hawaiian honeycreepers became extinct in the last decade of the nineteenth century, representing 0.08 per cent of all bird species.

A Hawaiian honeycreeper, the iiwi
Vestiaria coccinea

1. Biological Groupings

Biologically, in relation to their population dynamics, animal and plant species can be divided into five groups:

B 1 Species which are comparatively few in number and slowly increasing, while establishing themselves in a new environment, as for instance all introduced and and newly invading species in their early years.

B 2 Species which are rapidly increasing and occupying a new environment, e.g. the cattle egret and the Mexican house finch in North
America, and the neotropical daisy relative *Galinsoga parviflora* in
many temperate and subtropical parts of the world.

B 3 Species which are in a steady state, to include upward and
downward fluctuations of roughly 25 per cent over 10- or 20-year
periods; a group that includes the great majority of the world's
species up to the mid-twentieth century.

B 4 Species which have decreased by roughly 25-75 per cent from their
peak, to the point where stocks are seriously depleted compared with
their original levels, e.g. the sperm whale, the hooded seal and the
medicinal leech. These can be termed *depleted species*.

B 5 Species which have fallen below 25 per cent of their former
abundance and seem likely to become extinct if the downward trend
is not reversed, e.g. the wild Monterey pine in California and the the
sokake tortoise *Geochelone radiata* in Madagascar. These are clearly
endangered species.

These biological groupings must be borne in mind when considering the
categories related to threats discussed below. Biologically rare species can,
of course, occur in B 1, B 3, B 4 and B 5 quite independently of current
threat factors.

Deborah Rabinowitz has discussed the attributes of rarity, considered
purely as a biological problem. She points out that the status of a plant
depends on three factors (which are equally applicable to animals):
geographical range (GR), habitat specificity (HS) and local population size
(LPS). From this, she has constructed an eight-cell table where all but one
cell represents a different kind of rarity. (The examples given are not
necessarily those used by Rabinowitz.)

R 1 GR large, HS wide, LPS large : e.g. common plants and animals,
such as bracken, one of the five commonest plants in the world, or
red deer.

R 2 GR large, HS wide, LPS small : e.g. sparsely distributed plants and
animals, such as foxtail bristle-grass *Setaria geniculata* or barn owl.

R 3 GR large, HS narrow, LPS large : e.g. the mangrove *Rhizophora
mangle*, the limpet *Patella vulgaris*.

R 4 GR large, HS narrow, LPS small : e.g. American yew, Eurasian
otter.

R 5 GR small, HS wide, LPS large : e.g. *Fuchsia procumbens*, New
Zealand.

R 6 GR small, HS wide, LPS small : this is the category believed by
Rabinowitz not to exist, but the last surviving population of the
passenger pigeon would presumably have qualified.

R 7 GR small, HS narrow, LPS large : e.g. endemics such as the crucifer
Shortia galacifolia in the Appalachians and the Galapagos marine
iguana.

R 8 GR small, HS narrow, LPS small : e.g. endemics such as the Texan
wild rice *Zizania texana*, which occurs only in unusual alkaline
conditions along 2.4 km of the upper San Marcos River in Texas,
where water temperatures vary only 5° annually, and Queen
Alexandra's birdwing butterfly, the world's largest butterfly, which

Gallant soldier,
Galinsoga parviflora

Queen Alexandra's birdwing butterfly

is restricted to lowland rainforest in or near the Popondetta Plain, a small area in northern Papua New Guinea.

Furthermore, J. L. Harper has pointed out that rarity varies both in time and space. Rarity in time is reflected in the B 1 - B 5 groupings, rarity in space by the R 1-R 8 set. Thus the passenger pigeon moved from B 3 and R 1 in North America at the beginning of the last century, successively through B 4 and B 5, and the whole gamut of R groupings, to actual extinction in the wild by the 1890s.

Frankel and Soulé have listed three factors that contribute to the extinction of species:

1. Biotic factors: competition, predation, parasitism, disease;
2. Isolation;
3. Habitat change: slow geological change, climate, catastrophe, human interference.

These factors, of course, relate to all population changes. It is because they never stay constant that equilibrium is never actually achieved, but is more like a goal towards which animal and plant populations trend. Though these factors largely consist of natural components, man may be a factor in almost all of them.

Man influences the biotic factors in various ways:

By himself acting as a predator, as in harvesting seals, birds' eggs, wild fruits and edible fungi;

By introducing alien animals and plants, which compete with native species, e.g. the guava, which is colonising moorland in the Galapagos Islands; and the North American mink, which has decimated waterfowl stocks in Iceland;

By altering the food supply, e.g. by removing for human consumption so many deer, gazelles or other ungulates that the natural predators, such as wolves or lions, are driven to prey on domestic stock, leading to their depletion or extermination by outraged farmers;

By polluting the air, water or soil with toxic substances;

By introducing disease into the environment, either deliberately, as with the myxoma virus which decimated rabbit stocks in Europe, or accidentally, as with the Dutch elm disease fungus which has severely depleted the elms of much of eastern North America and England.

Isolation, on marine or freshwater islands, on mountain tops or in scattered patches of forest, often leads to population decline and ultimate extinction, for two reasons. On the one hand, small populations are more vulnerable to climatic or catastrophic hazards: the eruption of Mont Pelée in 1902 wiped out the Martinique rice rat, and recent hurricanes have gravely endangered the already tiny populations of the pink pigeon of Mauritius. On the other hand, the smaller the population the greater the danger from genetic drift, which may actually change it into a new species or subspecies, as has repeatedly happened in archipelagos, notably in Hawaii and the Galapagos. Nevertheless many quite small populations are known to have survived for centuries.

Moreover, it has now been abundantly demonstrated that the smaller any isolated patch of habitat, the more rapidly its animal and plant populations become locally extinct. The natural rate of both speciation and extinction on islands, and especially small islands, is consequently much greater than elsewhere. Even continental land-bridge islands as large as Great Britain,

Guava

Mauritius pink pigeon

Ceylon, Tasmania and Borneo have suffered from the fact that when such populations die out, it is more difficult, or even impossible, for them to be replenished from the mainland. Thus, J. M. Diamond has shown that land-bridge islands off New Guinea have lost up to 90 per cent of their non-marine bird species, and that the rate of loss clearly depends on the size of the island. This is partly because habitat diversity also depends on island size. Where habitats have been artificially created on Caribbean islands, bird species have also increased through successful invasion. However, all this natural extinction does not absolve mankind from trying to save species from extinction. For mankind accelerates the rate of extinction while doing little or nothing to increase the rate of speciation, unless indeed the rising waters of the oceans as a result of the 'greenhouse effect' (see p. 56) were to produce a large number of new land-bridge islands towards the end of the next century. By then, however, the genetic resources left as a basis for fresh speciation might well be greatly impoverished, and in any case such speciation could hardly have much effect before the year 2200. In theory accelerated extinction should in turn speed up speciation, as niches become vacant, but this applies mainly to extinction by direct destruction; for when habitat is destroyed, most of the niches go too, leaving only farmed and waste lands that are already fully occupied by species adapted to such man-made habitats.

Human interference with the habitat is the major influence, together with direct predation, on the decline or loss of natural animal and plant populations. Man does not contribute to such natural catastrophes as Krakatoa and Mount St Helens, but we cannot be sure that his tinkering with the planet, if, for instance, the Russian plan to divert the waters of the River Ob were ever carried out, might not unintentionally trigger off much greater natural catastrophes, such as long-term desertification or flooding. The impact of the Aswan Dam on the Nile valley and delta is some indication of what might happen on a larger scale.

Nor can we be at all sure that human interference will not extend, again unintentionally, to climatic change. Already it is being claimed that the worldwide destruction of the rainforests may be a factor in the increasing drying up of the Sahel and other semi-arid regions. Some climatologists also warn us of a possible long-term warming of the world's climate, due to the so-called 'greenhouse effect' produced by the carbon dioxide that results from the widespread burning of fossil fuels; this rise in temperature could be enough to melt all or part of the Antarctic ice cap, leading to cataclysmic flooding along low-lying coasts all over the world. Moreover, in the US, the Environmental Protection Agency and the National Academy of Sciences have each issued an independent report, showing that the greenhouse effect has already started and by 1990 will be dramatic; in the last decade the sea level has risen by some 10-12 cm. Indeed, only slow geological change seems unlikely to be affected by man.

2. Degrees of Threat

We now turn from biologically-based categories to consider the classification of degrees of threat to the current status of animal and plant populations. These were defined by W. K. de la Mare in a paper prepared for the IUCN Species Survival Commission in 1983 and to be published in 1986. (The comments that follow each definition are not de la Mare's; the references to the B and R series are explained on pp. 52 and 53.)

> T 1 An *unendangered species* is widespread and abundant, adapted to a variety of habitats and known to be at a level of abundance comparable with or greater than it had in historic times.
>
> This would include B 2, much of B 3, and R 1 to R 3. One problem here is our ignorance of the level of abundance achieved by many species in former times. We may think we know, for instance , that the common 24-spot ladybird *Subcoccinella vigintiquattuorpunctata* was as common 5000 years ago, or even 500 years ago, as it is today, but without positive evidence we shall never be certain.

> T 2 A *vulnerable species* faces no known threat, but should such a threat develop, it would probably be classified as endangered.
>
> This would include B 1, many species in B 3, and much of R 4, R 5 and R 7. Vulnerable species are mainly those with populations apparently stable, but small or very small because they are confined to a limited habitat, such as an island or a mountain top, and so subject to inevitable genetic erosion. Mount Athos in Greece has many endemic plants not at present known to be threatened, but a

herd of grazing goats might well decimate or eliminate some of them.

T 3 A *threatened species* is either likely to decline in abundance, if present trends continue; or, having once been classified as endangered, is now known to be increasing but has not yet reached its former level of abundance.

This includes elements from both B 3 and B 4, as well as from R 4 to R 8.

T 4 An *endangered species* is in danger of becoming extinct if present trends continue and no action is taken in time to be effective.

The great bulk of the species listed in the IUCN Red Data Books belong here. T 4 applies especially to B 5 and R 8.

T 5 A species of *indeterminate status* is not perceived to be vulnerable, threatened or endangered, but equally is not known positively not to belong to one of these three categories.

In the present rudimentary state of knowledge of an enormous number of known species, notably plants, invertebrates and fishes (not to mention the even more numerous unknown species), this could well be the largest category of all, covering perhaps the majority of species which are, or are believed to be, in B 3, together with B 1 and R 1 to R 3.

De la Mare gives five examples of how of his classification applies to vertebrates. The blue whale in the Antarctic is a severely overexploited species (B 5, R 4), which has now been protected for some fifteen years, but still shows no positive sign of recovery. It is therefore clearly endangered (T 4). The vicuña, on the other hand, is also severely depleted, but in Peru and perhaps in parts of Chile has responded well to protective measures, and is only threatened (T 3), though still endangered elsewhere in the Andes (T 4).

His second example is the Atlantic puffin in the Lofoten Islands off Norway. This population (until recently B 3 and R 3) has decreased so dramatically, apparently due to competition from industrial fisheries for its staple diet of sprats and sand-eels, that it might become extinct in about 20 years. It is therefore threatened (T 3) at present, but will become endangered (T 4) if nothing is done within five years.

The controversial harp and hooded seals, the next two examples, both rank as threatened (T 3) under this classification, being depleted (B 4, R 3) though present in very large numbers; the harp seal is still harvestable without being threatened with extinction as defined in T 4. However, the factual basis for fixing the quotas of the hooded seal is so uncertain that it should be seriously considered as a candidate for endangered status (T 4), the harp seal being left for the present in T 3 (threatened). If it seems unreasonable to classify an animal between one and two million strong as threatened, the passenger pigeon, which plunged from millions to extinction within 30 years, is a good reminder, while the American bison nearly suffered the same fate.

De la Mare's final example, the North Sea herring, suffered a catastrophic decline of 90 per cent in its biomass, from 2,000,000 tonnes in the 1950s (when it was B 3, R 3) to 200,000 tonnes in 1976, entirely due to overfishing (see p. 69). No catching regulations were introduced until the 1970s, and when these failed to stem the decline, herring fishing had to be banned altogether. As with the great whales, the fishing nations allowed the resource to be destroyed for short-term gain rather than conserving it for the long term. The herring is a dynamic species, and may well soon recover

Hooded seal

Ghost orchid

Wild peony of Steepholm

from endangered (T 4) to threatened (T 3), in which case limited harvesting can be allowed again. If the harvesting is well managed and the North Sea nations can control their fishermen, it is not impossible that the herring will recover to a point where it is again unendangered (T 1). But unless a quota regime is then enforced, the sorry tale of the 1950s and 1960s, when a valuable European resource was destroyed, will be repeated. It is entirely possible, however, that the herring stocks will never regain their former numbers.

The sardine fishery around Monterey, California, described in Michener's *Cannery Row*, has never recovered from a similar collapse. The sardine has not become extinct, but has struck a new balance with smaller numbers. Several points of balance are possible in many, if not most, wild populations interacting in a natural community.

Perring and Farrell have made an interesting attempt to provide a quantitative basis for allocating priorities to endangered species. In the first volume of the British Red Data Book (RDB) they calculate 'threat numbers', to indicate the degree of endangerment, using six parameters: number of one-kilometre squares where the species occurs; number of such squares where it occurred in the past; a subjective estimate of its attractiveness to man; the proportion of its localities that are in nature reserves and other protected areas; and two measures of accessibility: geographical remoteness, and actual on-site accessibility, e.g. a rarity growing on a cliff on an offshore island would be inaccessible in both senses. To qualify for the British Plant RDB, a rarity has to occur in no more than 15 one-kilometre squares, and each qualifying plant is given a threat number in the range 1-15. Of the 317 species listed, 19 are already extinct and a further 25 fall into the two top groups of endangerment, with threat numbers of 12 and 13. On this basis, the seven most endangered plants in Britain include the ghost orchid *Epipogium aphyllum*, the Plymouth pear *Pyrus cordata* and the fen ragwort *Senecio paludosus*, which recently reappeared in a roadside ditch in Cambridgeshire, after being considered extinction, while the St Kilda wren *Troglodytes t. hirtensis* has quite happily

The key definition in all this, because of its impact on the administration of endangered species legislation, both national and international, is that of 'endangered' (T 5). Many attempts have been made to define this term, both scientifically and legally, and especially to fix some number below which a species or other discrete population can be regarded as in danger of extinction. But this is clearly futile, since an overexploited population of hundreds of thousands of whales, seals or crocodiles may be in danger of extinction, while the St Kilda wren *Troglodytes t. hirtensis* has quite happily existed on a small Hebridean island for probably several thousand years with a population of around 230 pairs. The St Kilda wren is clearly T 2 (vulnerable) rather than T 5 (endangered), as are also many mountain-top endemic plants, such as *Potentilla robbinsiana* on the White Mountains of New Hampshire, and such highly localised rarities as the wild peony on Steepholm in the Bristol Channel, which has a Perring and Farrell threat number of 9.

The most widely used definition of endangered has been that of the IUCN Red Data Books: 'in danger of extinction and whose survival is unlikely if the causal factors continue operating'. This, however, is almost a tautology, and without de la Mare's addition of a time scale provides no clear objective standards. A biologically sounder definition comes from the IUCN/SSC Crocodile Specialist Group, which calls a species endangered when the death rate in its populations consistently exceeds the birth rate; but this, too, embodies a subjective element in the word 'consistently'. Moreover, it fails to account for threats to the existence of a whole population, such as the flooding of the shores of Lake Pedder in Tasmania by a dam, which in one local catastrophe destroyed the great majority of the seventeen endemic animal and plant species of the lake. Nor does de la Mare's definition allow for this kind of threat. The administrators of the US endangered species legislation use a third definition: an *endangered* species is one whose prospects of survival and reproduction are in immediate jeopardy, due to one or many causes; it must have help to avert extinction.

3. Attempts to Reverse Extinction

Whether a species is extinct or not may in fact be quite hard to establish with certainty; the fen ragwort mentioned on p. 58 is a case in point. The seeds of this species probably lay dormant in the fen peat for upwards of a century, before disturbance enabled them to germinate. Other supposedly extinct species have just been overlooked. It was the rediscovery of the takahe, a large moorhen-like bird, in 1948, that gave rise to the classic remark by a New Zealand minister that 'this species must never be allowed to become extinct again'.

Even the normal definition of extinction, the total and irreversible disappearance of a species or stock, has been challenged. Recent plans by American and Russian scientists to resurrect the long extinct woolly mammoth, which probably disappeared some 10,000 years ago, have raised the question of whether extinction can be reversed. Is extinction really forever? The plans involve extracting a full complement of undiminished chromosomes from the frozen cells of a mammoth yet to be located in the permafrost of Arctic Siberia; transplanting them into an enucleated egg of an Asian elephant; stimulating that new 'hybrid' egg to develop; and finally implanting the resultant embryo into the womb of a healthy female Asian elephant, where it could be carried to full term.

But there are difficulties, and not too much reliance should be placed on achievements with domestic animals in the laboratory. Since freezing a mass of meat as large as a mammoth is a relatively slow process, there is every likelihood that its cells will have partly decomposed, so modifying the genetic information in their chromosomes. Moreover, scientists have yet to demonstrate that they can even identify when a female Asian elephant is about to ovulate, let alone remove an egg from so large an animal without killing it. Even if these formidable obstacles were overcome, and a mammoth embryo were actually planted in the womb of the surrogate elephant mother, there would still be no guarantee of success, witness the problems that have been encountered in perfecting the 'test-tube' technique used to fertilise and implant human mothers.

Even if all these odds were overcome, and a baby mammoth were actually born to an elephant, it would be a unique event unlikely to be repeatable with any other species, except in the highly improbable event of finding another frozen extinct animal with living relatives that could provide the precise biochemical and physiological environments demanded by the developing egg, environments that cannot yet be duplicated artificially. What is more, two mammoths, a male and a female, would be needed, to actually perpetuate the reconstituted species.

Laboratory advances in genetic engineering – synthesising genes, splicing together dissimilar genes and chromosomes, creating new genes – while they may yet result in the creation of entirely new species, at present hold out little hope of man ever being able to recreate extinct ones, even though DNA has already been recovered from extinct mammals, such as the mammoth and quagga. Each gene is only one in an array of genes within a

Takahe

chromosome. Each chromosome is itself one of a set. Each set is one of two in the normal body cell of an organism. That cell needs the correct internal and biochemical mix before it will develop and grow. Above all, the mass of detailed information needed to construct the hundreds of thousands of genes, the sets of chromosomes, the cells, the unique biochemistry, and much of the data on ecological and behavioural requirements of the species, will have disappeared along with the whole organism when the species became extinct. Thomas Carlyle was able to rewrite his *French Revolution* after the original manuscript was accidentally burned, because it all remained in his head. He could not have reconstructed the last beetle in the world if he had accidentally trodden on it.

Aurochs

Nor can the very interesting 'breeding-back' experiments by Heinz Heck at the Tierpark Hellabrunn in Munich 40-50 years ago, with the aurochs *Bos primigenius* (extinct since 1627) and the tarpan *Equus caballus silvaticus* (extinct since 1876), be genuinely claimed to have cancelled the extinction of these ancestors of our cattle and horses. From skeletal remains and contemporary pictures, Heck knew what the aurochs and tarpan looked like, so he chose modern cattle and horses showing one or other of the desired features to breed from. By crossing and recrossing their offspring, he produced remarkable facsimiles, which bred true. Since plenty of species pairs are virtually identical in their external appearance, these new stocks of cattle and horses could not possibly be anything other than facsimiles. Their chromosomes could not be identical with those of the stocks that perished in seventeenth and nineteenth century Europe. This is clearly demonstrated by the experience of Heck's brother Lutz, who later, at the Berlin Zoo, used quite different races of cattle and obtained results identical to his brother's. Undoubtedly, the modern cattle and horses the Hecks worked with did give them some genes closely related to those of the aurochs and tarpan. The vast majority of extinct species, however, have no such closely related descendants.

4. The Prevention of Depletion and Extinction

The rules which must be obeyed if wild stocks of animals and plants are to be preserved, and not first depleted, then endangered, and finally exterminated, are extremely simple, but their enforcement raises massive social, economic and consequently political problems. The first and overriding consideration is that this is a biological and ecological problem, and therefore the inescapable laws of biology and ecology must be given priority over man-made political, social and especially economic laws. Economists and financiers believe that their considerations are the important ones, and these are basically to ensure that a profit is made on any invested capital. If securing the profit involves the extinction of a natural population, so be it, so long as the investment has been recouped. It is this line of thought that has led to the carefully supervised commercial extinction of the great whales (see p. 163). Its rejection led to the equally carefully supervised recovery, and the profitable, and until recently sustained, utilisation of the Pribilof fur seal (see p. 181).

What, then, are the rules of wildlife conservation, as dictated by biology and ecology?

Basically, they are those of good husbandry:

1. Maintain the ecosystem.
2. Maintain the breeding stock.

To which may be added two more, one moral, the other practical:

3. Do not kill any animal or destroy any plant without some constructive
   purpose.
4. Make sure that all the people concerned understand what needs to be
   done, and why.

The implications of these rules will be discussed in the following chapters.

Indian elephant

4 Assessment and Monitoring

Clearly the first essential in launching any enterprise is to establish the facts, or, in the modern jargon, provide a data-base. Once the enterprise is under way, it is equally important to monitor progress. In the past, information on the status of animals and plants has been collected more or less haphazardly. Surveys on any scale have only been possible using the resources of established institutions, such as the Royal Botanic Gardens, Kew, the Botanical and Zoological Surveys of India, and the Smithsonian Institution in Washington DC. Only exceptionally do we find such special efforts as the seminal 1873 voyage of HMS *Challenger*, which founded the science of oceanography. Even so, a remarkable body of facts was amassed in the nineteenth century's first flush of enthusiasm, and the twentieth century until quite recently has rather tended to rest on these laurels. As Gren Lucas, Curator of the Kew Herbarium, has noted, progress in completing the big regional floras, such as *Flora Zambesiaca* and the *Flora of Tropical East Africa* is still tantalisingly slow. However, in 1980 a consortium of the University of Mexico, the Missouri Botanical Garden and the British Museum (Natural History) announced plans for a flora of Middle America, from southern Mexico to Panama.

With birds, although Salim Ali and Dillon Ripley completed their ten-volume *Handbook of the Birds of India and Pakistan* in the decade up to 1974, the seven-volume *Handbook of the Birds of the Western Palaearctic*, which began to appear in 1977, has only reached Volume 4 and is unlikely to be finished before the 1990s. An immense amount of information has also been gathered by amateur naturalists worldwide, but needs to be systematised and co-ordinated if it is to be usable for the conservation of genetic resources.

During the past twenty years, and especially in the past six or seven, IUCN has built up a massive network of data-bases for the assessment and monitoring of wild genetic resources. An entirely separate system, mainly funded by FAO, operates for cultivated or domesticated genetic resources. In fact, modern attempts to assess and monitor endangered species began in 1931, when the new American Committee for International Wild Life Protection started to assemble facts about endangered mammals and birds throughout the world. This pioneer effort produced Glover M. Allen's *Extinct and Vanishing Mammals of the Western Hemisphere* in 1942, followed by volumes on the mammals of the Old World (1945) and the birds of the world (1958). In 1949, the first technical meeting of IUPN (as IUCN then was) at Lake Success in New York State was presented with lists of fourteen mammals and thirteen birds stated to be 'in need of emergency action if they are to be saved from extinction'. Twenty-five years later I judged that most of them were still endangered, and at least two of them, and perhaps five, were actually extinct.

It was soon realised that there were many more than 27 seriously endangered mammals and birds, but not until 1964 did work begin on Sir Peter Scott's brainchild, a series of 'red data books' (RDB) to list all endangered animals and plants, together with enough information to show what needed to be done to save them. The first to appear, in 1966, was the *Red Data Book: Mammals*, compiled by Noel Simon, with a revised edition in 1972. It was followed, also in 1966, by the *Red Data Book: Birds*, compiled by Jack Vincent for the International Council for Bird Preservation (ICBP), with a revised edition in 1978/79. These first two books were in loose-leaf format, updated annually by batches of new and revised sheets. The third loose-leaf RDB, on reptiles and amphibians, was edited by René Honegger, and appeared in 1968, with a third edition by 1979. The first RDB to appear as a bound book dealt with plants, and was published in 1978 by the Threatened Plants Committee of IUCN's Survival Service Commission. This was also the first volume to come to terms with the burgeoning number of species known to be threatened, by deliberately including only a selection.

By the mid-1970s, it was clear that to cope with the increasing volume of data, and to ensure the completion of the projected comprehensive series of Red Data Books, computers would have to be used. This led, in 1979, to the creation of IUCN's Conservation Monitoring Centre (CMC) at Cambridge and Kew, UK. The Centre now has four operational units, together with a computer which processes their data: the Species Conservation Monitoring Unit (SCMU) for animal species conservation; the Threatened Plants Unit (TPU) for threatened plants; the Wildlife Trade Monitoring Unit (WTMU) for wildlife trade; and the Protected Areas Data Unit (PADU) for protected areas.

CMC's main aim is to provide the accurate, up-to-date and reliable information needed to develop realistic conservation and development policies worldwide. It performs its function of continuously collecting, analysing, interpreting and disseminating the necessary data by integrating its four units. The primary data sources are the worldwide networks of scientists and other informants linked with IUCN either directly or through its commissions, notably, of course, the SSC for species and the Commission on National Parks and Protected Areas for protected habitats. CMC's specialist staff collect information both through this network and from the scientific literature, including many unpublished reports from IUCN/WWF and other projects. They then critically assess and summarise the resulting data and store it in CMC's computerised database, both as text and in coded data files. CMC's unusually flexible database enables it to produce reports and publications to meet the special needs of many institutions concerned with development and conservation; it is used by both the World Bank and the Council of Europe. CMC is part of UNEP's Global Environmental Monitoring System (GEMS) and, as special consultant to the Convention on International Trade in Endangered Species (CITES), provides technical and scientific advice to the CITES Secretariat. It also cooperates with Unesco, WWF and ICBP.

The Species Conservation Monitoring Unit (SCMU) at Cambridge, which brought together the various vertebrate RDB compilers, was the first of CMC's units to be set up. It covers all animals, except birds, and has so far produced new RDB volumes for mammals, reptiles and invertebrates. The first volume of the new Mammal RDB, published as a book in 1982, deals with 155 species or subspecies in the Americas and Australasia. The second volume will deal with Africa and Madagascar, and the third will cover Eurasia. There will also be special volumes on regions, such as Madagascar, and groups of species, such as antelopes, cetaceans, primates and cats. The ultimate aim is to include in the data-base all mammals, not just the threatened ones.

The Bird RDBs continue to be a joint undertaking of CMC and ICBP in Cambridge. The first volume of the new Bird RDB, for Africa, was published in 1985, and will be followed by others for Australasia and the Pacific, Eurasia and the Americas.

The first of the new reptile and amphibian RDB volumes appeared in 1982. This covers crocodiles, marine turtles, tortoises and the tuatara, which is a unique Triassic relic with an ancestry covering Europe and North America some 200 million years before the dinosaurs, and surviving on a few islands off New Zealand. One more volume is planned for 1986, to cover African reptiles (snakes and lizards) and amphibians (frogs, toads, newts, salamanders). Work on RDBs for fishes has been slower, because so much less is known about their distribution.

Even less is known about most invertebrate groups. The first volume of this RDB, published in 1983, therefore presents only selected examples – 124 molluscs, 70 insects and 60 species from eleven other classes or phyla – to illustrate the conservation problems involved. A special volume on swallowtail butterflies (Papilionidae) appeared in 1985, and volumes on coral reefs and molluscs will follow. To date, information on some 700 invertebrate taxa, mainly from Europe and North America, has been fed into the computer, yet more than a quarter of a million beetle species alone have been described, and the status of the vast majority is quite unknown.

Tuatara

The pioneer in international endangered plant research was the late Ronald Melville of the Royal Botanic Gardens, Kew, who in 1970 produced for the SSC the first sample plant RDB, confined to angiosperms (flowering plants). In 1974, the SSC set up its Threatened Plants Committee, which developed into the present Threatened Plants Unit (TPU), a component of CMC located at Kew. This unit has compiled not only the first volume of the new-style Plant RDB, but also lists of rare, threatened and endemic plants in Europe, and of threatened plants held in botanic gardens. Work continues on further RDB volumes, but since there are so many plant species in the world, and the proportion in danger is likely to be at least one-tenth, this is inevitably a slow process. A volume on plant sites is scheduled for 1986.

The original IUCN Red Data Books stimulated similar efforts on a national scale all over the world. One of the earliest was on vascular plants in Britain, issued in 1977, which went into a second edition in 1983. Two more RDBs, for the USSR and New Zealand, were presented at the IUCN General Assemblies in those countries in 1978 and 1981. The movement is spreading, and today a Red Data Book is almost a status symbol for new nations, just as national parks have become. By mid-1984, at least 154 RDB's for animals had appeared in various parts of the world, together with an unknown number for plants.

The Wildlife Trade Monitoring Unit (WTMU), also located at Cambridge, started life as the TRAFFIC Specialist Group of the SSC, with the aim, which it still retains, of providing detailed information on wild animals and plants in trade. TRAFFIC stands for Trade Records Analysis of Fauna and Flora in Commerce. WTMU's major output is the TRAFFIC Bulletin, published five times a year, which carries its special trade reports and analyses, and recent trade news. It has also prepared identification manuals on parrots and birdwing butterflies, and a checklist of internationally endangered mammals.

The fourth constituent of CMC is the Protected Areas Data Unit

Continued on p. 65

◁ **1.** Oakwood, Shropshire, England. *G. I. Bernard/Oxford Scientific Films.*

2. Soil erosion due to overgrazing by goats, Chaco, Argentina. *C. M. Perrins/Oxford Scientific Films.*

3. Goat browsing in tree, Morocco. *M. J. Coe/Oxford Scientific Films.*

4. Saguaro cactus in Saguaro National Monument, Arizona, USA. *T. Middleton/ Oxford Scientific Films.*

5. Coniferous forest by mountain stream, West Himalayas, India. *Ardea London.*

◁ 2

◁ 3

4 ▷

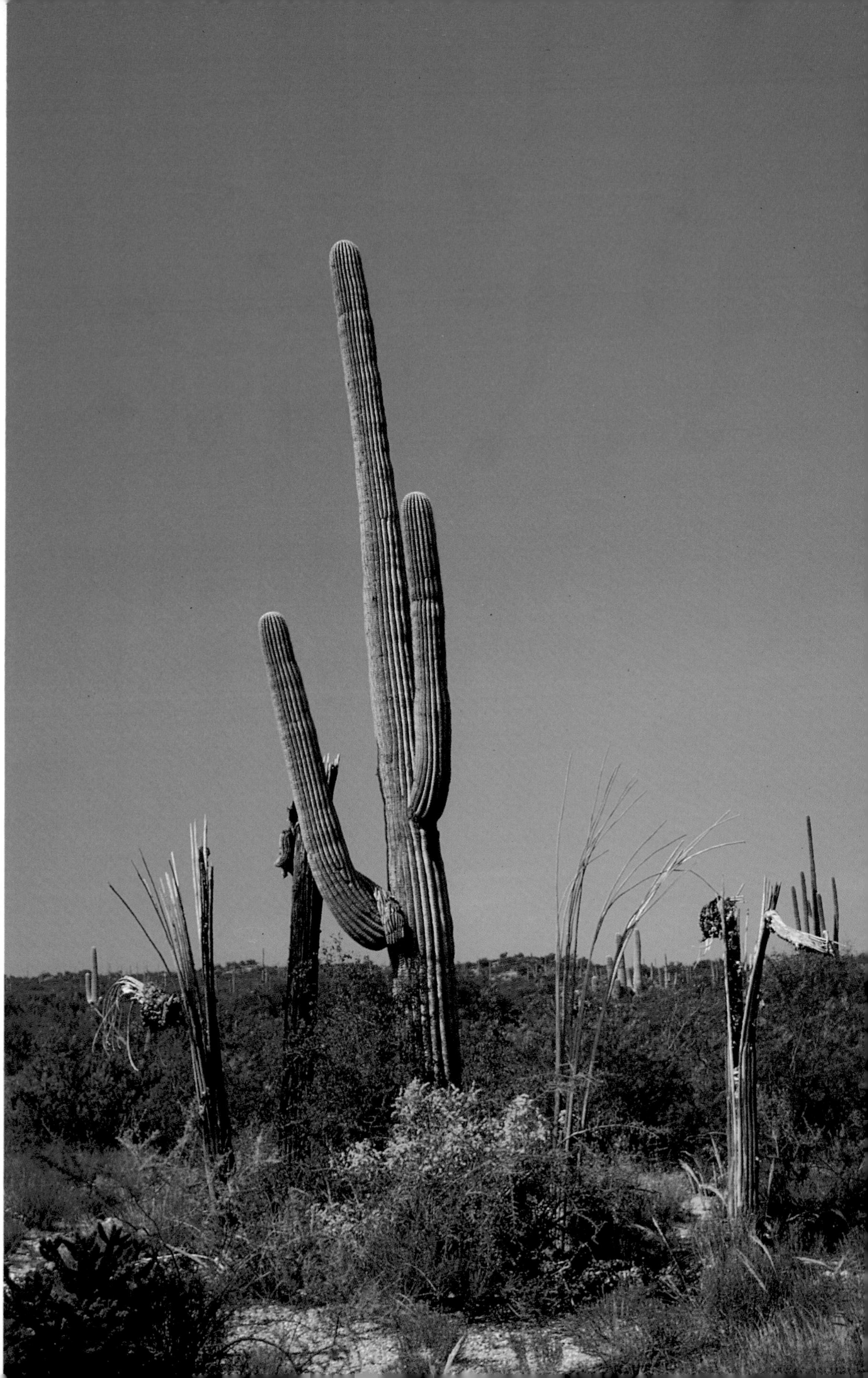

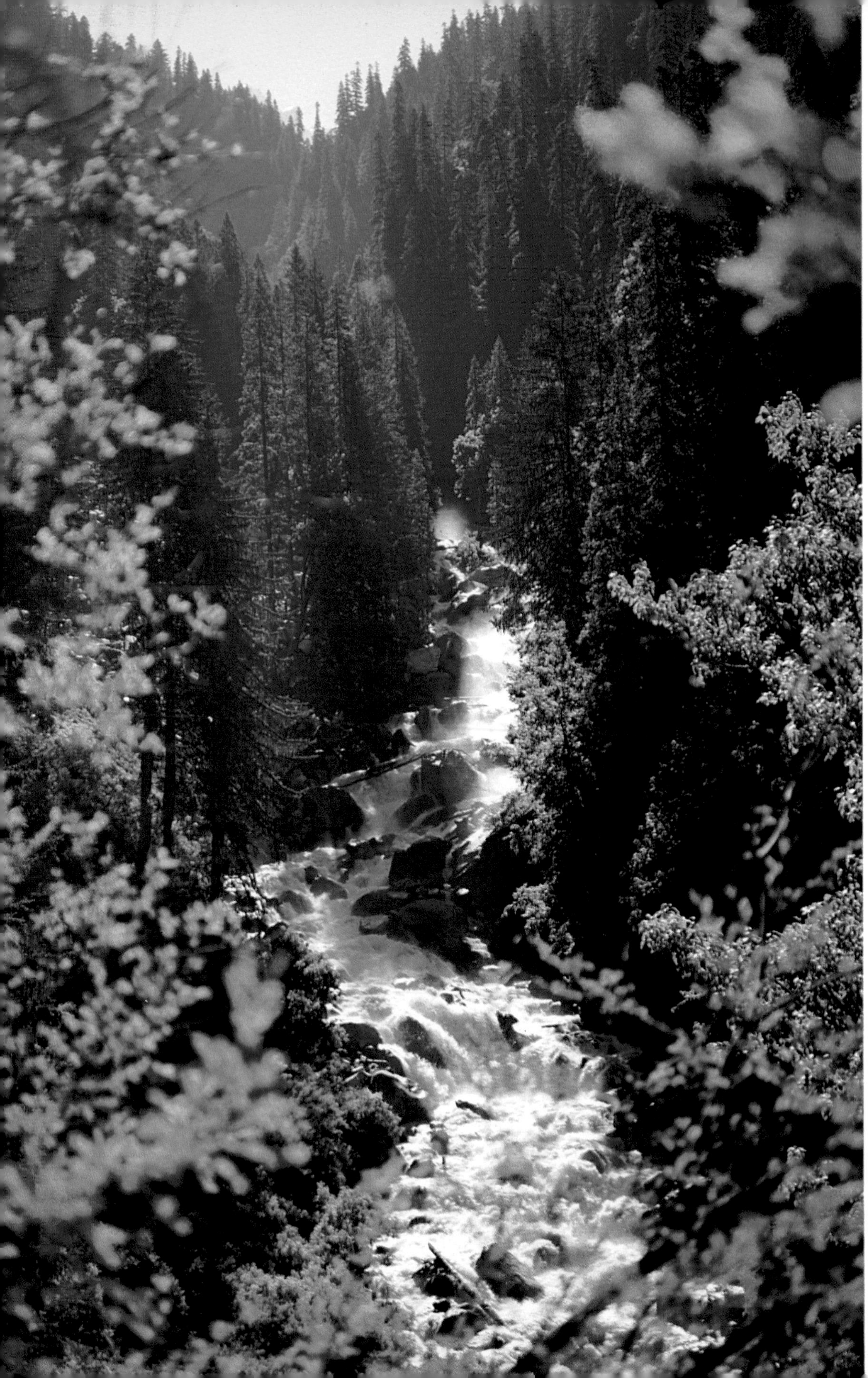

◁ 5

6 ▷

2

6. Bats leaving a cave at dusk, Pelabuan Ratu, Java, Indonesia. *Sylvia Yorath/World Wildlife Fund.*

7. Emperor penguins, Brunt ice shelf, Antarctica. *Doug Allan/Oxford Scientific Films.*

8. Hillside pattern produced by selective burning of heather to stimulate food supply of red grouse, Dumfries-shire, Scotland. *R. Mearns/ Nature Photographers Ltd.*

9. Pollution in the Rhine: detergent foam at a weir, Frankfurt-am-Main, West Germany. *Ralph Lewin/Oxford Scientific Films.*

10. Coral reef, Red Sea. *Laurence Gould/ Oxford Scientific Films.*

13 ▷

14 ▷

11. The wildebeest migration, Masai Mara, Kenya. *Paul Sterry/Nature Photographers Ltd.*

12. Mangroves. *Nancy Sefton/World Wildlife Fund.*

13. Chalk downland turf, Great Cheverill Down, Wiltshire, England. *Bob Gibbons/Ardea London.*

14. Opalescent pool in black sand basin, Yellowstone National Park, Wyoming, USA. *M. R. L. Fogden/Oxford Scientific Films.*

15. Wicken Fen, Cambridgeshire, England. *J. L. Mason/Ardea London.*

◁ 17

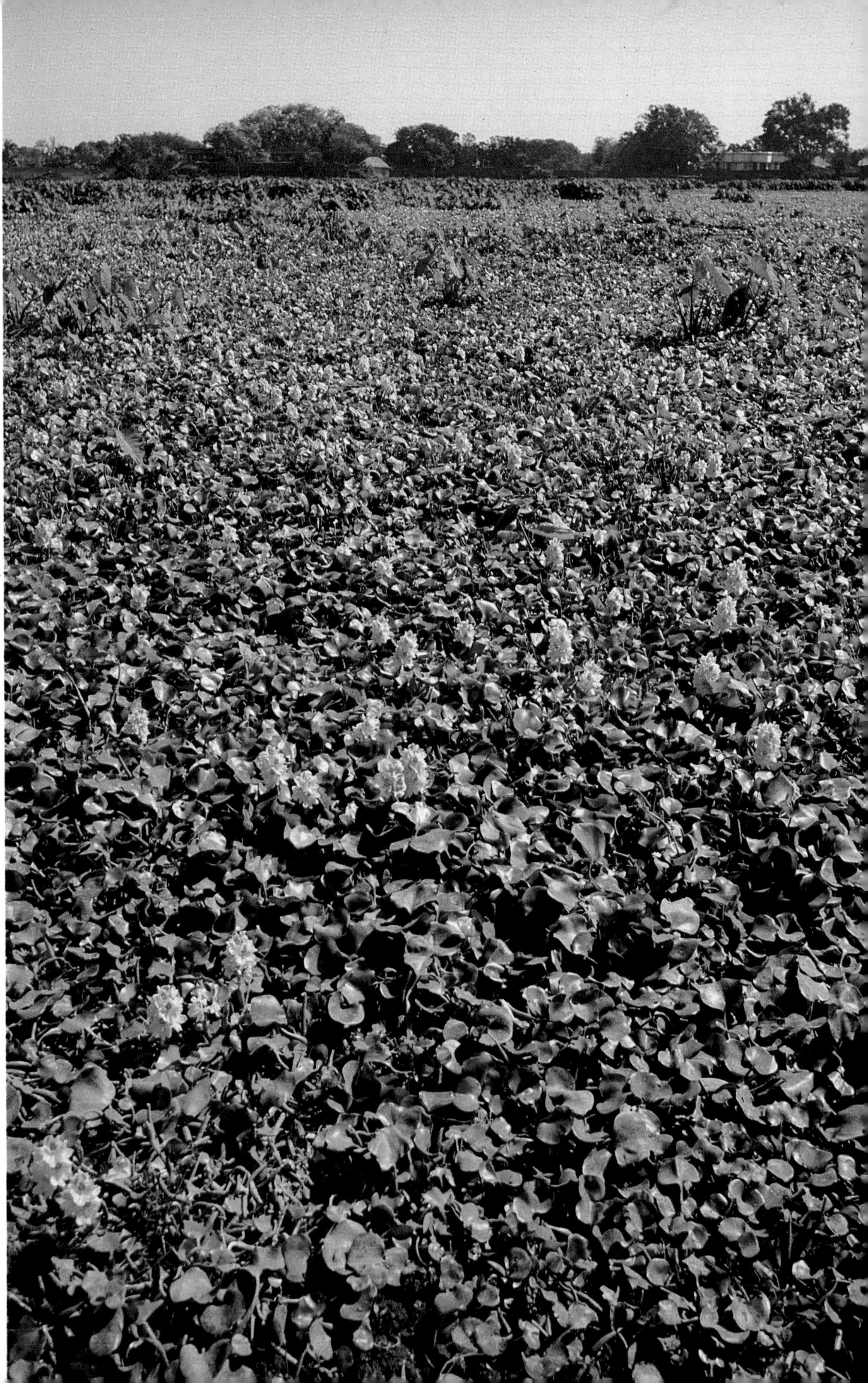

◁ 18

19 ▷

(PADU), now based at Cambridge, whose origin dates back to the first *World Directory of National Parks and Protected Areas*, published by IUCN for the United Nations in 1971. The Unit was set up in 1981 and is planning directories for the protected areas of each of the eight biogeographical realms, and special publications on, for instance, tropical rainforests. The first directory, on the Neotropical Realm, appeared in 1982, followed by the Afrotropical Realm in 1986.

Another data bank of great value for species conservation is ISIS, the International Species Inventory System, sponsored by the American Association of Zoological Parks and Aquariums, and located at the Minnesota Zoolog"cal Garden. This is a computerised catalogue of more than 53,000 animals in zoos and primate centres worldwide, together with the births, deaths and breeding records of another 40,000 animals, which are the parents or ancestors of some of the 53,000. This information is vitally important in enabling zoos to plan breeding programmes with the best available genetic information. ISIS is linked with the SSC's Captive Breeding Specialist Group through the latter's Chairman, Dr Ulysses Seal. This group advises zoos on the safest way of using their breeding stock of endangered animals in order to minimise inbreeding, and to perpetuate those species.

The Royal Botanic Gardens, Kew, and Oxfam have jointly set up a computer-based Survey of Economic Plants for the Arid and Semi-arid Tropics, which so far has listed some 6000 arid plants of economic importance, from which one can find out, for instance, that 28 species of grass with edible seeds are found in Ethiopia alone. One of these, *Panicum turgidum*, also has the following uses: (shoots) thatching, traps, fuel, fibre matting; (leaves) grazing and fodder for domestic animals; and (whole plant) sand stabilisation and soil improvement.

An International Legume Database and Information Service for the 17,000 species of Leguminosae has recently been established at Southampton University, UK.

The World Data Centre on Micro-organisms, located at the University of Queensland, Brisbane, maintains an important culture collection of microscopic algae, bacteria, fungi, protozoans, yeasts and animal and plant viruses. It also houses the master copy of the World Directory of Collections of Micro-organisms, which has registered 441 collections from 65 countries.

Individual countries are now beginning to create their own equivalents to IUCN'S Conservation Monitoring Centre. Peru recently created a Conservation Data Centre, which monitors the whole of the country's natural heritage. Britain's Biological Records Centre, which concentrates on collecting facts about the distribution of wild animals and plants, was started even before CMC.

Two national fact-finding projects may also be mentioned: Project Linnaeus, which is listing the 170 endangered plant species of Sweden; and the Eastern England Rare Plant Project at the University Botanic Garden, Cambridge, which has gathered detailed information on the distribution of rare plants in eleven English counties.

It is perhaps worth noting that this chapter deals almost entirely with species that have been described scientifically and have also had, or are in the process of having, their conservation status assessed. It therefore applies, at most, to one-sixth of all species in the world, though probably to the majority of vertebrates.

20. *Tropical rainforest with tree ferns, Java, Indonesia.*
Tom Moss/World Wildlife Fund.

A Note on Monitoring

There is currently some confusion as to the meaning of the word
'monitoring'. As a verb, 'to monitor' did not feature in the *Concise Oxford
Dictionary* 50 years ago, so it is not surprising that differing usages have
grown up. Like 'data-base', it has become an in-word, sometimes used to
persuade grant-giving bodies that they are doing something different and
more up-to-date than just collecting data. But however it is described, the
collection of information continues to be an essential adjunct to practical
species conservation.

Some papers in *The Biological Aspects of Rare Plant Conservation*, edited
by Hugh Synge (1981), illustrate the confusion that arises from using
'monitoring' as a new all-purpose word. Davy and Jefferies, for instance,
extend the term monitoring from ascertaining the status of particular
species or populations to 'a more fundamental type which yields a
predictive understanding of population structure and function'. This
means, presumably, research into population dynamics. Monitoring of
both kinds is carried out by many bodies, both official and voluntary, but it
seems desirable that the term should be restricted to its primary meaning
rather than extended, perhaps to meet the wishes of grant-giving bodies, to
basic research. Synge's book gives many examples of plant monitoring
research of both kinds, in Australia (desert plants), Britain (Upper
Teesdale) and the USA (national parks and reserves), and on a species basis
into terrestrial orchids, mesembryanthemums, the juniper in Britain and
the Cape endemic *Staavia dodii* (Bruniaceae) in South Africa.

Causes of Depletion and Extinction: Overexploitation

5

Some 25,000 plants, well over 1000 vertebrate species and subspecies and an immense number, so far unestimated, of invertebrates are today threatened with extinction. Still greater numbers of both animal and plant species and populations are depleted, many severely. Estimates suggest that at least a million species, all bearing genes of potential value for man's future welfare, will have become extinct by the year 2000, and some scientists would put the figure much higher. Such a loss of genetic resources would be a major human disaster. It is, unfortunately, a disaster the human race is at present contemplating like a rabbit transfixed by a stoat.

The two prime causes of the depletion, endangerment and eventual extinction of species, are habitat destruction and overexploitation. Until about 1950 overexploitation was the more important of the two; it still is the more important for species already being used by man, such as whales, fur seals and many marine fishes. Habitat destruction, which is now much the more important adverse factor, has a greater impact on potential than on currently exploited genetic resources, especially on the great array of species whose potential value to man has yet to be assessed. Habitat destruction, the subject of Chapter 6, is taken here to include not only direct actions such as felling forests, draining marshes and ploughing prairies, but also changes in the environment due to pollutants and competition from introduced species for food and breeding niches.

Overexploitation is discussed first, since it came first historically. In the past, overexploitation has led to many spectacular depletions and extinctions, notably the American bison, the quagga , the passenger pigeon, the dodo and the great auk. The whole range of wild populations – mammals, birds, reptiles, amphibians, fishes, invertebrates, trees, other flowering plants, fungi – have been and are being overexploited. Given the chance, the commercial harvester grabs all he can get, before someone else appears. Preserving the habitat is thus not enough; direct exploitation must also be controlled. Of course, many present methods of exploitation, of the tropical rainforests for instance, involve not only overexploitation of species, as with the trees felled for timber, but the destruction of their habitat along with that of all the other species.

1. Food

Man's use of wild animals and plants for food or drink has caused most of the major extinctions or severe depletions of the past. To the five animals

Dodo

Quagga

just mentioned we can add the saiga antelope of the Central Asian steppes, traditionally hunted for food and eventually overhunted to the point when in 1919 only some 1000 animals survived. Its recovery is discussed on p. 179. We must assume that some 10,000-12,000 years ago a similar fate befell the mammoth, the woolly rhinoceros and the rest of the lost larger fauna of Palaeolithic Europe, so graphically depicted in the cave art of southern France and northern Spain. The first Americans also appear to have killed off all the numerous large animals that inhabited their prairies when they arrived a few thousand years later, except for the analogues of the two that survived in Europe: the bison and the pronghorn antelope. The first human colonists of Madagascar, who arrived about 500 AD, also killed off many animals, notably fourteen species of lemur, two giant tortoises, the elephant bird *Aepyornis* and a pigmy hippo, as did the Maoris with the moas when they arrived some 1500 years later still. Indeed, since man emerged as *Homo sapiens* some 35,000 years ago, he appears to have exterminated more than half the world's large land animal species, i.e. those weighing more than 80-90 kg as adults.

Pre-industrial people, living close to the land, kill large animals mainly for food and to make artefacts from their skin and bones. Once the agricultural revolution appears, and cultivation destroys the habitats of the large ungulates, these become crop predators and so are also killed to protect the new and precious crops.

Even in the modern industrial world, overexploitation of wild animals for food continues apace in many parts of the tropics, for instance in West Africa. In Liberia where, until recently, hunting was quite uncontrolled, there may be one gun for every dozen inhabitants; hence no game animals survive within ten kilometres of the main highways and, as there is an extensive road network, undisturbed places are few. In Niger, all antelopes are threatened or endangered, except in Park W; even here there is both heavy poaching and illegal grazing, and the scimitar-horned oryx is expected to become extinct by 1988. In the buffer zone of the Pendjari National Park in Benin and Upper Volta (now Burkino Faso) nearly two-fifths of the topi were shot in 1979 alone.

Topi

In East Africa, overhunting in the politically disturbed years of the later 1970s wiped out 90 per cent of Uganda's elephants and almost all its black rhinos. In the Queen Elizabeth National Park, elephants were reduced from 30,000 to a mere 150, and buffalo and hippo stocks fell by nearly half; the racks of poached buffalo and hippo meat showed why. In the more accessible areas of the Ruwenzori Mountains leopard, duiker and tree hyrax were exterminated, and leopard and duiker probably in the remoter parts too. Similar stories of poaching for meat come from Botswana, Sudan and many other parts of Africa.

Nor is overhunting by any means confined to Africa. Both Asiatic and North American brown bears are being hunted, and often poached, to supply the increasing demand for bear paw dishes in the Far East, and even in California. The Guam restaurant trade has heavily depleted many island populations of flying foxes in the Pacific; the Guam flying fox is probably already extinct, but Guam continues to import huge numbers of bats from elsewhere. In Papua New Guinea the fruit bat *Aproteles bulmerae* appears to have been virtually wiped out by hunters. The proboscis monkey in Sabah and the babirusa in Sulawesi are only two of innumerable South-east Asian animals to be heavily depleted for the same reason; the babirusa, a wild pig, was recently reported almost extinct.

Fruit bats

Apart from the great whales, catastrophically depleted by an international system set up specifically to conserve their stocks (see Chapter 9), the most generally overexploited animals have been the fishes and reptiles.

At least 25 of the world's most valuable commercial sea fisheries have either collapsed or substantially declined as a result of overfishing, and even now up to half the commercially important fish species are being overexploited; the remaining 40 are fully exploited. Depleted species include cod, haddock, herring and mackerel off north-west Europe; and California sardine, Pacific hake, Atlantic salmon and Alaska pollack off North America. What is more, for technical economic reasons, all kinds of regimes, pre-capitalist, capitalist, socialist and communist, have overexploited fish stocks in the past and continue to do so.

In the north-east Atlantic, overfishing dates back to at least 1890, when North Sea plaice yields began to fall, despite enhanced fishing effort. After World War II, several important fish stocks were eliminated in quick succession. One was the herring stock in the Barents Sea between Norway and Iceland, once by far the largest in the region, five times the North Sea stock. Gross overfishing, at first by traditional trawling methods, reduced the catch from 1.4 million tonnes a year in the mid 1950s to half a million in 1960 and, after a spurt to 1.7 million due to the introduction of more efficient purse seines, down to 300,000. At this point fishing was banned. In Icelandic waters, herring catches fell from 400,000 tonnes in 1963 to 80,000 tonnes, when this too had to be stopped. Further south the Dogger Bank stock, the basis of Great Yarmouth's prosperity, was fished down from 300,000 tonnes a year in the early 1950s to only 10,000 in 1966.

Atlantic salmon

It is hardly believable that advanced countries such as Britain, the Netherlands, Norway, Denmark and Iceland should have allowed their fishermen to destroy their own livelihood in this way, but Japan too allowed its fishermen to destroy its own Hokkaido herring fisheries. The reason lies partly in the biology and partly in the economics of fisheries. Herring stocks in particular fluctuate widely, and both fishermen and governments have tended to take the optimistic view that lower catches were due to natural causes rather than their own overfishing. It is difficult too for fishermen with substantial capital invested in their fleets to accept that, for the sake of their future livelihood, they must not use it because scientists counsel caution - after all scientists are not always right. This is where governments have failed the fishermen, for they ought to (but rarely do) take a longer view.

A particularly glaring example of a fish stock currently being destroyed, with the full awareness of all concerned, is the Atlantic bluefin tuna, which is steadily being driven to commercial extinction by a combination of Japanese overfishing and ineffective US fishery regulations. Modern tuna boats use fearsomely efficient longlines that stretch across 20-40 kilometres of ocean, with thousands of hooks on secondary lines. Not many small tuna are seen in the fishery today, showing that too few are surviving to spawn and provide the next year's stock. These bluefin tuna are being airlifted to Tokyo to satisfy the Japanese demand for *chiai*, the strip of blood-red meat along the bluefin tuna's side that is believed by many Japanese to contribute to their financial success, longevity and sexual potency. The Japanese fishermen maintain that they are not really fishing for bluefins at all, but for the still numerous yellowfin tuna and the Atlantic bigeye tuna, but in 1981 the incidental catch of bluefins, by seventeen boats fishing off Florida, amounted to 8000 fish, almost as much as that of all the other tuna in the fishery together.

Atlantic bluefin tuna

Another major commercial fishery faced with extinction is for pilchards off Namibia. The first quota fixed, 470,000 tonnes in 1977, had to be more than halved, despite fierce opposition from the Walvis Bay fishermen, when scientists proved that the stock was in real danger.

Yet another example was the almost deliberate destruction of the haddock fishery off George's Bank, New England, by Russian fishermen using intensive box-fishing techniques. They drove up a steady catch of 50,000 tonnes a year to 150,000 tonnes in 1966, but by 1974 it had fallen to 10,000. Russian and Polish fishermen have also helped to overexploit Antarctic fish stocks. Indeed the whole South Atlantic has been overfished, notably around South Georgia, the South Orkneys and the South Shetlands. Off South Georgia the standing stock of one million tons was reduced by 90 per cent in five years of intensive international overfishing in the late 1970s, and similar collapses have occurred around Kerguelen and other subantarctic islands. In 1969/70 the catch of the Antarctic cod, which had previously averaged only 2000 tons, was 403,100 tons; three years later it fell to 800 tons, showing that the bulk of the stock had been wiped out. In 1986 similar overfishing is in progress around the Falkland Islands.

Perhaps the most striking of all modern fish stock collapses was the anchoveta fishery off the coasts of Peru and northern Chile in the early 1970s. Here the anchovies simply disappeared, mainly because gross overfishing had removed the breeding stock, but partly because they had been driven into deeper water by El Niño, the periodic warm current which displaces the nutrient-rich cold Humboldt Current, on which the anchovies depend. In 1970 anchovetas were being harvested by 1500 modern fishing vessels at the rate of 100,000 tonnes a day, and the 1972 fishery caught almost the entire product of the spawnings of the two previous years, at a rate of up to 180,000 tonnes a day. Once again, both the amount of capital invested in the fleets, and the number of people with jobs at risk, made it politically impossible to act on the warning that the fishery was endangered, not by a natural fluctuation (which might recover naturally) but by human overfishing. By not so acting, the Peruvian government ensured the very outcome it was seeking to avoid.

All these lower yields are due to the removal of too many young fishes from each year class, before they have been able to realise their full breeding potential by contributing their full share to the next year class. Once the spawning stock is too low to sustain the previous level of recruitment to each year class, numbers begin to fall rapidly, and the fishery collapses. The basic cause of overfishing is that fish are common property, so that it is in each individual fisherman's short-term interest to catch as many fish as possible. No fisherman will voluntarily reduce his catch, without a cast-iron assurance that his competitors will do the same; this applies even more strongly in international waters. The responsibility for providing this assurance lies squarely with governments; their failure to do so has repeatedly led to the loss of commercially valuable fish stocks. The world has yet to find a way of solving the problems of fishery economics, and so preventing both fishermen from fishing themselves out of a living, and all nations from destroying their own and other nations' share of a common resource.

Freshwater fish can of course be overfished too. In Uganda, for example, the growth of fishing villages in the Queen Elizabeth National Park has both increased the demand for fish, and reduced stocks in Lakes Edward and George and the Kazinga Channel. In the Macarena reserve in Colombia, stocks have been severely depleted by commercial fishermen, using dynamite.

The totoaba, a large seatrout of the croaker family (Sciaenidae), spawns in submarine channels around the mouth of the Colorado River in northern Mexico. By 1975 its commercial catch was down to 2.5 per cent of the previous recorded maximum, leaving Mexico to close the fishery, and the United States to declare it an official endangered species and prohibit its import. The problem of restoring the totoaba is complicated by the loss of

Anchovies

some of its spawning grounds, dams upstream having reduced the Colorado's flow into the Gulf of California.

'Few animals are more misused than sea turtles', concluded a world conference on their conservation, in Washington DC, in 1979. Six of their seven species have been severely depleted by overexploitation, for both eggs and meat. The eggs are used locally, but the meat now often enters international trade. Turtle soup is a luxury food, which brings much needed foreign exchange to some Third World countries. The green turtle is the most widespread and still probably the most numerous marine turtle, numbering millions. However, a glance through the *Reptile Red Data Book* shows it widely listed as depleted or severely depleted – in the Cape Verde Islands, Cayman Islands, Colombia, Dominican Republic, El Salvador, Guyana, Haiti, Honduras, India, Indonesia, Israel, Jamaica, Japan, Kenya, Line Islands, Malaysia, Mexico, Papua New Guinea, Philippines, Seychelles, Sri Lanka, Tanzania, Texas, Thailand and Tokelau. For Papua New Guinea there is a suggestive remark that 'in areas where turtles are hunted population decline is now becoming obvious, with people having to go further afield to catch them. However, in areas where Seventh Day Adventism (which forbids the eating of meat) has become established, villagers report a noticeable increase in populations in the last 30-50 years'. Likewise in the Cayman Islands: 'in the old days Caymanians used to make a living catching turtles, gradually sailing further afield as numbers declined'.

Green turtle

Green turtles, though depleted, are still a valuable natural resource, which will continue to benefit mankind if harvested sustainably. Kemp's ridley, on the other hand, is a classic instance of a natural resource destroyed by overexploitation. Although common in the Gulf of Mexico, its breeding ground was unknown until in 1947, after years of searching, Professor Archie Carr learned of a nesting site at Rancho Nuevo on the almost uninhabited coast of Tamaulipas, Mexico. There he found the ridleys crowded ashore to lay their eggs on a 145-kilometre stretch of beach, these assemblies, known as *arribadas*, being perhaps 'the most concentrated breeding aggregation of any vertebrate animal in the world'. In the late 1940s, some 40,000 ridleys came up the beach at each *arribada*; over the next fifteen years so many fishermen swarmed into the area to exploit the new resource that by 1963 only some 3000-4000 females were breeding sporadically, and by the 1978-81 seasons, only 1000 nests could be found. The demise of Kemp's ridley was almost as swift as that of Steller's seacow, which was hurried to extinction by a similar ugly rush within 27 years of its discovery by George Steller off Kamchatka in 1741. On the Pacific coast of Mexico the olive ridley turtle has also been seriously overexploited; indeed virtually all known marine turtle rookeries have been overexploited.

If the large land tortoises had developed on continents instead of small islands, none of them might have survived for western zoology to describe, any more than the elephant bird in Madagascar, or the moas in New Zealand. As soon as they did become known to marauding western navigators, they were, like the marine turtles, treated as a convenient way of transporting fresh meat. Horrifying stories are told of the wretched animals being piled up on their backs in ships' holds to be killed off at seamen's convenience. The result was the extermination of all the Indian Ocean giant tortoise species, except on Aldabra, where a population of some 150,000 has miraculously survived; and the severe depletion of most island populations in the Galapagos, to a low point from which they are at last being rescued by the Ecuadorian authorities and the Charles Darwin Research Station. Almost all the large tortoises on continents have been overexploited too.

Giant tortoise

Tuatara

Passenger pigeon

Geochelone radiata on Madagascar, one of the world's rarest tortoises, owes its desperate plight partly to being considered a local delicacy.

A similar fate has befallen many of the larger freshwater turtles or terrapins. In the mid-seventeenth century, in the Amazon and Orinoco basins, people living where the arrau *Podocnemis expansa* occurred 'never knew what hunger was'; its great numbers impeded the passage of canoes and smaller boats. For the first 300 years of western colonisation, the arrau was a primary food source and the basis of the economy along the two rivers. It was killed both for meat and for oil, which was used both as edible fat and for lamps, while the eggs were collected in heaps up to seven metres high. This reckless exploitation, coupled with destruction of the nesting beaches, so reduced the stocks that by the mid-nineteenth century the arrau was rare all over its original range. Today it breeds only in a few areas in Brazil, Bolivia, and the Amazon and Orinoco headwaters, whence, however, thousands of hatchlings are still exported for the pet trade.

Another overexploited South American river turtle is the terecay *P.unifilis*. Its eggs are a highly esteemed food that also yield a cooking oil; and its hatchlings go to the pet trade. Since little if any effort is being made to conserve the stocks of these turtles, a valuable resource of the region's inhabitants is being squandered. Similarly the painted batagur *Callagur borneoensis*, a large estuarine turtle of south-east Asia, is much depleted from overcollection of its eggs for human consumption.

Even that celebrated reptilian living fossil the tuatara, now well protected, was once exploited for food. This had disappeared from the two main islands of New Zealand before the British arrived early in the nineteenth century; as its remains have been found in Maori middens, it is assumed that the Maoris, who had come seven or eight hundred years earlier, and perhaps also their dogs, were responsible.

Two amphibians that have been badly depleted by overcollection for food are the large bullfrog *Leptodactylus fallax*, known as the 'mountain chicken', of mountain streams on eastern Caribbean islands from Montserrat to Grenada, which is often sold to hotel restaurants; and the Indian bullfrog *Rana tigrina*, exported, especially from Bangladesh, in increasing quantities to Europe and elsewhere.

Since the well-known and spectacular extinctions of the dodo, the great auk and the passenger pigeon, all killed primarily for food, overexploitation of birds and their eggs for food has continued widely, and has depleted many populations. In the Seychelles, overharvesting of sooty tern eggs led to an official British Government report in the 1950s. In Bali and elsewhere in South-east Asia the nests of the swiftlets used for bird's-nest soup are widely overexploited.

It is estimated that the 25 million migratory birds killed each year around the Mediterranean, very largely for food, represent 10-15 per cent of the available stocks. Up to one and a half million small birds are trapped in Malta alone and there are now only thirteen breeding species on the island. On Cyprus some half to three-quarters of all migrant birds are taken. There has been much argument as to whether or not this substantial Mediterranean harvest is depleting the breeding stocks in northern Europe. Certainly it does severely deplete the numbers of some migrant species in these areas, notably skylarks on Malta, quail and turtle doves in Egypt, and bee-eaters in Cyprus. So in any case the harvesters lose their resource.

Molluscs likewise provide valuable protein and are also frequently overexploited. Abalones are a striking example. In California in the early 1970s, the abalone harvest was less than a third of what it had been twenty years before; this was mainly due to overfishing, though the fishermen tried to blame the sea otter. Much of the Californian and Mexican harvest is

Great auk

canned and some is exported across the Pacific. The ormer, the European abalone, used to be fished in Guernsey, but has now almost vanished from the whole English Channel.

Off Long Island, New York, trawlermen began dredging for the surf clam, source of the celebrated New England clam chowder, in the 1950s; they quickly overfished the resource, and were forced to move south, first to New Jersey and then to Virginia. Commercial dredging for scallops began in Tasmania in 1919, but by 1960 the beds were exhausted. In Chile, the mussel *Mytilus chorus* has almost disappeared from its natural beds. In the western Pacific, Taiwan has seriously overfished giant clams; their adductor muscles are removed for their meat and the rest is left on the reef to rot. In Philippine, Palau, Fijian and Australian waters, illegal fishing has markedly reduced the populations of the clams *Tridacna gigas* and *T.derasa*.

Among land molluscs, the queen or pink conch has been overharvested in the Bahamas, both for food and for sale to tourists. The Roman snail, a gastronomic delicacy in Europe, still eaten in its millions, has become extinct or rare in many areas including Poland, Switzerland and the Netherlands. In Thailand, a promising commercial venture based on the introduced giant African snail failed from overharvesting.

There are fewer instances of overharvesting wild plants. In 1799, after the botanist William Curtis had created a fashion for eating sea kale, the wild populations around the British coasts were substantially reduced. The early settlers of North America provided a classic recipe for impoverishing the stock: to obtain pecan nuts, they simply felled the trees bearing the most nuts.

Giant African snail

2. Other Everyday Uses

In almost all the many material uses to which animal and plant products are put, such as clothing, fuel, building materials and drugs, the overfishing syndrome, unless rigorously guarded against, appears sooner or later.

Sea otter

Mammal skins have been used for human clothing from the dawn of man's emergence as a thinking and tool-using species, though nowadays furs have become a luxury in most parts of the world. Only since the arrival of 'civilisation', however, has their use become a significant cause of depletion of animal stocks. Beavers in most parts of Europe in the Middle Ages, and sea otters on the Pacific coast of North America more recently, both disappeared largely due to the demand for their fur. The otter stocks were discovered in the Aleutian islands in 1741 by the Russian navigator Vitus Bering, at a time when furs were what gold became a hundred years later and diamonds later still. So first the Russians ruthlessly pillaged them; then, on the sale of Alaska to the United States in 1867, they were harvested even more vigorously by the free enterprise buccaneers of America.

Fur seals have also been grossly overexploited for their pelts. The Kerguelen fur seal has the melancholy distinction of having been exterminated commercially three times over: first in the 1820s, at a time when one and a quarter million skins were being harvested annually; again 50 years later, when the colonies had revived enough to encourage more sealing, only to collapse after sixteen years; and finally in 1921, when a short-lived enterprise harvested 800 skins from Prince Edward Island in the southern Indian Ocean. Similarly, the Juan Fernandez fur seal was wiped out 150 years ago and regarded as extinct, until some were rediscovered on Alexander Selkirk Island off Chile as recently as 1965. Today, as described on p. 181, southern fur seal stocks have substantially recovered, and there is little doubt that, but for the present outcry over the harvesting of seals off eastern Canada, sooner or later an attempt would be made to restart southern sealing too. This outcry, by promoting boycotts, is currently restricting the market for sealskins, and is likely to continue at least until public opinion in Europe is satisfied that seals can be killed humanely.

In the North Pacific, a similar story can be told of the destruction of the northern or Pribilof fur seal stocks. In 1786, when the Russian navigator Gerassim Pribilof discovered the islands that now bear his name, some two and a half million seals may have been breeding there. But the sealers of Russia and North America set to work, and within twenty years had almost destroyed the resource. In 1805 the Russian authorities imposed the first of a series of stop-go bans that lasted through the nineteenth century. Because only males were allowed to be killed, reasonable seal stocks remained until the 1880s, when British and Canadian sealers took to pelagic sealing. Hunting on the high seas is especially destructive, since a great many seals sink when they are shot. This nearly finished the seals off, until the present conservation regime, described on p. 164, was established.

Today, the only wild land mammals being exploited on any scale for human clothing are those, discussed in the next section, whose furs, skins or feathers are primarily used for adornment.

Many wild animals exploited for meat – whales, seals, sea turtles, penguins – also yield fats and oils, which are used for fuel as well as food. The main difference between whale and seal exploitation has been that the whalers set up machinery to control it, but failed. So the whale resource has been destroyed, most notably the great whales of the southern oceans: the blue whale, the largest animal that has ever existed, and the fin, sei and humpback whales. In the southern oceans the total biomass of the great whales is believed to have fallen from 40-50 million tons to about five million. Before this, five other whales had already been hunted near to extinction. As long ago as the Middle Ages, English and Basque whalers had exterminated the Biscay stock of the North Atlantic right whale (so called because it was the 'right' whale to catch), which still remains very rare. Whalers in the Pacific almost exterminated both the gray whale and the bowhead or Greenland right whale, while the North Pacific right whale and the southern right whale were also overhunted. These five whales were all slow enough to be caught by seamen in sailing or even rowing boats; none became biologically extinct, but all were critically endangered and even after years of protection some stocks are still extremely small.

Few wild animals seem to have been depleted or exterminated for their value as draught animals, except perhaps the wild ancestor of the dromedary. In Burma, the only country that uses work elephants on any scale today, the 200 that have to be captured each year to maintain the work force may represent a major drain on the surviving wild population of 3000-6000.

Dromedary

Trees and shrubs have always been major sources of both fuel and building materials, and have frequently been overexploited. Thus, most of the surviving trees in the old Caledonian pine forest in the Scottish Highlands were felled to provide fuel and timber during the eighteenth century; and in southern England the iron foundries of the Weald eventually failed because they overexploited the oak timber on which they depended for fuel. On remote St Helena in the South Atlantic, most stands of the now very rare ebony *Trochetia melanoxylon* were felled, to provide fuel to burn the lime needed for mortar, for fortifications during the Napoleonic Wars. The pencil manufacturers of the United States have so depleted the red cedar *Juniperus virginianus* forests of the southern states, that they have had to turn to incense cedar *Libocedrus decurrens* from the west coast.

The present-day destruction of whole forests for their timber is discussed on p. 102, but the 23 tropical hardwoods known as mahoganies are one group of trees that have suffered especially severely from demands

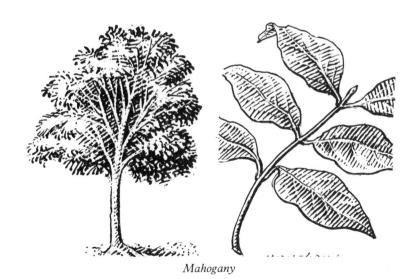

Mahogany

Grey hornbill

for building timber and furniture. If present trends continue, these trees may well be commercially extinct by 1990. Unfortunately, no mahogany plantations have yet proved viable. True mahogany is *Swietenia mahogani* from northern South America, but much mahogany in recent use has been African mahogany from *Khaya ivorensis* (both Meliaceae). Supplies of both these have fallen off so much that most of the mahoganies used in trade today, under the name of Philippine mahogany, are dipterocarps, mainly *Shorea*, from South-east Asia. Many species of ebony, and other hardwoods often called ironwood, are also being harvested faster than wild stocks are being replenished. Rattans, too, are falling victim to the twin dangers of overexploitation and forest clearance; as they become scarce in the wild, villagers are driven to poach, often from national parks and nature reserves, both their own supplies and what they sell commercially. Massive felling of mangroves is occurring in Sarawak, Sabah, India, Venezuela, Madagascar, and elsewhere in the tropics: in Asia mainly for export to Japan as wood chips for the manufacture of pulp and rayon; and in Madagascar for firewood, charcoal, tannin and lumber.

In Sri Lanka, where exploitable limestone, needed for building, is scarce, coral reefs are quarried for their lime content. In the Maldives and the Comoros, huge blocks of living coral are prised from the reefs by hand, and either moulded into building stones or burned to make mortar. Even when dead coral is dredged, many living corals are also destroyed, and with them the innumerable other creatures that compose the coral reef community.

Demands on wild stocks for the supply of drugs were discussed on p. 24 The medicinal leech, for instance, is now severely depleted all over Europe, except in Hungary, by a combination of overexploitation and habitat pollution. In the Gir Forest in north-west India the grey hornbill was exterminated comparatively recently because of its supposed medicinal value. The metre-long giant salamander *Andrias japonicus*, which inhabits rushing mountain streams in Honshu, the main island of Japan, is now greatly depleted because so many have been used in traditional Japanese medicines; and also because dam construction and the channeling of rivers into concrete banks, has greatly reduced its available habitat. The same fate has befallen its Chinese relative *A.davidianus*. A combination of direct killing with habitat destruction is the surest way of destroying genetic resources.

The demand for rhino horn, and other rhino products, in oriental medicine has been a major factor in stimulating the poaching that has brought all five rhinoceros species into the *Red Data Book*. The reduced supply due to this catastrophic fall in rhino numbers, coupled with restrictions on trade due to the CITES convention, have at last begun to divert some of this demand to other products such as saiga horn and even, in Hong Kong, to fake 'rhino hide', which actually comes from the water buffalo. However, although Japan and Hong Kong have banned rhino horn imports, Singapore and South Korea have not; so there has recently been an upsurge in poaching the great Indian rhino in Assam, the horn being smuggled out of Calcutta to Singapore. Similarly, the demand for musk from both traditional Asian medicine and the cosmetics industry has led to the disappearance of the musk deer from many parts of the Himalayas, even in protected areas such as the Sagarmatha National Park around Mount Everest. Kathmandu is the centre both of the illegal trade and of its poaching squads, currently operating in Bhutan and Sikkim. The fact that the sale of a few musk pods covers all the living costs of an Indian hill family for a year goes far to explain why the musk deer is now endangered.

In Mexico, the black turtle, the local race of the green turtle, once nested on the Pacific coast in millions. One reason why it now numbers only thousands, which are still being steadily poached away, is that its meat and blood are locally believed to lead to health, vigour and sexual potency. The eggs, valued as an aphrodisiac, command very high prices in the cities.

Among medicinal plants depleted by overcollecting, are the yam species, which provides the diosgenin used in birth-control pills; the Eurasian sweet flag *Acorus calamus*, an aroid whose rhizomes contain an essential oil with insecticidal and sedative properties; and ginseng, valued as an aphrodisiac, which is heavily poached in the Shenandoah and Great Smoky Mountains National Parks in the south-eastern United States.

3. Ornamentation

More species are at risk today from the demand for their skins or other parts for ornamenting and adorning people or their domestic environment, than for such utilitarian purposes as food or fuel. Thus in Colombia most of those larger animals whose skins were in great demand for luxury goods only a decade ago are now on the endangered list: spotted cats, otters, deer, peccaries and caimans. In Yemen a quite recent fashion among newly oil-rich Arab males for rhino-horn dagger handles, the *djambias* traditionally worn as a symbol of manhood, has severely threatened the two African rhinos.

By 1980 numbers of the black rhino had fallen to 14,000-15,000 throughout the continent, already a severely depleted figure; four years later they had fallen by a further 40 per cent to 9000. By 1984 the black rhino was extinct in Uganda and nearly so in Botswana, Chad, Ethiopia, Malawi, Rwanda and perhaps also Somalia; Mozambique had lost half and Angola and Sudan two-thirds of their black rhinos in those years when the world had already been fully alerted to the plight of the black rhino due to poaching. In the Central African Republic, Sudan and Uganda the northern white rhino appears to have been exterminated by the same well-armed poaching gangs, largely supplying this market, as are steadily extirpating the black rhino, leaving only a tiny remnant of the northern race, fewer than twenty, still alive in the wild, in the Garamba National Park in Zaire. Though Yemen has now banned the trade, rhino horn continues to be smuggled in, mainly from Khartoum despite Sudan's signature of the CITES convention.

A similar demand for those mammalian teeth large enough to rank as ivory, especially from elephants and walruses, is the main reason, together with habitat destruction, for the serious decline in the numbers of both Asian and African elephants. The increasing shortage of Asian ivory and consequent rise in price has played havoc with the ivory carving industry in India, concentrated especially in Kerala and the Delhi area, and the old Hindu custom of brides wearing ivory bangles has almost died out, except in Gujarat and Rajasthan.

North of the Sahara, elephants were extinct by the early Middle Ages, but to the south of it upwards of a million still exist. Estimates of the number of African elephants killed illegally each year for their ivory differ widely. Iain Douglas-Hamilton has suggested it is between 50,000 and 100,000; Ian Parker and Esmond Bradley Martin put it at 40,000. In *Ivory Crisis* (1983) Parker maintains that the part played by ivory poaching in the decrease of African elephant stocks has been exaggerated, but in 1984 the SSC Specialist Group on African elephants concluded that the ivory trade had indeed been largely responsible for the population collapse. Even the lower estimate of elephants killed annually for their tusks can mask a serious impact in some areas. In Uganda, admittedly an extreme case, 90 per cent of the elephants were killed in the 1970s, mainly during the

Sweet flag

Black rhino

turbulent Amin years and their aftermath; this reduced total numbers from 30,000 to 2000, half of each total representing the elephants in Murchison Falls National Park. Indeed, the poached elephants are too often those in the national parks that ought to be most securely protected, but which are as easily found by poachers as by tourists. In the Manovo-Gounda-St Floris National Park in the Central African Republic, for example, one-tenth of the 2000-3000 elephants were poached in the first half of 1980 alone.

The root of the ivory problem is the gain to be made by killing even one elephant: a large pair of tusks may weigh 200 lb and fetch more than $30 per lb. Nor is it any longer just a case of local tribesmen adding to their small incomes; the poaching gangs are large, well armed and aggressive. However, the ivory trade is aware of the risk of losing its African sources of supply, as has already happened in Asia, and its more responsible members are anxious that the resource should be properly managed.

One of the more unpleasing phenomena of the 1970s was the misuse of the concept of 'fun furs', which was originally intended for mink and other ranched furs, so as to consign many wild mammals to their deaths at the whim of fashion designers in New York, Paris and London. To conservationists, the most troublesome of these fashions was the sudden, but luckily short-lived, mania for wearing leopardskin coats. We have never had any really reliable facts about the impact of this craze on the world stocks of leopards, jaguars, ocelots, and other spotted cats; but at the very least it must have depleted or exterminated many local stocks, before it was more or less suppressed by the use of the CITES convention. Certainly the disappearance of the bobcat from much of the eastern and central United States is at least partly due to the undiminished demand for its skins.

The widespread destruction of the stocks of the vicuña for the sake of its extremely fine wool, now very much at the luxury end of the market, is another case in point. Since Peru has successfully rehabilitated the wild population, notably in the Pampa Galeras reserve, it is further discussed on p. 180

A few mammals have been endangered by the tourist souvenir trade, notably the bumblebee-sized Kitti's hog-nosed bat *Craseonycteris thonglongya*, the smallest mammal in the world, found only in or near Sai Yok National Park in western Thailand. By 1981 demand for its corpse as a souvenir had reduced it to one cave only, where as few as 30 bats remained from some 200 only nine months earlier.

Kitti's hog-nosed bat

At the turn of the century the plumage trade was a serious threat to several bird populations, notably egrets (whose plumes were confusingly called osprey) in Florida, but this has been largely stopped. The threats from the millinery trade to several species of gull and tern, which became almost extinct in New England, has long gone. The reasons why the present world population of the short-tailed albatross is so low, about 200 birds remaining on Torishima in the North Pacific Bonin Islands, is that between 1887 and 1903 plume hunters nearly exterminated it. By 1939 only 30-50 birds were left, and ten years later it was mistakenly reported extinct. The drain on rare bird stocks for their feathers still continues, however, for in 1983 the US authorities uncovered a smuggling business, worth one million dollars a year, of bald eagle carcasses and plumage that were used to make replicas of Indian artefacts such as fans, whistles, rattles and head-dresses. Eighteen other species were also involved. In the Guianas the red feathers of the threatened scarlet ibis are used to make 'feather flowers' for tourists; as a result the bird no longer breeds in French Guiana. Feathers can, however, be harvested without destroying the resource: similar ornaments are made in East Africa from moulted flamingo feathers.

Greater bird of paradise

In Papua New Guinea, although the skins and feathers of birds of paradise have acquired a semi-monetary function, they have been harvested for thousands of years without harming the stocks. But in the last 30-40 years, when tribal war has steadily diminished, tribesmen have been able to travel further afield and have considerably stepped up their hunting of birds of paradise. Since they have also acquired firearms, and a demand for bird of paradise skins has appeared in world trade, stocks are now potentially threatened with depletion. Fortunately no bird of paradise has yet had to be included in the *Bird Red Data Book*, thanks both to the great care taken of their plumes by the Papuans, and also to the control of international trade in most of the species by the CITES convention.

Crocodiles have been depleted all over the world, sometimes, as with the gharial in India and Nepal and the Cuban crocodile, almost to the point of extinction. Although there are local uses for the meat and skins, the main economic motive for hunting them – as distinct from the desire to kill a dangerous wild animal – has been the supply of their hides to the luxury leather trade. This has seriously depleted the estuarine and marsh crocodiles all over south-east Asia; the American and Morelet's crocodiles in the Caribbean; and the black and spectacled caimans on the South American mainland. The American alligator was declining quite sharply in the south-eastern United States, but since it was protected in 1969 it has recovered to the point where it is no longer included in the *Red Data Book*, and harvesting is allowed again in certain states.

American alligator

Crocodile hunting patterns usually follow the classic overfishing syndrome. The first species hunted are the large ones in open-water areas such as rivers and lakes, and usually only the larger specimens are taken. When these supplies are exhausted, and they are invariably short-lived, attention turns to the juveniles, and to the stocks living in more difficult areas to hunt, such as reed swamps. When these supplies too are gone, the tanning industry develops a method of tanning the hides of a second species, which has previously been ignored because it was economically worthless. The same procedure is then followed until it no longer pays to hunt the second species, by which time all crocodiles are rare, or attention turns to a third.

Crocodile leather provides a serious dilemma for conservationists, who have deprecated its use on the ground that the poaching of wild stocks cannot be adequately controlled while the luxury demand persists, as in Togo, where the shops are still full of tourist goods made from the skins of crocodiles, pythons and monitor lizards. On the other hand, well-run crocodile farms are an acceptable way of exploiting this valuable resource, as those in Papua New Guinea, Zimbabwe and South Africa show, both providing income for local people and bringing in valuable foreign exchange. The Zimbabwean Minister of Natural Resources has said that without the economic justification these farms provide, the government would have found it hard to justify the widespread conservation of crocodiles. The crux of the matter rests on adequate arrangements for preventing poached crocodile skins from getting on to the market, which in many countries is virtually impossible to achieve. The dilemma remains: how to protect the wild stocks and at the same time secure a market for the farmed skins. The same dilemma applies to leopard skins legitimately obtained by African game departments in the course of stock protection, which as a result of decisions at the CITES meeting in Botswana in 1983 may now again enter international trade.

Green turtle

As crocodile leather becomes scarcer, it is replaced by leather from marine turtles. In 1979 the Sea Turtle Conservation Strategy declared that the leather trade 'constitutes an intolerable drain' on marine turtle stocks, especially of the olive ridley and green turtles. The worst overharvesting was on the Pacific coasts of Ecuador, where it has now been banned, and of Mexico, where it continues under the aegis of a state-owned processing plant. Some 1.4 million olive ridleys were killed on the beaches of three western Mexican states between 1966 and 1977. The turtle shell most in demand comes from the hawksbill. Every year more than a quarter of a million hawksbills are taken for tortoiseshell jewellery and polished carapaces, the Caribbean stocks being the most heavily exploited. The hawksbill is listed in Appendix I of CITES, but Japan, which consumes the great bulk of the tortoiseshell in international trade, has entered a reservation for it and two other sea turtles so that imports can continue.

The most gratuitously wasteful killing of sea turtles, especially of young hawksbills, is for stuffed souvenirs. The Sea Turtle Conservation Strategy says flatly that 'this totally unnecessary luxury trade is having a serious impact on hawksbill stocks and should cease forthwith'. Between 1962 and 1977 Japan alone imported at least 600,000 young hawksbills; this takes no account of the souvenirs sold to tourists in the countries of origin, which never enter into international trade. A similar frivolous luxury trade afflicts young crocodiles and caimans. Although Colombian law forbids the export of caiman skins less than 150 cm long, the majority of skins listed in the export documents examined by the leading South American turtle expert, the late Professor Federico Medem, proved to be shorter.

Snakes and lizards, especially monitors, are also heavily exploited for their skins, which are all too often traded illegally. An estimated $60 million worth of snakeskin is smuggled out of India every year, and many snake and other reptile skins are believed to leave Sri Lanka in tourists' baggage. Snakes are still illegally killed and their skins tanned and sold openly all over India. As a result, sixteen species, including the cobra, the krait and three species of viper are now classed as endangered. The Indian python is locally extinct in many areas, and both the checkered keelback water snake, perhaps the commonest snake in India, and the rat snake have been locally exterminated by intensive collection for the skin trade.

Cobra

Invertebrates that enter the jewellery and curio trade include brightly coloured tropical butterflies, corals, sea urchins and many molluscs. Most of these are at a greater or lesser risk of overexploitation, the most threatened today being the birdwing butterflies of South-east Asia and the black corals of the Caribbean. Though seven species of birdwing are legally protected in Papua New Guinea, trade in them and in the more ornamental shells of land molluscs continues illegally, while on one Philippine reef overcollecting has reduced the six commonest coral species by three-quarters. The tree snail *Papuastyla pulcherrima* of Manus Island north of New Guinea, the only large, bright green tree snail, is in serious trouble from a combination of overcollection and habitat destruction. Not only is it in great demand from amateur collectors, but it is losing its habitat because the islanders cut down trees to collect it. It seems highly unlikely that such a drain can continue indefinitely without at least local depletions and extinctions.

The pearl-bearing freshwater mussel in Europe and the various species of pearly mussel in North America have both been seriously overexploited. Pearl fishing has been banned in parts of Scandinavia and Germany, but in Britain treasure-seekers still take many mussels, so that juveniles now form no more than five per cent of the population, a sure sign of a stock about to plummet. In the nineteenth and early twentieth centuries pearl mussels were the basis of thriving button and pearl industries in the upper Mississippi basin, but massive overexploitation and water pollution destroyed them. In 1929 the shell output of Lake Pepin, Minnesota, was only four per cent of what it was in 1914, and by 1946 the shelling industry in the Mississippi below Muscatine, Iowa, was extinct. Nevertheless, poaching continues, and in Kentucky in 1981 poachers were caught with an illegal catch of 10,000 mussels.

In Indonesia both the pearl oyster *Pinctada margaritifer* and the top shell *Trochus nilotica* have been stripped from most reefs by divers who subsist solely on collecting shells, and like so many fishermen have fished themselves out of a living. Overfishing has also affected the mother-of-pearl fishery in New Guinea, so that a moratorium had to be imposed on top-shell collecting. Off California, abalones have been overexploited for both their shells and their meat. In many parts of the world there is an enormous trade in tropical marine shells and corals, with between 5000 and 10,000 retail outlets in Florida alone. The Philippines, where Cebu City is

Black corals

known as the coral and shell capital of the world, export over 4000 tonnes of shells and over 1800 tonnes of coral a year. In Jamaica too, illegal collection of corals, molluscs, sponges and gorgonians is prevalent; even in the Montego Bay Marine Park few colonies of the pillar coral *Dendrogyra cylindricus* are undamaged.

Black corals (Anthipathidae), greatly valued in the jewellery trade, have been overharvested throughout the Caribbean, as well as in Hawaii, Galapagos, the Red Sea and off New Zealand. Around St Lucia and Curaçao the resource is believed to be virtually extinct. Even where, as in southern Baja California, Mexico, attempts are made to manage the fishery, these are often frustrated by 'pirate' divers. In Hawaii too the harvesting of black corals is now controlled as a result of their protection by CITES.

Sandalwood *Santalum album*, a parasitic tree of southern Asia, is greatly valued for its hard, close-grained, scented and oil-rich heartwood, which is used both to carve such items as trinket boxes and and to distil an aromatic oil with medicinal uses. In India, trade in sandalwood is a Government monopoly, but such is the scale of poaching and smuggling, often by gangs who live off the land, that wild-growing stocks are described as 'vestigial'. One Kerala forester is said to have woken up to find that all the sandalwood trees growing inside his compound had been felled and removed during the night. Dead flower-heads of the sea oat *Uniona paniculata*, valued for decoration in the eastern United States, are harvested commercially. At the north end of their range wardens of some national seashores have to guard against piratical raids in which whole pick-up loads may vanish overnight.

4. Sport

Just as hunting for food and commercial gain led to overharvesting of stocks, so did hunting for sport. Even 300 years ago, King Charles II and other landowners in southern England were overshooting the grey partridge and had to supplement the stock with imported red-legged partridges from southern Europe. Ironically, today the red-legs are proving the better adapted of the two to modern chemical agriculture, and over much of southern and eastern England they are now the commoner species. Replenishment of depleted native game stocks from elsewhere has now become a worldwide practice, sending, for instance, ring-necked pheasants from Asia to western Europe and thence to North America and even New Zealand; California quail to Argentina; and wild turkeys from North America to Hawaii. In New England eastern cottontails *Sylvilagus floridanus*, a hardy hybrid rabbit stock imported by sportsmen from all over the eastern United States, now supplant the native cottontail *S. transitionalis* wherever the two come into contact. Wild turkeys were also successfully reintroduced into the north-eastern United States, where the original stock was overhunted by the nineteenth century.

California quail

Various deer species too have been transported about the world, either to augment stocks or to improve their genetic basis, because of the deer hunter's inveterate habit of shooting the males with the finest antlers, which leaves only those with poor antlers to pass their genes to the next generation. (In Alaska this abuse, permitted by the state Fish and Game Department, has reduced the proportion of bull moose in the Kenai National Wildlife Refuge to 13 per 100 cows.) Thus there are now sika deer from the Far East in Britain, Indian sambar and hog deer in Australia, and both elk (wapiti) from North America and chamois from the European Alps in New Zealand.

Heavy shooting pressure in West European countries means that before the opening of each season, the wild or feral stocks of game birds, especially ring-necked pheasants, have to be copiously augmented with large numbers of farmed birds. Some parts of North America are so overhunted that the birds are only released on the day of the shoot, and in some private US reserves wild turkeys, bobwhite quail and mallard are all released 'in front of' hunters.

The sport-hunting pressure on wildfowl is also very high in many countries. In the USSR upwards of 30 million ducks, geese and even coots (by no means a gourmet's bird) are shot every year, and in Sweden sport hunters shoot more than 70 per cent of each year's crop of mallard. Wildfowl stocks, especially of mallard, have to be replenished annually in many countries by releasing farmed birds, although in North America breeding stocks are well enough protected by the national wildlife refuge system to allow upwards of twelve million wild birds to be shot each year. Yet, although the black duck has declined by 60 per cent since 1955, many hunters are resisting attempts to reduce bag limits. The Labrador duck was actually exterminated by hunters, the last known specimen being shot in New York state in 1875. That similar attitudes prevail in Australia was shown when 290 out of a flock of 400 of the endangered freckled duck, protected in all seven states, were shot on the first day of Victoria's 1985 shooting season.

American elk or wapiti

Waders (shorebirds) are also shot for sport, though less than formerly because so many species are protected. The Eskimo curlew of eastern North America, however, nearly joined the Labrador duck; in the mid-nineteenth century immense flocks of this Arctic-breeding bird wintered on the Texas coast, and as late as 1863 more than 7000 migrating birds were shot in one day on Nantucket Island, Massachusetts. By 1900 very few indeed were being seen in New England, and since then only singletons or very small parties have been sighted at long intervals down the east coast; one was actually shot in Barbados in 1964.

Threatened non-game species, even when protected, can still be depleted by shooting. In the Pyrenees trophy hunters have destroyed entire breeding colonies of griffon vultures, and sport-shooting is also a serious threat to the red-billed chough in Brittany. In 1982 alone twelve brown bears, although protected, were shot in and around the Abruzzi National Park in Italy. It was in the same spirit that Arab hunters invading the Empty Quarter from Qatar and Abu Dhabi eventually succeeded in 1962 in exterminating in the wild the white or Arabian oryx, an animal held in especial esteem in the Arab world.

Arabian oryx

The widespread shooting of Mediterranean birds (see p. 72), though mainly for food, is also a sport. In Malta, where one in eight of the male population is a licensed hunter, shooting small birds is so deeply embedded in popular culture that the hunters recently petitioned the Government to allow hunting in two small bird sanctuaries up to noon on weekdays and until 9 a.m. at weekends. In Lebanon too, the mass shooting, estimated at 15-20 million birds a year, appears to be largely a way for men to prove their virility as well as, apparently, an outlet for anger and frustration over the civil war. In Greece, men and boys scour the countryside with cars and mopeds, and even kill such relatively inedible birds as golden orioles, cuckoos and red-footed falcons.

As Frank Graham of the National Audubon Society once said: 'many people feel an uncontrollable urge to shoot any large, colourful bird they see'. Or, in Sir Frank Fraser Darling's memorable words, 'the human race, particularly the mass of the so-called civilised part of it, has shown itself too often quite unfit collectively to care for a population of wild creatures that have a trophy value'.

Soldiers, being trained to kill, have a particularly bad record of wanton disturbance or destruction of wildlife. Thus the last flamingo colony on Andros in the Bahamas came to an end in the late 1940s, after persistent buzzing by Royal Air Force pilots for 'fun'. However, the British armed forces have made amends during their recent spells of duty in the Falkland Islands, enforcing strict regulations against any kind of disturbance of the wildlife.

When United Nations troops occupied Zaire in the early 1960s, they invaded the southern sector of the Upemba National Park and killed large numbers of antelopes, zebra and other animals. Their example was followed by Katangan gendarmes, the Zairois National Army, commercial operators and eventually the park guards and local villagers. As a result the formerly teeming game herds of the park were reduced within seven years to a few timid survivors, fleeing at the first sound of a vehicle. In 1978 there was a fearful slaughter of animals in Uganda, when Amin's retreating soldiers passed through the national parks. They used their sophisticated weapons to devastate the stocks not only of elephant, but also of black and white rhinos, topi, Jackson's hartebeest, Uganda kob and defassa water-buck. In 1979 alone, three-quarters of all the game animals in Murchison Falls National Park were killed. In both Israel and Jordan the gazelles were nearly wiped out before the military could be brought under control, and the edmi gazelle *Gazella cuvieri* has suffered in the same way in Algeria. Lebanese soldiers during the civil war have been using eagles and other migrating raptors for target practice; the endangered scimitar-horned oryx has been a major target for heavily armed military convoys in Chad; and the extremely endangered Persian fallow deer is reported to have been wiped out during the Iraq-Iran war in one of its two last localities in the wild, the Karkheh wildlife refuge in Iran. In southern Sumatra the military have been blamed for the virtual extermination of all the larger wildlife except monkeys and pigs.

Falconry has two impacts: on the hunting hawks or falcons, and on the hunted prey. It is a minority pursuit in western Europe, but a major one in the Middle East. The consequent demand for gyrfalcons, peregrines and other raptors leads to serious predation on nests by poachers who seek to supply the Arab and German markets. If not checked, this could undoubtedly lead to local extinctions. The prey species most in danger is the houbara bustard, whose stocks Arab falconers have severely depleted in

Flamingo

Houbara bustard

the Arabian peninsula and are now steadily depleting in Pakistan, where the government is unfortunately not controlling this pressure on the birds, mainly from the USSR, that winter in their country. Between 1965 and 1980 the number breeding in Kazakhstan fell by 75 per cent.

A form of trophy hunting that involves eggs rather than birds is obsessive egg collecting. Though it is very much a minority pursuit, it can seriously harm rare and endangered birds. Thus the nest of one of the first few Ross's gulls to breed in Canada was robbed; the eggs are said to have been sold for $10,000. The first pair of ospreys to return to breed in Scotland in the 1950s was robbed more than once.

Freshwater fishing is another sport that takes an excessive toll. Most of the three million anglers in Britain can only pursue their pastime if they heavily restock the waters they fish, sometimes with native species, such as brown trout or roach, but often with aliens, such as rainbow trout. The Atlantic salmon is not only a top sport fish, but has great commercial value, especially when caught in bulk in the sea. Consequently there has been gross overfishing, especially off Greenland and the Faeroes, and this, coupled with widespread poaching from rivers, has seriously reduced the breeding stock on both sides of the Atlantic, where it is extinct in many once fine salmon rivers, even in Finland, where catches have fallen from 150 to only 2-3 tonnes a year. One sport fish which actually became extinct was the relict population of the Arctic grayling in Michigan. Overfishing, such as the removal, in a fortnight, of 3000 fish from a single river, the Manistee, for sale in Chicago, exterminated the grayling in that river by 1935 and in the rest of the state not long afterwards.

A by-product of sport-fishing that is ecologically particularly unpleasing is the poisoning of rough or coarse fish to make way for game fish, as when 450 miles of the Colorado River in Utah and Wyoming were treated with rotenone in 1962. Now several of the target species, such as Colorado squawfish, razorback sucker and bonytail, are officially endangered and are being reared in a fish hatchery for restocking the river. As recently as 1981 a 55-mile stretch of the Feather River in California was similarly treated, and elsewhere in the United States rough fish have been trapped and barriers put into rivers to restrict their movements.

Spearfishing has likewise had disastrous results, notably the virtual extinction of such large fish as the cernier *Polyprion americanus* and the merou *Epinephilus gigas* in the Mediterranean and their relatives in Jamaica and the Philippines. These groupers, as well as parrotfishes and wrasses, mature as females, and only become males when older and larger. So if spearfishermen kill all the large specimens, as they so often do, these species cannot breed, however many smaller females survive. In Indonesia the large fish appear to have an unexpected protector: 'sharks soon learn to associate spearfishermen with an easy meal'.

5. Incidental Losses

Animals and plants are killed incidentally in the course of many kinds of human social and economic activity. Fishermen in particular are responsible for huge losses in non-target populations. Tuna fishermen use the dolphins and porpoises that school with the tuna shoals to lead them to their quarry, and as a result also catch them along with the tuna and drown them in their purse seine nets. At one time in the Pacific US fishermen alone killed more than 100,000 dolphins a year. Legislation has substantially reduced this kill, but in 1984 US tuna fishermen still caught nearly 21,000 unwanted small cetaceans, while the numerous Japanese and Taiwanese fishermen are quite uncontrolled. Off Sri Lanka some 17,000 porpoises a

Brünnich's guillemot or thick-billed murre (see p. 86)

year are believed to perish in a gillnet fishery established with FAO aid. Gillnet fisheries appear to cause most harm to both seals and cetaceans, which often cannot detect the monofilament nets by either eye or ear.

Incidental catch is indeed a very widespread problem, involving such endangered or vulnerable species as estuarine crocodiles (barramundi fishery, Australia), Kemp's ridley turtles (shrimp fishery, Gulf of Mexico), leatherback turtles and Hawaiian monk seals (Japanese squid fishery, north-west of Hawaii), the Saimaa seal (fishing nets, Finland), the beiji river dolphin (sturgeon fishery, China), dugongs (widely in the tropics) and even otters (lobster creels, Outer Hebrides; abalone fishery, California). In Queensland one fisherman accidentally caught 23 dugongs while working a seagrass bed in an estuary, and many dugongs, dolphins, turtles, rays and other marine creatures are caught in shark barriers. A turtle-excluder device attached to nets has proved very effective in the Gulf of Mexico.

Seabird stocks too suffer severe drains from incidental catch. In the Danish gillnet salmon fisheries off West Greenland, some half a million thick-billed murres (Brünnich's guillemot) perish every year, along with a great many razorbills and other diving seabirds. In the 1970s the Japanese gillnet fishery in the North Pacific is believed to have caught about 50 million salmon, and although Japan publishes no figures, US scientists estimated the resultant annual seabird mortality at between 280,000 and 750,000. This means that since the fishery began in 1952, Japanese fishermen could have destroyed some 4.7 million seabirds, 58 per cent of them murres (guillemots), 27 per cent shearwaters and 9 per cent puffins. Some of these shearwaters had migrated from as far afield as Australia, New Zealand and Chile. Nearly 600 dead seabirds were found entangled in the ground nets used by fishermen along 12 kilometres of the Polish Baltic coast in one recent winter, and similar mortality is believed to occur along the whole coastline. Freshwater fishermen and anglers create similar hazards for swans and other birds by abandoning nylon fishing line.

Moreover, purse-seine fisheries can be very wasteful of fish, even of the target species, as the eminent Swedish conservationist, Kai Curry-Lindahl, has pointed out. Hauls of shoal fishes, such as mackerel, are often too large to be handled by the boat, so that nearly all are thrown back. Entire catches are also 'slipped' if they contain too many fishes of unwanted species or even target fishes of the wrong size. Moreover, most of the dumped catch, often juveniles of commercial species, die from shock, suffocation or injury. About 7 million tonnes of fish are believed to be wasted in this way worldwide every year. In shrimp trawls non-target species form some 80 per cent of the catch, so that several tonnes of 'trash' fish, crabs, sponges and marine plants die for every tonne of shrimps caught and frozen. Even common species can be made locally extinct, as the common skate has become in the Irish Sea because it was a 'by-catch' in another fishery. Similarly, whalers, who are supposed to catch only male sperm whales, often take a by-catch of females because of the difficulty of sexing sperm whales at sea.

Ocean fishing can also kill by delayed action: fishermen often abandon their nets at sea, creating the so-called ghost fishery: floating islands of trawl net and vast invisible submerged spiderwebs of nylon, made up of thousands of tons of lost and discarded fishing nets. Some 18 kilometres of net are believed to be lost every night in the North Pacific alone, and these are believed to be responsible for the deaths of some half a million seabirds and 10,000 Dall's porpoise each year. They are also one of the factors blamed for the recent fall in the numbers of the Pribilof fur seal, perhaps accounting for as many as 150,000 seals a year. The Hawaiian monk seal and several seals of the southern oceans may also be victims of the ghost

Mackerel

Common skate

fishery, but the evidence in all these cases is inevitably largely circumstantial. The dynamiting of fish near coral reefs likewise involves a great incidental destruction of corals and many other creatures. Nearly half the Pacific countries report reef damage from illegal dynamiting and poisoning for fish.

A side effect of overfishing, which is only just beginning to be realised, is its impact on the food supply and so the numbers of fish predators: fewer Alaska pollack mean fewer Pribilof fur seals; fewer sand-eels mean fewer auks in British Columbia; and fewer pilchards mean fewer South African jackass penguins. The converse of this is the increase in the southern oceans of seals, seabirds and perhaps minke whales, all krill feeders, because the overfishing of the great whales reduced their predation on krill. Similarly the overfishing of white fish, herring and mackerel off northern Europe in the early twentieth century led to a population explosion of their sand-eel prey, which in turn resulted in an increase in the puffins and other seabirds that prey on sand-eels, and perhaps also of the grey seal, now known to be a great sand-eel predator.

Even the provision of bait can lead to overexploitation; in Chile, the removal of protection from sealions has led to hundreds being killed as bait for the king crab fishery.

Farmers have always persecuted certain wild animals as potential competitors for their crops and stock. In Australia kangaroos, especially the big red and grey kangaroos, and flying foxes or fruit bats suffer in this way. The kangaroos are accused, not wholly accurately, of competing with sheep for grazing. The flying foxes are persecuted even more speciously for alleged damage to fruit, a charge that was disposed of by the biologist Francis Ratcliffe 60 years ago. Nevertheless, flying foxes, which play a vital part in the pollination of fruit and other economically valuable trees, have been constantly harried and in Queensland have even been recently deprotected. Once there were many roosts containing millions of bats – one is known to have held 30 million – but now only a few roosts hold more than 100,000.

In Rwanda in 1975 the entire adult elephant population was killed and all the juveniles were moved to the Akagera National Park, because of the threat they represented to cultivated areas. The endemic wild pig of Iriomote has been nearly exterminated on this island in the extreme south of Japan, largely because it damages crops, coupled with habitat destruction, and a skin disease derived from domestic pigs; it is also good to eat. In some parts of Java too, poisoning, partly for crop protection, has greatly reduced the number of Javan pigs *Sus verrucosus*.

Grazing wild geese are seen in many parts of the world as competing with farm stock for crops and grass: barnacle geese in Scotland, Canada geese in Wisconsin, and upland geese in the Falkland Islands. As a result, farmers persecute all these species, sometimes even when they are protected. Ironically, we now know that geese are often beneficial to grassland, since their droppings contribute to a rapid turnover of organic matter that both improves and conserves the soil.

Stock-rearers likewise campaign against mammals and birds they accuse of taking lambs: the coyote and the golden eagle in western North America, the white-tailed sea eagle in Norway and the wedge-tailed eagle in Australia. Political pressure by western cattlemen has for many years obliged the US Government to engage in an expensive predator control programme that has certainly reduced the numbers of the cougar and some other predators, and exterminated the wolves of Yellowstone National Park. In New Mexico too, the National Park Service has recently been forced by sheep farmers' complaints to agree to the killing of cougars in

Upland goose

Carlsbad Caverns National Park. In strictly economic terms all this has been a substantial waste of public money, ineffective in reducing coyote numbers, but destroying many non-target species and domestic pets. In Mexico ranchers who feared attacks on their stock actually exterminated the local race of the grizzly bear. Dingos in Australia and hyaenas and jackals in Africa have all, at times, been victimised. In East Africa hunting dogs *Lycaon pictus* have also been killed in national parks, on the spurious grounds that they harm the other animals.

Ever since the Middle Ages, bounties have been a favourite method of attempting to control predators, and even in the 1960s lions were exterminated in the north of Upper Volta (now Burkina Faso) by a bounty programme. However, even the official mind is at last coming to accept what scientists have been telling governments for many years, that bounties are much too often an open-ended commitment, almost an outdoor-relief programme for the trappers, which rarely achieve their aim, and sometimes actually stimulate population growth in the target species. Moreover, it is all too easy for trappers to claim rewards for animals they have not killed.

Fishermen are no less keen to kill supposed competitors for their fish. The last known colony of Caribbean monk seals was exterminated by fishermen in Yucatan, Mexico, in 1911. The collapse of a squid and yellowtail fishery 320 kilometres north of the Japanese island of Iki, due to overfishing, seems to have led to the dolphins, mainly Risso's and bottle-nosed, moving southwards. The fishermen, who had formerly revered the dolphins, turned on them with an annual battue, which draws the attention of the world's press; in 1979 as many as 1600 were killed. In the Black Sea too, Turkish fishermen kill 50,000 porpoises and dolphins every year, partly as a crop, but also accusing them of depleting the fish stocks.

In Peru, when the warm El Niño current drove the grossly overfished anchovetas out to sea, which cut their already diminished catches still further (see p. 70), the frustrated fishermen turned on their fellow predators the guano birds, even though the birds they were killing are also the basis of a lucrative industry. In the Danube delta in Rumania pelicans, including the endangered Dalmatian pelican, accused by fishermen of eating up to 50 lb a day of their fish, were recently being 'mercilessly shot by fishermen's cooperatives'.

Pressure is likewise building up to allow Californian abalone fishermen to kill some of the endangered sea otters, which are accused of depleting the abalone beds the fishermen themselves have overfished. In Canada fishermen and civil servants have tried to strengthen the case for harvesting harp and hooded seals by alleging that the seals are depleting local fisheries, which again have been overfished by man. A similar situation exists in Scotland with regard to the grey seal, but new scientific evidence shows that these seals do not at present eat significant quantities of commercial fish. In none of these cases had the wild predator depleted its prey before human predators arrived.

Sport hunting also has important secondary effects, the most serious being the control of mammal and bird predators, accused of killing game species or taking their eggs, in the supposed interests of preserving those species. Thus in Poland the President of the Hunters' Association, Professor Krupka, has recently recommended that brown bears and wolves should be controlled in order to increase game stocks in Mongolia. The Alaska Fish and Game Department is currently seeking to reduce the number of wolves, on the ground that they are competing with man for moose and caribou. Birds of prey are now protected in many countries, but many sportsmen and gamekeepers still kill them illegally. Game preservation is generally blamed for the severe decrease in numbers of raven,

Grey jungle fowl

buzzard, red kite, pine marten and polecat in Britain in the nineteenth century, many of them becoming actually or virtually extinct in the south-eastern half of England.

A minor side effect of angling is the demand for feathers to make trout flies; this was one of two severe drains on stocks of the grey jungle fowl until India banned the export of its feathers. The other demand was for its feathers to make capes. Until stopped by better import controls, these capes were being illegally imported into the US.

A few other important incidental effects may be mentioned. Ungulate populations in Botswana have been severely depleted, because the veterinary fences erected to prevent the spread of foot-and-mouth disease bar their traditional annual migrations to water-holes. As a result, out of between one and three million wildebeest, an even greater number of springbok and many thousands of red hartebeest and other antelope that once ranged the Central Kalahari, fewer than half a million are now believed to remain. Ironically, informed opinion no longer believes the fences are needed to control the disease, but influential local cattlemen find them too convenient a method of limiting competition with their cattle for scarce water supplies. This is an excellent example of man's too frequent inability to use wildlife rationally: the antelopes, if harvested appropriately, would yield far more protein for human consumption than the cattle do. Instead, the once vast herds are simply being allowed to die of thirst and their flesh rots. More recently, a thousand buffalo were shot in Zimbabwe just to satisfy foot-and-mouth disease regulations for beef imports to Europe.

Some years ago a campaign to control rodents in Israel with extremely poisonous thallium and organophosphorous compounds inflicted enormous damage on the very large numbers of birds of prey that migrate southwards from eastern Europe through Palestine to Africa. Many thousands of raptors died from eating the poisoned rodents. Egyptian and lappet-faced vultures and black kites were reduced to a tenth of their former numbers. In Sicily in 1965, the griffon vulture actually became extinct, after poison bait was put down to control rabies in small mammals.

In northern South America, the campaign against the vampire bat led to a vast incidental slaughter of millions of other, often beneficial bats. The bat caves were mist-netted, so that all bats were killed indiscriminately. Since the bats are the least studied mammal group, especially in the Neotropics, it is more than likely that this has actually exterminated several bat species before they were known to science. Another hazard for bats is disturbance while guano is being collected from their caves for use as a fertiliser. In Jamaica this has led to the desertion of at least one cave.

Vampire bat

Up to the mid 1960s wild ungulates were extensively slaughtered in many parts of Africa in attempts to control tsetse fly, most notably from 1922 in what is now Zimbabwe, from 1945 in Uganda and later in Sudan and Zambia. Tsetse flies, which transmit the parasitic protozoans *Trypanosoma* that cause the disease variously known as nagana (in animals), sleeping sickness (in man) or trypanosomiasis (in both), have prevented man from inhabiting up to ten million square kilometres of sub-Saharan Africa, because of their impact on the numbers and productivity of cattle, sheep and goats. Killing wild ungulates for tsetse control has caused a great many temporary local extinctions, such as the elimination for a time of all the buffalo, eland, waterbuck, oribi and warthog in the Ankole district of Uganda, but has never had such a long-term impact as the actual spread of agriculture, with its total habitat destruction. Fortunately, this method of tsetse control is now generally recognised to be ineffective and a waste of money. All too often the politicians and administrators allowed the area so

Tsetse fly

laboriously and distastefully 'reclaimed' to go back to bush; it was then reoccupied by both the animals and the tsetse.

Modern tsetse control by pesticide spraying, on which FAO has spent upwards of $1 billion, must have had some harmful effect on other insects and invertebrates, but so little is known about these that we cannot say how severely their populations may have been depleted. There have undoubtedly been some local extinctions and declines, for instance the almost complete disappearance of orchids and Asclepiadaceae from the Umfolozi reserve in Natal because their pollinators were eliminated, and a decrease in both honeybees and bee-eaters in Somalia. What does seem reasonably certain is that, in the long term, largely because of failure to introduce an integrated land-use policy, this will prove no more effective a method of controlling tsetse fly than the now discredited slaughter policy.

6. Predation by Introduced Species

Whether alien species are introduced to new territory deliberately, as with the rabbit in Australia, or accidentally, as with the fire ant in many parts of the Americas, they have many adverse effects on native species. Direct predation is important, but habitat degradation or destruction, discussed on p. 125, may be even more so. The newcomers usually also compete with the natives for space or food and may transmit to them various parasites and diseases. Birds, reptiles, smaller mammals and fishes are all especially prone to predation by introduced predators to which they are not adapted.

Smaller introduced carnivores, especially feral dogs and cats, are particularly dangerous to smaller native vertebrates. In settled areas they may do no more than replace native predators that were exterminated by agricultural or other development, and so have no great impact on native animals that are adapted to cope with these predators. But on islands, they may have a devastating effect on birds and reptiles that have had no predators to adapt to. The classic instance is the Stephen Island wren, a small songbird of a family (Xenicidae) endemic to New Zealand, and not known to science until 1894; in the same year it was exterminated by the lighthouse keeper's cat. In the late nineteenth century cats were released on Mangere Island in the Chatham group east of New Zealand, to control the rabbits. This they did effectively, but before they died out themselves they killed off twelve bird species, three of which were endemic and so became extinct. Even more recently, South African meteorologists have released cats on Marion Island in the South Atlantic, with disastrous results. The Seychelles magpie robin is now reduced to 24 individuals on Frigate Island, supposedly due to feral cats. However, though all the cats were removed in 1981, the birds have not so far increased, so there may also be habitat problems. Cats are also blamed both for the extinction of a once abundant rodent, the hutia *Geocapromys brownii thoracatus*, on Little Swan Island off Jamaica within a few years of their arrival in the early 1960s, and for the decline of the banded iguana and several other lizards in Fiji. In the Caribbean too, several ground iguanas have been endangered or exterminated by feral cats and dogs. Feral dogs have also destroyed several colonies of the Galapagos land iguana, and are threatening both the kagu, a heron-like bird in a sub-order of its own, in New Caledonia, and the maleo fowl in Sulawesi.

Mongooses, stoats and other mustelids released on islands have done immense harm. Indian mongooses *Herpestes edwardsi* were brought to several West Indian islands to control rats in the sugar plantations. At first they killed enough rats to save Jamaican planters £150,000 a year, but then the rats took to the trees and the mongooses went on to decimate endemic

Hutia

Maleo fowl

lizards and ground-nesting birds. On Martinique and St Lucia they all but eradicated the fer-de-lance snakes *Trimeresurus atrox* and *T.lanceolatus*. In Iceland introduced North American mink have done substantial harm to breeding wildfowl stocks.

Rats too can be serious snail predators, and in New Zealand have been blamed, along with introduced European hedgehogs and house mice, for putting greater pressure on the native snail *Paraphanta* than does its only native predator, the weka rail. They are also responsible for the giant Orthoptera known as wetas *Deinacrida*, once widespread on North Island, now being confined to four offshore islands. These remarkable insects, 8.5 cm long, have evolved in the absence of rodents to fill many of their niches, and are known as 'invertebrate mice'. *Dryococoelus australis*, a phasmid related to the stick-insects and leaf-insects, was likewise exterminated by rats on Lord Howe Island, off eastern Australia.

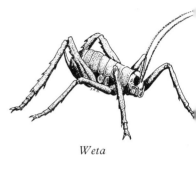

Weta

Rats, especially that hardy pest the brown or Norway rat, are notorious pillagers of eggs and young birds, and the list of birds whose island populations they have decimated or exterminated is a long one. Black or ship rats are largely responsible for the endangered status of both the dark-rumped petrel in the Galapagos and its relative the cahow in Bermuda. They have also been blamed for the extinction of several island forms of rice rat *Oryzomys* in the Galapagos and of a whole family of insectivores (Nesophontidae) and some endemic rodents in the Caribbean. On some of the smaller Galapagos Islands, black rats have helped to reduce the giant tortoise populations by killing their vulnerable young, and feral pigs are an additional hazard to both eggs and young. Pigs are also major predators of iguana eggs in the Caribbean.

Grazing and browsing by introduced ungulates can severely deplete or even exterminate plants. The European wild hogs that infest the Great Smokies National Park at the southern end of the Appalachians dig up many tubers. They are blamed for the local disappearance of the orange-bell lily *Lilium grayii* and feed so heavily on spring beauty *Claytonia* that even this common plant may be threatened.

The Australian brown tree snake and the Philippine rat snake, both bird and egg eaters, have been introduced to Guam since World War II and are now believed to be the primary cause of a dramatic fall in the numbers of native forest birds, first noticed in the 1960s; the Guam rail is down to fewer than a hundred.

Introduced fishes are another serious hazard. Large-mouth bass, introduced by anglers to Lake Atitlan, Guatemala, eat the chicks of the highly endangered giant grebe, which is confined to this one lake, and are a major factor in its serious decline. In South Africa alien brown and rainbow trout prey on an endangered minnow, the maluti *Oreodaimon quathlambae*. In East Africa, introduced Nile perch *Lates niloticus* have almost exterminated many cichlid fish species in Lake Victoria. The viviparous fish *Gambusia gaigei*, confined to Big Bend National Park, Texas, is constantly endangered by exotic mosquito fish *G.affinis* from the neighbouring Rio Grande. The Colorado squawfish is a large predator itself, but one reason for its dramatic decline in the Colorado basin is believed to be the large number of exotic fish competing with it for food and probably preying on its young.

Large-mouth and small-mouth bass

Many invertebrates are affected by introduced aliens. For terrestrial molluscs in the South Pacific, the introduction of the cannibal snail *Euglandina rosea* was a complete disaster. The cannibal, which in its native Florida preys on *Liguus* snails, was brought in to control the also alien giant African snail *Achatina fulica*, the world's largest terrestrial snail, reaching over 15 cm in length. The giant snail, originally confined to Africa and

Madagascar, had been brought to Réunion in the Indian Ocean early in the nineteenth century, supposedly to make soup for the Governor's mistress. Within a few years it became a serious pest of cultivated plants. Later it reached India, colonised much of the Asian mainland, and spread to Indonesia, New Caledonia, the New Hebrides, Tahiti, the Hawaiian chain and other Pacific islands. Eradication proved very difficult, and one of the more unsuccessful attempts at biological control was the introduction of carnivorous snails. One of these, *Euglandina*, was released on many Pacific islands, although it quickly became clear that it much preferred the smaller endemic land snails to the giant pest. Brought to Hawaii in 1955, it shares the blame for the extinction of 21 of the 41 *Achatinella* tree snails endemic to Oahu, and the endangerment of the rest. Shell collectors, the burning and felling of highland forests and rat predation also helped the disaster along.

In 1978 *Euglandina* was brought to Moorea in the Society Islands. Here it is spreading rapidly and is expected soon to cover the whole island; it preys heavily on the endemic *Partula* snails, which have provided invaluable material for genetic research because of their high level of speciation. Since one *E.rosea* can consume four *Partula* in 24 hours, there are fears that the nine described *Partula* species on Moorea, and possibly others still undescribed, face imminent extinction. A rescue operation has been mounted; specimens of six species were brought to Britain to establish a captive breeding colony, from which it is hoped that Moorea can eventually be replenished. Unfortunately, *Euglandina* is still being spread to yet more islands by misguided government agencies.

Introduced ants are another serious threat to endemic island species, especially the notorious fire ant *Wasmannia*. This reached the Galapagos Islands some years ago, and has removed a native iurid scorpion *Haduroides maculata galapagoensis* and two web-building theridiid spiders, *Theridium calcynatum* and *Tidarren sisyphoides* from some of the islands. On Oahu, Hawaii, not only have alien ants contributed to the demise of *Achatinella* tree snails, but the African ant *Pheidole megacephala* has wiped out many other endemic snails and insects. The same ant is blamed for the decrease, from thirteen to two, in the number of entodontid snail species on Rarotonga in the Cook Islands between 1870 and 1965. In Upolu, Western Samoa, *Thaumatodon hystrellicoides*, a snail that was common in 1865, was a century later found only on high mountain peaks the ants had not yet reached. In Bermuda a succession of alien ants, most recently *Iridomyrmex humilis* from Argentina, have radically changed the local invertebrate fauna.

All countries fear the import of plant diseases, which can wreak havoc among trees and crops. Many of the worst outbreaks arise from alien fungi being somehow imported. *Coryneum cardinale*, the canker affecting the Monterey cypress in California in 1928, later spread to Europe, Australia and Argentina by human agency. The blight *Endothia parasitica*, which destroyed the American chestnut at the beginning of the century, originated in China. Dutch elm disease in North America arose from a combination of the fungus *Ceratostomella ulmi* from Asia and its vector, the bark beetle *Scolytus scolytus* from Europe. Sooty bark disease of the sycamore in Britain, on the other hand, is due to the saprophyte fungus *Cryptostroma corticola*, a parasite of sugar maple, being imported on timber from North America in the 1940s.

Several rare Hawaiian plants have been endangered by introduced insects, including *Abutilon menziesii* and *Hibiscadelphus distans* (both Malvaceae) by the Chinese rose beetle *Adoretus sinicus*, which cuts large holes in their leaves, and the legume 'ohai *Sesbanea tomentosa* by the black

Partula sp.

stinkbug *Comptosoma xanthogramma*, which only arrived in 1966. The gypsy moth, the great defoliator of North American hardwoods, came from France in 1869. Bermuda, in four years from 1947, lost 96 per cent of its dominant forest cover of Bermuda cedar *Juniperus bermudiana* due to attacks by an imported scale insect (Coccidae). The introduced rhinoceros beetle *Oryctes rhinoceros* is one of the threats to the endemic and monotypic palm *Neoveitchia storckii* in Fiji.

Animal diseases, imported and spread in the same ways, are usually caused by some bacteria, virus or other microscopic form of life. Domestic animals often infect wildlife with their imported diseases. The Chilean huemul, an Andean deer, can acquire foot-and-mouth disease, coccidiosis, intestinal worms and the louse *Bovicola caprae* from domestic cattle, sheep and goats, as well as the bladderworm *Cysticerus tenuicollis* from dogs' faeces. This is thought to be a significant factor in its recent decline. Desert bighorn sheep in the south-west of North America are debilitated by lungworms, picked up from domestic sheep that graze on their range. Horse sickness picked up from domestic horses and asses is thought to affect the herd of endangered Indian wild asses in the Little Rann of Kutch. Many endemic birds in Hawaii and Guam are believed to have died, and to be still dying, from diseases such as avian malaria imported with the numerous alien birds. In Hawaii an introduced mosquito *Culex quinquefasciatus* is a major disease vector, and avian pox can also be spread by mites and by direct contact between birds. In Scotland sheep carry the ticks which transmit the 'louping ill' virus to red grouse, so that stocks may sometimes fall to the point where shooting is not worthwhile.

In North America the rainbow trout was seriously affected by the imported European virus that causes viral haemorrhagic septicaemia, which has now colonised many fish farms.

Chilean huemul

7. Pets, Zoos and Gardens

From a conservation viewpoint it makes little difference whether animals or plants are removed from a wild stock alive or dead. The pet trade and the supply of animals or plants taken in the wild to zoos or gardens is thus potentially as harmful to the species as if the animals or plants were actually killed. Enormous numbers of tropical fish and cage-birds, and smaller but still significant numbers of tortoises, monkeys and other animals are captured every year, mainly in the less developed countries, to be sold in the more developed countries as pets. India, for instance, is a major bird exporter, averaging some 1,345,000 individual birds a year. Nowadays zoo animals are mainly bred in captivity (90 per cent of all new zoo animals in the US in 1983) and the tiny proportion of the animals in international trade that go to zoos (2 per cent of US imports) makes little impact on the wild stocks, except where the animal is endangered, e.g. with some cetaceans or the occasional mountain gorilla that finds its way to European zoos. A recent attempt to smuggle the extremely endangered golden-headed tamarin from Brazil to Belgium was fortunately thwarted by the vigilance of conservation-minded European zoos.

There is little positive evidence of this trade's effect on wild stocks, although the removal of such substantial numbers has caused local extinctions of some species, such as the two Mediterranean tortoises *Testudo graeca* and *T. hermanni*, which used to be exported to western Europe in very large numbers – over 450,000 to Britain in 1967 alone – and are now locally extinct in many parts of North Africa. In a 40-day journey in Algeria in 1981, a herpetologist saw only one small *T. graeca*. It is also

Frilled lizard

Golden dragon or emperor fish

Rothschild's starling or Bali myna

highly suggestive that by 1982 Britain was only issuing 35,000 import licences a year for these tortoises, and those actually imported all came from one area of Turkey.

In 1984 a Japanese television commercial depicting the frilled lizard promoted a craze for keeping this striking looking reptile in captivity. TRAFFIC (Japan) has established that 56 specimens were imported, often having been illegally exported from Indonesia and Papua New Guinea and smuggled into Japan. Several ended up on display in department stores and amusement parks, although they were supposedly imported for scientific research.

Coral fishes are among the most popular tropical fishes for home aquaria, and the large-scale collection of such species as clownfish *Amphiprion* spp. is depleting their stocks in Malaysia and elsewhere. The extremely high prices now offered in Singapore for specimens of the golden dragon or emperor fish *Scleropages formosus*, which cannot yet be bred in captivity, also point to a very depleted population.

Some parrot populations have also been sharply reduced, and many rare species, notably from Australia, fetch very high prices when smuggled out. The golden-shouldered paradise parakeet, one of whose subspecies may now number fewer than 250 in the wild, is still being illegally trapped and exported to unscrupulous aviculturists. Many of the seventeen species of the large, long-tailed neotropical parrots called macaws, especially the scarlet, red-fronted, blue-headed and hyacinth macaws, are also in danger from the pet trade. Some 21,000 were exported in the 1970s to the United States alone, and a great many also went to Japan and western Europe. For each macaw sold in a US pet shop, eight are estimated to die on the way there.

A similar threat faces the beautiful, pure white Bali myna or Rothschild's starling, confined to the island of Bali, where only 230-280 are believed to remain in the wild. Despite its protected status, the Bali myna is still being caught with decoys and birdlime in the Bali Barat reserve set aside for it, and can be readily bought in the markets of Bali, Djakarta and Sourabaya. Like other endangered birds it is also threatened by habitat destruction - fuelwood has been cut on a very large scale in Bali Barat. Although some of these endangered birds are protected by the CITES convention, so many countries (notably Singapore) are still outside CITES that the trade cannot be completely suppressed. Moreover, unluckily for the Bali myna, CITES does not control internal trade.

A particularly frivolous misuse of a threatened wildlife resource afflicts the chimpanzee; more than 150 of them are currently being used as photographers' models on Spanish beaches from the Costa Brava to Tenerife. People are photographed holding the animal, usually a juvenile, whose capture represents a serious drain on the already depleted wild stocks, especially as several females are usually killed in the process of securing one live baby chimpanzee. A similar practice has recently been detected on the south coast of England, using squirrel monkeys.

By no means all the pet trade involves export. One of the worst fates for a rare animal is to become a status symbol as a pet in its own country, as has happened to the orang-utan in South-east Asia. (The fate of the Philippine eagle is worse, because its stuffed corpse is the status symbol.) Many wretched small orphaned orang-utans, whose mothers were killed when they were captured, still languish in the households of high civil and military officials in South-east Asia. Yet few rare animals are so comprehensively protected by all kinds of national and international legislation as the orang-utan.

Conservationists are only just waking up to the huge scale of the international trade in wild plants, which threatens greatly to increase the number of depleted and endangered species. Around ten million plants are believed to have been imported into the United States alone each year in the late 1970s, and the American appetite for house plants can be judged from the *legal* import into the US in 1977-78 of a staggering 6,850,000 cacti from more than 50 countries - many more were smuggled in.

The plant groups under the greatest pressure from this trade are cacti, other succulents, cycads, orchids, cyclamens, lilies and other bulbous plants. The plants are collected from the wild, sold through a variety of middlemen, and end up in the small greenhouses of enthusiasts in the United States, Japan and western Europe, some of whom actually demand wild rather than nursery-raised specimens. In the early 1970s many thousands of cacti, mainly of the popular barrel shape, were sent to Europe from the arid parts of South America. Almost the whole known population of the bamboo cycad *Ceratozamia hildae* in Mexico and 70 per cent of the cactus *Pediocactus knowltonii* in south-western USA have also been removed by collectors during the past five years.

Though cacti may sell at $1000 each, wastage can be massive. The golden barrel cactus *Echinocactus grusonii* of Mexico and Arizona forms barrels up to a metre or more high, and is greatly valued by collectors, yet heaps of mature specimens have been seen discarded and dying by the roadside in Mexico. Alhough, or perhaps because it is common in cactus collections throughout the world, the golden barrel cactus is now either extinct or critically endangered in all its known wild localities. Like many cacti, it is easily propagated, so there is no reason, apart from short-term profit to individuals, to collect any more from the wild. It was in Mexico too that Japanese commercial cactus collectors, posing as scientists, were arested in the Tehuacan Valley in 1982, loading uprooted cacti into trailers in quantities far exceeding those specified on their suspect permits. On the other hand, most of the cacti smuggled out of Arizona are probably sold within the US; in the eastern states the thieves can double or triple their money. Cacti legally exported from Arizona are valued at $1.8 million per annum, and the illegal trade is thought to increase the total by one-quarter or one-third.

Orchids, cyclamens and insectivorous plants also suffer greatly from predation by plant fanciers. One recent American trade catalogue lists 700 orchid species from three continents. A single shipment of half a million of the rare and spectacular slipper orchids *Paphiopedalum* spp from Asia was recently sent to a dealer in California. On the other hand, 20,000 native orchids were smuggled out of the US in 1980 under bogus permits, mainly to the Netherlands, and in England even in the mid 1980s misguided collectors are digging up or stealing the seed-pods of rare and protected orchids, presumably in the vain hope of growing them in their gardens or greenhouses. In Kenya also much harm has been done by gardeners tearing epiphytic orchids off trees and digging up succulents. Over half of the more than three million cyclamen tubers exported from the Netherlands in 1984 were of wild origin; many of them had been imported from Turkey, where local botanists have warned that exports of many wild plants are above the levels needed to maintain the wild supplies.

Venus's flytrap *Dionaea muscipula*, an insectivorous plant related to the sundews, which Charles Darwin called one of the most wonderful plants in the world, is threatened both by collecting and by habitat change and destruction. It traps insects between two hinged lobes of its leaf, but nobody really understands why, when the 'trigger' hairs are touched, the lobes should rapidly close up. The plant grows in the two Carolinas, only one of which protects it. The rarest of the pitcher plants *Nepenthes rajah*,

Golden barrel cactus

Slipper orchid

Venus's flytrap

found only on Mount Kinabalu, Sabah, is also being seriously depleted by illegal collecting.

An indication of how quickly plants can be endangered by trade is provided by *Sternbergia candida*, an endemic bulbous plant with a very restricted distribution in Turkey, and the only white-flowered *Sternbergia*. It was first discovered among rocks at the edge of cedar forests in 1976, described as new to science in 1979, and advertised in British horticultural journals in 1980. The first plants in trade are known to have been dug up in the wild. Similarly, enormous numbers of the golden slipper orchid *Paphiopedalum armeniacum*, first described in 1982, had two years later been collected from its only known site, a limestone mountain in southern Yunnan, China, and sold in California, Taiwan, Japan and Britain.

Nor is this a novel phenomenon. The Franklin tree *Franklinia altamaha* was discovered along the Altamaha River in Georgia in 1765 by John and William Bartram. Its beautiful white flowers attracted horticulturists, who by 1790 had made it extinct in the wild. Luckily William Bartram had collected both seeds and specimens, which were grown on in Philadelphia, so that today the Franklin tree is widely available from American nurseries. In Britain too, a local nurseryman eradicated the lady's slipper orchid from a wood in north-west England as early as 1796.

Wild plants can be threatened by picking the flowers, as well as by uprooting the whole plant. Thus the very beautiful marsh rose protea *Orothamnus zeyheri* of the Cape flora was reduced by picking for the Cape Town markets to only 68 plants before the pickers were controlled. Indeed, when a plant is very rare even picking a single flower or branch, for whatever reason, may represent a threat. Two of the extremely threatened woody plants of Rodrigues in the Indian Ocean are at risk in this way; *Ramosmania heterophylla* (Rubiaceae) and *Hibiscus liliiflorus* (Malvaceae) are both represented by single specimens, yet both have recently suffered the loss of some of their few remaining branches, picked by local people, perhaps for propagation, perhaps for some quite irrational motive, but still risking the survival in the wild of the last known specimen of the plant.

8. Scientific Research

Collecting by scientists, both amateur and professional, often with the loftiest motives, has sometimes reduced rare species or populations to near or actual extinction. Much the worst case has been that of the Galapagos giant tortoise. Four expeditions to the islands between 1897 and 1901 took what they supposed to be the last survivors from Pinzon, and the California Academy of Sciences expedition in 1905-6 took 86 more alleged last survivors from the islands. More than twenty years later, the New York Academy of Sciences removed no fewer than 180 tortoises, with the unsuccessful aim of establishing breeding colonies in zoos. So even the well meant efforts of the early twentieth century scientific community harmed the future of the species. Smaller rare reptiles and amphibians, such as the Panama golden poison frog *Ateropus varius zeteti* are also often endangered by overcollecting by scientists.

From the 1950s to the 1970s, biomedical research caused a most serious drain on certain primate stocks, especially in India, East Africa and Amazonia. Although some rare species suffered, the main brunt inevitably fell on such very common species as the rhesus macaque and the neotropical squirrel monkey, because the contemporary demands were for large numbers of animals. During the 1960s, when upwards of 200,000 rhesus (85 per cent of them juveniles) were exported annually from India alone, whole areas of Uttar Pradesh, for instance, were being denuded of their juveniles, so that the adult breeding stocks could not be maintained. Indeed one survey showed that nearly two-thirds of all village and town colonies had been lost over five years. At this period, some 400,000 primates were being traded worldwide each year, and the losses between capture and arrival in the importing country (estimated at 80 per cent in the pet trade, but probably lower in the laboratory trade) meant that at least a million primates a year were being taken from the wild. A quite recent estimate suggests that 70 per cent of all crab-eating macaques trapped in Indonesia die before reaching their destination country. However, the trade has fallen substantially since the mid 1960s, because not only did the exporting countries begin to protect their resource, but the demand fell at the laboratory end, thanks, for instance, to more efficient methods for testing and producing polio vaccine.

Nevertheless there is still some overexploitation of primates for biomedical research, most notably of the threatened chimpanzee, despite its protection by the CITES convention in most countries. In Sierra Leone, where only 2000 chimpanzees are left, it has recently been used as a symbol of endangered wildlife on the postage stamps; yet commercial exploitation of wild-caught animals continues, both for export to Japan, and more recently for a research centre to be set up inside Sierra Leone, allegedly in order to circumvent the CITES prohibition of their entry into Austria. Entomologists too have a reputation for overcollecting. They were responsible for the extinction of both the native English stock of the large copper butterfly in the Fens, and of the small geometrid moth *Sterrha humiliata* from the Isle of Wight. It was not collectors who finally exterminated the large blue butterfly *Maculinea arion* in the west of England, but they certainly persecuted it so much that conservationists, despite desperate efforts, could not save it from extinction. One private collector had no fewer than 770 specimens in his collection in the mid twentieth century. The Colorado hawk-moth *Euprosperpinus weist* has the unhappy distinction of being the first animal known to have been exterminated in the course of an ecological study, when the Colorado Department of Agriculture inadvertently sprayed the last known colony in 1980.

The handsome large metallic-green ground beetle *Carabus olympiae* has been harried to near extinction by collectors twice since it was discovered in Piedmont, northern Italy, in 1855. Across the Atlantic, overcollecting by scientists has been blamed for the endangered status of the tiny amphipod *Stygobromus hayi* in its sole known site, one small spring in the National Zoological Park, Rock Creek, Washington DC. In the Pacific, overcollecting at the beginning of the century began the decimation of the endemic *Achatinella* snails of Oahu, Hawaii, that was later compounded by habitat destruction.

Rare plants, especially orchids, are subject to similar hazards. In 1934, in a misguided attempt to save the species, a collector removed the whole known population, nearly 50 plants, of the cactus *Mammillaria wrightii* in New Mexico. There are no records of their survival in cultivation, but fortunately other sites have since been found. When the brown bog-rush *Schoenus ferrugineus* was discovered on the shore of Loch Tummel, Perthshire, in 1884, botanists flocked to the spot to stock their herbaria. One party came away with 22 complete plants and 88 separate flowering stems. Not surprisingly, by 1900 'not a plant was to be seen', though fluctuations in the water level may have contributed too.

Chimpanzee

Ground beetle Carabus olympiae

9. Overexploitation due to Fear or Superstition

Animals which are a real or supposed direct danger to man, such as the larger carnivores and crocodilians, are of course liable to be killed for human security. The tiger in India, the wolf in Europe and North America, and crocodiles and snakes throughout the tropics, have all suffered local extinctions for this reason. In Cuba, for instance, the zoologist Luis Varona reports that all snakes are killed at first sight. Even when the main reason why such animals are killed is stock protection (see. p. 87), protection of the villagers themselves from personal danger is an important ingredient. Indeed animals that represent any kind of threat to human health and welfare, such as vampire bats and biting insects, are bound to be severely reduced in numbers in any area inhabited by man. Much the same applies to plants such as the North American poison ivy, and in Europe deadly nightshade is often destroyed for fear its luscious poisonous berries should tempt a small child.

Fear is understandable, but superstition tends to arouse irritation in those who do not share the often deeply-held beliefs it may represent. A classic instance of an animal endangered by superstition is the aye-aye, a lemur which is the sole surviving member of its family (Daubentoniidae); fewer than a score may now survive in its only known habitat, an island off north-east Madagascar. Unfortunately, the Malagasy people see it as a witch, whose presence near a village will bring ill luck and even imminent death; to touch it is also believed to hasten death – and of course such beliefs are liable to be self-fulfilling. To propitiate the 'sorcerers' and ward off the ill luck, villagers used to protect aye-ayes, which made them very tame and, as with other protected animals, changed their natural habitat preference by encouraging them to live near villages. But in this century some factor has made the villagers change their tactics and strike back at their supposed oppressors, killing them on sight. Indeed for a quarter of a century the aye-aye was believed to be extinct, but in 1957 Dr Jean-Jacques Petter found some in a remote east coast forest and was able to translocate nine to the small island of Nossi Mangabe, where they have now bred.

The bonobo or pygmy chimpanzee in Zaire is also threatened by, among other factors, predation by villagers who believe its bones provide superhuman strength. In parts of Sicily, where there is a large annual migration of honey buzzards, the male citizens are said to believe they will be cuckolded if they do not shoot one each year.

As mentioned above (p. 38), superstition can also be benevolent and a protective influence, as with the aye-aye in the past; cows and monkeys, especially rhesus macaques and hanuman langurs in India; the cattle egret in Liberia, where it is protected by a taboo; and the birdwing butterflies of Malaysia, whose larvae the Asli villagers believe to be harmful and so do not touch. The survival to the present day of innumerable ancient sacred groves in Asia shows the value of sacred status, but of course it is not easy to create either benevolent feelings or sacred status.

Superstition is by no means confined to Third World countries. The effect on tuna stocks of the irrational beliefs of Japanese males was mentioned on p. 69. The concept of 'good' or 'useful' species as opposed to 'bad' or 'harmful' ones, such as the plants in the wrong place which we call weeds, developed in the nineteenth century even among conservationists, and lingers on today despite data showing that all species have a role to play in their ecosystem. Predators are readily seen as villains, and so are any animals and plants that impinge, in however small a way, such as even a midge bite, on human economic or other interests. Although there is no documented record of unprovoked attack by wolves on man in North

Aye-aye

America, European settlers who brought their fear of wolves (justified by the presence of rabies in Eurasia) established a tradition of killing wolves whenever they could. Hyaenas were often shot in colonial Africa and India because the white settlers thought they 'looked cowardly'. A supposed belief in the 'nobility' of the horse appears to be a factor in the irrational opposition to controlling the feral mustangs of the western United States.

Poison ivy

6 Causes of Depletion and Extinction: Habitat Destruction

Habitat or ecosystem destruction is the major source of species depletion and extinction today: destruction not only of the primeval climax eco-systems that had evolved before agriculture was invented, but also of the secondary or successional habitats produced by primitive farming methods, such as slash-and-burn in tropical forests and sheep grazing on temperate calcareous grassland. (The concepts of climax and succession were explained in Chapter 2). The destruction of secondary habitat is often as important as that of climaxes, for most of our present wildlife has perforce had to adapt itself to these habitats. In settled areas, such as Europe, North America and much of India and China, virtually all wildlife habitat, woodland, moorland, heathland and grassland is successional. Even in the tropics enormous areas of rainforest and other apparently completely virgin habitats have been subjected to slash-and-burn many times over the past few millennia. In what follows no distinction will be made between climax and successional destruction, because both entail some displacement of wildlife. However, the animals and plants of climax ecosystems are less likely to be able to adapt themselves for survival than are those of successional or pioneer habitats, which are, by definition, pre-adapted to change.

Habitat destruction can take many forms. The World Conservation Strategy lists them as:

Replacement of the entire habitat by settlements, harbours and other human constructions, e.g. the building of Brasilia and Canberra, the construction of any airport or major highway, the projected major oil installation on the former US national wildlife refuge, St Matthew Island in the Bering Sea.

Replacement of the entire habitat by cropland, grazing land or tree plantations, as has happened over the greater part of western Europe and the central plain of North America and is now continuing into many parts of Africa, even in national parks, e.g. Dinder National Park in Sudan.

Replacement of the entire habitat by mines and quarries, e.g. in open-cast mine workings in Wyoming and on Mount Nimba in Liberia, and the phosphate mining on the Indian Ocean Christmas Island, which is destroying the rainforest where the last remaining colony of Abbott's booby breeds.

The effects of dams: blocking spawning migrations, drowning terrestrial habitat, altering chemical or thermal conditions, e.g. the Aswan Dam,

Egypt; Lake Pedder, Tasmania; and the multiple dam projects on the Mekong, Ganges and Columbia Rivers.

Drainage, channelisation and flood control, as in many rivers throughout the United States.

Chemical, nutrient and solid waste pollution, of domestic, agricultural, industrial and mining origin, which is widespread, e.g. the Rhine in Europe, the Cuyahoga River in Ohio, and until recently Lake Baikal in Siberia.

Overextraction of water, for domestic, agricultural and industrial purposes, which lowers water tables, e.g. the excessive demands of Los Angeles on Mono Lake, California, which led to the loss of the world's largest colony of California gulls.

Removal of materials, such as vegetation, sand, gravel and stones, resulting, for instance, in the disappearance of mangroves from northern Puerto Rico, extensive sand mining on the beaches and rivers of Sri Lanka, and flooded gravel pits throughout southern England. Topsoil from Colombian forests is on sale in town nurseries.

Dredging and dumping: in south-west England the china clay industry has covered parts of the sea-bed with a largely sterile white detritus, the marine counterpart of the nearby terrestrial spoil-heaps dubbed the 'Cornish Alps', and in Scotland a pulp mill has similarly carpeted the bed of Loch Eil with detritus, which has been colonised by polychaete worms, and has also produced anaerobic conditions.

Overgrazing and overbrowsing by domestic stock, which has created deserts all over the tropics and subtropics, notably in the African Sahel.

Erosion and siltation, which has denuded large parts of the hills of the Mediterranean basin, California, the Himalayan foothills of Nepal and many other regions, of almost all their soil.

The introduction of alien animals and plants, which in large parts of North America, Australia, New Zealand and many oceanic islands, have largely replaced the native species in and around human settlements.

California gulls

Man as a hunter was part of any ecosystem he inhabited, whether in the rainforest of the Zaire basin, the semi-deserts of Australia or the ice floes off Baffin Land. As soon as agriculture was invented, some change in ecosystems was inevitable. It has taken men some 7000 years to bring the accumulated changes to the point of impending disaster, a disaster which only forty years ago was hardly foreseen at all. Two of the few who did so were Fairfield Osborn, who wrote *Our Plundered Planet* in 1948, and William Vogt, whose *Road to Survival* appeared a year later.

The complexity of the pressures summed up in the phrase 'habitat destruction' are well shown in a recent survey of wildlife in Himachal Pradesh, northern India, by a Canadian biologist, A. J. Gaston (WWF Project 1674). He found that all the major vertebrate species of the western Himalayan temperate forest zone still occur, but most stocks have declined in the past hundred years because human disturbance of the forest has reduced the suitable habitat. The four main adverse factors are livestock grazing, timber cutting, road building and hunting, three involving habitat destruction and one overexploitation, but all interrelated. Thus herdsmen often cut firewood and fodder in the forest and, because they carry guns to protect their livestock, frequently take the opportunity to poach. Overgrazing by domestic livestock appears to be the most serious problem, followed

Cougar

by road building: both lead to severe soil erosion on the steep slopes and open up new areas for timber cutting. The whole situation is aggravated by rapid human population growth, which increases the demand for land to farm, wood for firewood and building, and yet more roads.

Indeed, most conservation problems boil down to too many people for the available resources: 'more people and less swamp', as an old Floridian said when asked why the cougar had disappeared. The population of the world, which was only 1.5 billion in 1900, had doubled by 1960 and risen to 4.3 billion by 1980, with forecasts of five billion by 1990 and six billion by 2000, a quadruple increase in a century. In Bangladesh alone, where there are some 1700 people per square mile today, there are expected to be three times as many by the middle of the next century. How all this affects forests can be seen in Kalimantan, the Indonesian part of Borneo, where in the early and mid-twentieth century Dayak tribesmen practised shifting cultivation with small plots scattered along the rivers, and harvested rattan and house-poles from the riverine forest. But the rapid increase in logging since 1970 has led to much larger settlements spreading up the rivers, and the World Bank is financing the transfer there of 2.5 million people from overcrowded Java – Indonesia is the fifth most populous country in the world. These new settlers will have to farm the poor Kalimantan soils; these, the World Bank surprisingly does not seem to know, soon become leached of their nutrients when the forest cover is removed. So genetic resources which were maintaining the Dayaks happily will be destroyed by Javanese settlers funded by the World Bank.

Finally, war can be one of the greatest destroyers of habitat, as witness the extensive defoliation by herbicide spraying of forests in Vietnam and Laos in the late 1960s and early 1970s. Governments have not encouraged surveys to assess the impact of nuclear tests on wildlife, but there is every reason to suppose that tests such as those on the islands of Eiao and Hatutu in the Marquesas in the 1970s must have made any endemic forms extinct. Nuclear war, it becomes increasingly clear, would mean the end of all life over wide tracts of land, even over whole continents. A nuclear winter brought about when clouds of smoke and dust shut out the sunlight would quite literally obliterate species throughout the northern hemisphere.

The remainder of this chapter discusses how species are affected by the various ways in which habitat can be destroyed.

1. Forests and Woodlands

The world's forests and woodlands are currently being destroyed at a rate that can only be described as insane. The 76 tropical countries alone, which still have nearly 3000 million hectares of natural woody vegetation, are losing 11.3 million of them each year, or 0.58 per cent of the total area. Put in another way, ten hectares of virgin forest disappear every minute. Yet only one-tenth of the area felled each year is being replaced by new plantations. Australia, for instance, has lost two-thirds of all its forests and three-quarters of its rainforests since it was first settled 200 years ago; in Java 95 per cent of all lowland forest (below 1000m) is now cleared; Sabah's forest cover fell from 61 per cent to 27 per cent in the decade 1971-80; western Madhya Pradesh, India, is now practically devoid of forests; and Cuba and Haiti are respectively left with only 12.7 and 10 per cent of their original forest cover. This incessant destruction is an important factor in the world's annual loss of eight per cent of its topsoil, the medium in which higher plants need to grow properly. This is a suicidal trend that no amount of chemical fertiliser will ever be able to rectify.

Some of the methods employed by logging companies might almost be designed to do maximum damage to the ecosystem. The yarding system used in Sumatra and Kalimantan, for instance, not only destroys a large part of the forest and the young trees, but guarantees soil erosion and landslides. When a valley with the most valuable trees has been located, all mature trees on the slope are felled and hauled to the highest point of the hill with cables attached to the tallest or strongest tree. Roads for extracting the timber are made by tractors simply pushing their way through the forests. Although these roads are supposed to have regard to the landscape, the loggers in fact do not hesitate to blow up parts of the hill to make easier or shorter roads.

When an area is deforested, whether for its timber or for cultivation, the primary losses are, of course, the forest trees, together with the numerous other plants and their associated invertebrates that can only live in rainforest, gallery forest, temperate forest or some other kind of woodland. Thus in the nineteenth century both red cedar *Toona australis* and white pine *Pinus strobus* were almost all logged out of the forests of Australia and North America respectively. Today the Chinese coffinwood tree *Taiwania cryptomeriodes* and the endemic leguminous tree *Amherstia* are both endangered by logging in Burma, while only a few trees of the fir *Abies nebrodensis* survive in the wild, high in the mountains of northern Sicily. If nothing but timber is extracted, and the logging trails have not encouraged small farmers to invade, the forest may recover, but this secondary forest often contains different species of both animals and plants, those which need a continuous high canopy giving way to species more at home on the woodland edge.

The search for fuelwood has deforested enormous areas. Indeed the difficulty of finding firewood near villages is one of the current crisis points in the Third World, forcing villagers to walk many miles each day. In Himachal Pradesh, northern India, villagers may have to climb several kilometres through snow, and up to 1000m above their villages to find firewood. It takes 360 woman-days each year to gather enough for one family in the Gambia; elsewhere in West Africa the collection of 130,000 tonnes of wood each year, to dry 40,000 tonnes of fish, has deforested the countryside for 100 km around. Villagers first collect any dead wood, but are soon driven to lop living branches, and then to felling the whole tree, finishing up by digging out the stump. And when the trees go, so does first the water supply and then the soil. Nor is this a new problem. It was Benjamin Franklin, in mid-eighteenth-century Pennsylvania, who wrote that 'wood, our common fuel, which within these hundred years might be had at any man's door, must now be fetched near one hundred miles to some towns, and makes a very considerable article in the expense of families'.

Grazing by goats and other domestic animals is a main cause of forests failing to regenerate. Indeed the bare, rocky, treeless appearance of much of the Mediterranean basin and large tracts of Africa and southern Asia is largely due to goats. The first stage can be seen today near many villages in Himachal Pradesh, where sheep and goats have removed most of the forest understorey, which both provided the cover needed by large mammals, pheasants and other wildlife, and ensured that when the mature trees die, none will take their place.

When foresters are faced with felled woodland, they are less likely to encourage it to regenerate than to replant it with commercially valuable trees. This may result in anomalies such as plantations of Mexican pine *Pinus patula* on mountains in Sri Lanka, which can actually increase the risk of erosion, and the deliberate poisoning or removal of surviving native trees in Uganda or oaks in English woodlands, because neither is considered profitable enough. But whatever succeeds the original high

Australian red cedar

forest, the ecosystem is irretrievably changed, and great numbers of climax species, some of the tropical ones probably undescribed, are lost.

Deforestation of both marine islands and their terrestrial equivalent, mountain tops, leads to a particularly high loss of endemic species, as discussed on p. 46. Most of the endemic flora of Madeira was lost as early as the fifteenth century, when the Portuguese settlers deliberately burned the forest. The small Indian Ocean island of Rodrigues (109 km²) provides another poignant example. Of 40 endemic flowering plants, the pitiful remnant of the flora of a once fully forested island, 36 are today in danger of extinction, and of these five are represented by no more than five individuals. One is a tree, *Ramosmania heterophylla* (Rubiaceae), whose sole remaining specimen has only three small branches, due to continual filching by superstitious local people. On St Helena we may be just in time to save a few of the endemics, such as the redwood *Trochetiopsis erythroxylon* (Malvaceae) and five other species which are down to no more than ten individual plants each. On Mauritius the only surviving specimens of the tambalacoque tree *Calvaria major* (Sapotaceae) are all believed to be over 300 years old.

A great many vertebrates depend on forests for their survival, and with mammals, of course, the larger they are, the more extensive the tract of forest needed to keep a viable population. Primates are especially at risk, and so are such large mammals as tapirs and the Sumatran rhino. The great apes and many monkey species will all virtually disappear in the wild if, as is freely predicted, all tropical forest outside national parks and protected areas disappears within the next 20-30 years. This has been demonstrated in particular for the orang-utan and the proboscis monkey in Borneo and for the woolly and spider monkeys in Amazonia. The coastal and mountain forests of East Africa and the lowland forests of eastern Brazil are among the areas noted for their endemic primates, birds and other species. The classic instance of the highly endangered golden lion tamarin was mentioned on p. 46.

In North America the woodland caribou of the Selkirk range on the borders of Idaho and British Columbia is an example of a threatened large mammal in temperate woodlands. These last caribou in the lower 48 states have steadily diminished, down to about 150, as felling and fire destroy their woodland habitat, for they depend for winter food on up to 5 kg a day of arboreal lichens that festoon spruce and fir trees more than 100 years old.

A small mammal threatened by modern forestry practices, such as monoculture and thinning, is the flying squirrel in southern Finland. It has been declining almost continuously over the past 30 years and is expected quite soon to become virtually extinct. An even smaller mammal endangered by deforestation is the tiny bumblebee bat *Craseonycteris thonglongyai* of western Thailand (see p. 78).

Endemic birds are equally at risk. On Guam the endangered status of all the dozen species of native forest birds is largely due to the loss of a substantial part of their habitat, especially in the south of this Pacific island. Similarly, the rapid destruction of Arabuko-Sokoke, in Kenya, the only remaining large coastal forest of East Africa, could lead to the extinction of four endemic birds: the owlet *Otus ireneae* (only discovered in 1965), the pipit *Anthus sokokoensis*, the sunbird *Anthreptes pallidigaster* and the weaver *Ploceus golandi*, as well as local races of another owl and a tinker bird. In Tanzania too, the habitat of six endangered endemic birds in the Usambaras and four in the Ulugurus is steadily being whittled away. The Bali myna also suffers from the loss of its forest habitat, as well as being threatened by the pet trade. Its main range is now a mosaic of coconut plantations, cornfields and virgin forest, with an additional hazard in the

Flying squirrel

Owlet Otus ireneae

shape of competition from the black-winged starling, which is much better adapted to cultivated areas. Many other endemic animals and plants are, of course, also at risk in all these areas.

Nor is it only endemics that are in danger. Deforestation in the tropics is believed to be responsible for the now well attested decline in neotropical migrant breeding birds in the Appalachians and elsewhere in North America. Lower vertebrates at risk from deforestation include the viviparous Mount Nimba toad *Nectophrynoides occidentalis* in Liberia, the Michigan stock of the Arctic grayling and the asprete *Romanichthys valsanicola*, a small percid fish known only in three Danube tributaries in Romania.

Among a great many invertebrates at risk or already lost due to forest clearance is Queen Alexandra's birdwing, the world's largest butterfly, threatened both by logging and by the expanding oil-palm industry in Papua New Guinea. The magnificent spectacle of the monarch butterfly at its winter roosts in southern Mexico is also acutely threatened by logging. Virtually the entire monarch population of eastern North America congregates on the trees in a few small sites in Michocoan state, each of no more than 5-7 acres. These hidden valleys provide for the monarchs unique conditions, so far known nowhere else in the world, combining sharply defined temperature and moisture levels with lack of human interference. The millions of butterflies that take part in this, the only true butterfly migration in the world, festoon the trees in such numbers that they weigh the branches down.

Monarch butterfly

More than half the named species of *Achatinella* land snails endemic to Oahu, Hawaii, are extinct and the rest are rare or endangered. The major cause of extinction has been the loss of 85 per cent of the original forest cover, destroyed first by the native Hawaiians with their primitive cultivation methods, then by the American colonists, aided by the cattle, sheep and pigs introduced in the eighteenth century. Deforestation was intensified by the demand for sandalwood, and the problems of the snails have been compounded by fire, soil erosion and the planting of exotic trees. Hawaii has in fact suffered the full range of man's forest mismanagement. Less than half the *Achatinella* species have been seen on introduced vegetation, so the planted Australian eucalyptus, ironwood and Norfolk Island pine *Araucaria excelsa* are no more help to them than to the native birds, which have been similarly affected.

Earthworms too are at risk from forest clearance. In South Africa several species appear to be extinct as a result of the consequent soil erosion, and the giant earthworms *Megascolides macelfreshi* and *M.americanus* are both now restricted to a very few sites in Oregon and Washington, having lost most of their forest habitat to agriculture.

Even afforestation can help to deplete species. In Scotland, for instance, the planting of alien conifers over the past twenty years has cut the number of ravens in Galloway by more than half. It has also acidified the water in the upper reaches of the Forth and Tay, producing changes, usually adverse, in plankton, other aquatic plants and invertebrates - mayflies and stoneflies have been replaced by caddisflies and chironomid midges - and ending in the loss of fishes.

2. Grasslands

Most grassland habitats are secondary, maintained either by the grazing and browsing of ungulates, domesticated (cattle, sheep, goats) or wild (deer, antelopes), or by periodic burning. The three main ways in which grasslands are being destroyed, along with their wild genetic resources are:

(1) by ploughing for cultivation or afforestation, (2) by overgrazing, and (3), by excessive burning. Undergrazing may also create some problems.

1. *Ploughing*. Most of the world's croplands were grassland before being cultivated, though some were converted straight from forest as in slash-and-burn economies. In Madagascar, for instance, *tavy*, the Malagasy name for this technique, is a major environmental problem. Every year more than 10,000 hectares of forest are converted to farmland by burning, and since 80 per cent of the island has been treated in this way, the greater part of the countryside both looks like and to a large extent is a desert, the rivers running red with the soil that washes away with each rainstorm. In north-east Kenya, a very sparse grassland, dominated by Sodom apple *Solanum incanum*, follows slash-and-burn cultivation.

In Europe and North America most grasslands are now leys, being regularly ploughed and resown with cultivars of such grasses as ryegrass, cocksfoot and bent, so that few unploughed ancient grasslands remain; those few, unless actually designated as nature reserves, are under continual threat of ploughing, often grant-aided. In the nineteenth century such destruction was, of course, much more frequent. The ploughing up of the floriferous chalk grasslands near Cambridge, for instance, was vividly described in 1860 by C. C. Babington, Professor of Botany at the University:

> Until recently (within 60 years) most of the chalk district was open and covered with a beautiful coating of turf, profusely decorated with pasque flower, purple milk-vetch and other interesting plants. It is now converted into arable land, and its peculiar plants mostly confined to small waste spots by roadsides, pits and the very few banks which are too steep for the plough. Thus many species which were formerly abundant have become rare.

That this still goes on is illustrated by the fate of the palmate bird's beak *Cordylanthus palmatus* (Flacourtiaceae), until recently believed extinct, whose site, when rediscovered, was ploughed by the landowner before the US Fish and Wildlife Service could protect it. Both the only two known populations of the endemic Arizona cliffrose *Cowania subintegra* are endangered by overgrazing from domestic cattle. Similarly, the species-rich meadow of Ripon Parks in northern England was ploughed in 1982 with the aid of a government grant.

Moreover, arable cultivation, which is of course essential to human welfare, is often self-destructive. Thus in south-west Finland the exposure of arable soils after the autumn ploughing and during the spring melt is estimated to lead, in wet years, to the loss of as much as 7000 kg of soil per hectare. Clearly such soils would in the long run be more productive if they were left to yield what natural forces had been able to achieve – and their genetic resources would still be available. A similar situation would arise in Tanzania if the Government ever gave way to the constant pressure from villagers and its own agriculturists to replace the savanna grasses of the Serengeti National Park with wheat and cotton. The very light volcanic ash soil of these plains blows away as soon as the turf is broken by the plough.

Another striking example comes from the Mohave Desert in California, where Professor Vasek of the University of California has recently discovered what is believed to be the oldest living thing in the world, a ring of creosote bushes *Larrea tridentata* (Leguminosae) estimated to be 11,700 years old. Yet this invaluable and historic plant stands on a plot of land that is likely to be bulldozed into farmland or horse pasture. Other endangered plant populations in the US so threatened include the only remaining stock of the buckwheat *Polygonum pelinophilum* and six of *Frankenia johnstoni* in Texas and New Mexico.

2. *Overgrazing*. Over the greater part of the world, however, the major current threat to grasslands comes from overgrazing in semi-desert and low-rainfall areas, especially the African Sahel. On the south side of the Sahara, desert conditions are advancing rapidly, due partly to recurrent droughts, but also to overgrazing by domestic livestock in the unfavourable conditions created by the droughts. This situation has been well known for years, and was the subject of a UNEP conference in Nairobi in 1977, whose recommendations have been effectively ignored both by the governments concerned and by aid-donor governments and agencies. Again, mankind appears to watch the advance of the desert in a kind of collective trance. Overgrazing has, however, been dealt with successfully in the Amboseli National Park, Kenya, as shown on p. 172. The overgrazing problem is aggravated by the use of temperate-forest livestock species in arid areas. Cattle, sheep and horses do not belong to arid habitats; their water needs are too great. Hence they cluster round the few water-holes and trample the relatively sparse vegetation into the dust, as happened with an experiment in providing water-holes in Kenya in the 1960s. Arid-land ungulates, such as antelopes, are adapted to need little or no water, and so are obviously the best species to provide protein in these areas. By using cattle and sheep instead, farmers lose their best means of exploiting the land resource sustainably.

In the western United States too, the cattlemen use their political clout to enforce a damaging degree of overstocking on federal grazing lands and in national forests; sentimental animal lovers on the other hand frustrate all efforts to prevent mustangs and burros (feral horses and asses) overgrazing their ranges. This politically determined overgrazing is the single most important factor affecting the bighorn sheep in North America, where stocks have fallen from 1.5-2 million to 15,000-20,000 over the past 200 years. Especially in the alpine meadows, grazed by domestic sheep in summer and by the bighorns in winter, grasses and forbs (pasture herbs) are replaced by shrubs, and stunted shrubs at that. These would not provide adequate sustenance all the year round, so the bighorns normally browse them only in times of shortage. And of course the excessive numbers of cattle and sheep are also eating themselves out of adequate sustenance.

Bighorn sheep

Another North American animal threatened by overgrazing is the desert tortoise *Gopherus agassizi*, California's state reptile. Once widespread over the entire Sonoran and Mojave Deserts, it is now reduced to a few small, widely scattered populations, largely as a result of overgrazing by cattle. In one 35-square-mile area of the Mojave Desert in south-west Utah, which once held 2000 tortoises, only 350 survived by 1980. Yet when it was officially listed as critical habitat for this tortoise, the nine part-time ranchers who graze 425 cattle there immediately protested. Inevitably, in view of the power structure in America, the future of the tortoise was sacrificed to maintain the principle that on federal lands cattle grazing always comes first.

Overgrazing by domestic stock is also a serious threat to wildlife throughout India. In the Dachigam sanctuary in Kashmir overgrazing by domestic sheep has long been known to be the principal threat to the last known herd of the hangul, a race of the Eurasian red deer. In the Thar Desert, Rajasthan, competition with domestic stock leads to malnutrition and consequent disease in nilgai, blackbuck and chinkara gazelles.

Undergrazing, or undermowing, of grassland that has been maintained by grazing or mowing leads to the growth of scrub and eventual conversion to woodland. This was the fate of many calcareous grasslands in England in the 1950s and 1960s; since the cessation of sheep grazing 30 or 40 years earlier, they had been grazed primarily by rabbits. When the great myxomatosis epidemic of 1954 removed 80-90 per cent of the rabbits, the drastically reduced grazing pressure enabled many grasses and other plants to grow so tall that a great deal of short chalk and limestone turf, with its specialised flora and fauna, was lost. The large blue butterfly actually became extinct in Britain in 1979 for lack of grazing, but the reason was not discovered until too late. The butterfly's larvae are taken care of by the ant *Myrmica sabuleti* and by this ant alone. Because relaxed grazing pressure allowed the grass to grow longer, another common grassland ant, *M.scabrinodis* was replacing *M.sabuleti* in the butterfly's last known site.

Large blue butterfly

3. *Fire.* Burning is a method of stimulating grassland to produce an 'early bite' of nutritious shoots for the benefit of domestic stock that is widely used in Africa and elsewhere. Burning, originally from natural causes, is in fact probably the most important factor in the maintenance and spread of lowland dry savannas (prairies, llanos, steppes) all over the world. As 'muirburn', it is used in Scotland to maintain healthy stocks of red grouse, which eat the young shoots of ling heather. Used in moderation, it can be beneficial, but all too often nowadays it is not done in such a way as to conserve either the fertility of the soil or the natural genetic resources. On nearly all British uplands managed primarily for sheep grazing, burning and overgrazing combined have drastically reduced the cover of heather and related undershrubs, such as bilberry. They are replaced by such unnutritious plants as mat-grass, a prime indicator of infertile soil.

The original Polynesian inhabitants of Hawaii used annual fires to ensure a good crop of grass to thatch their houses. This, together with the maintenance of grazing, is also the reason for burning the thatch-scrub jungle of the Brahmaputra Valley in Assam, thus depriving two highly endangered species, the pygmy hog and the hispid hare of their prime habitat. In northern Mexico grass burning is one of the factors blamed for the endangerment of the endemic and very local aquatic box turtle *Terrapene coahuila*, and a disastrous fire in 1959 actually exterminated the Santa Barbara race of the song sparrow in the Channel Islands off California.

Pygmy hog

Burning not only greatly reduces the amount and variety of habitat, but isolates the remaining patches of unburned habitat so that other harmful factors concentrate on them. In fact, to quote Kai Curry-Lindahl:

> Fires may be useful as a management tool locally, and occasionally their short-term effect on the vegetation may also be beneficial. But in the long run, annual burning is detrimental to the soil, the vegetation and the animals. It reduces the nitrogen content and the organic matter in the topsoil, impoverishes the vegetation, and destroys a number of animals in and on the soil. It also leaves many animals without food. In short, annual indiscriminate burning slowly reduces the general fertility of the area.

This conclusion, of course, applies equally to the straw-burning with which most British cereal farmers, unlike those of continental Europe, currently afflict their neighbours.

3. Wetland Drainage and Reclamation

Wetlands are among the most productive habitats on earth. They comprise both freshwater marshes, fens, bogs, swamps, lakes and rivers, which can be drained, and coastal estuaries, mudflats and saltmarshes, which can be reclaimed. Draining or reclaiming a wetland usually annihilates an entire ecosystem; if there are no contiguous wetlands, almost all the genetic resources, except for birds and perhaps some flying insects, will then be lost, since most animals and plants of wetlands are ill adapted to migrating across dry land.

Some of the most fertile farmland in the world lies on drained or reclaimed wetlands. The English Fenland, for instance, was almost all drained between the 1630s, when the Dutch engineer Vermuijden constructed the 21-mile New Bedford River for the Earl of Bedford, and 1852, when the last great wetland, Whittlesey Mere, was drained. So a rural economy that depended on harvesting the plentiful fish, wildfowl, thatch and litter of the medieval Fens was ultimately replaced by one of the most highly capitalised groups of farming enterprises in Europe.

A Dutch engineer was chosen to drain the English Fens because, over the centuries, the Netherlands has specialised in this form of reclamation. Indeed, about one-fifth of its present territory has been reclaimed from the sea, six per cent of it from the Zuyder Zee within the past 50 years. This inlet of the sea, which had developed during the past 2000 years, became an inland lake, the Ijsselmeer, and 165,000 hectares of the sea-bed was reconverted to very fertile farmland. The process still continues in Europe: the Waddensee in Denmark, the Ebro delta in Spain and the Oosterschelde estuary in the Netherlands, along with their abundant wildlife, are all under various degrees of drainage threat. Some of the most contentious issues in current British conservation politics relate to the drainage of marshy grasslands, such as Halvergate Marshes in Norfolk and West Sedgemoor in Somerset, to secure higher grant-aided agricultural production. Western nations thus have to ask themselves some searching questions, in particular whether they are justified in continuing to destroy one kind of productive habitat in order to create another, whose products have to be stockpiled for lack of effective demand.

One large mammal may have been exterminated in the wild because its marshland habitat in China was drained for rice-growing: Père David's deer, which now survives only in captivity. The Jonglei Canal in Sudan, still scheduled for completion in the late 1980s, will partly drain the extensive swamps of the Sudd, and seems certain to reduce severely the herds of two antelope species, the half a million tiang (topi) and most of the total population of the Nile lechwe.

Waterfowl are naturally among the birds most acutely affected by wetland drainage, and greylag geese, common cranes and perhaps spoonbills were among the breeding birds lost when the English Fens were drained. In Asia no fewer than five species of crane, most notably the Siberian white crane, are at risk from the drainage of their breeding and wintering grounds, coupled with being hunted on migration. The snail-eating Everglades kite, the Florida race of a widespread South American bird, is endangered because Lake Okeechobee and much of the Everglades have been drained for agriculture; similar habitat loss further north in Florida led to the extinction in the wild of a local race of the widespread seaside sparrow.

Amphibians, aquatic reptiles and fishes are of course especially vulnerable to drainage. Four out of many species whose numbers it has severely

Père David's deer

Siberian cranes

Painted frog

Large copper butterfly

Natterjack toad

reduced are the painted frog *Discoglossus nigriventer* around Lake Huleh, Israel; the short-necked tortoise *Pseudemydura umbrina* in Western Australia; the aquatic box turtle *Terrapene coahuila*, which is confined to the Cuatro Cienagas basin in northern Mexico; and the garter snake *Thamnopsis sirtalis tetrataenia* around San Francisco Bay. In Britain frogs, toads and newts are at increasing risk from the disappearance of their breeding ponds. Over most of the south of England, about one-third of mapped ponds have been lost, at a fairly constant rate, during the past 20-25 years, with a loss of as many as 70 per cent in one area. In the Wirral peninsula in Cheshire almost half the 2500 ponds present in 1969 had been filled in ten years later. In Denmark too, frogs and toads have disappeared from more than half the sites they inhabited 40 years ago.

Channelisation, involving the extensive removal of vegetation from the beds and banks of rivers and streams, is an extremely destructive form of water management. Only one breeding stock remains of a dace *Moapa coriacea*, now confined to one area in Nevada, because almost all the springs which it inhabits have been lined with concrete and/or gravel, channelised, chlorinated and cleared of vegetation.

The very large number of invertebrate species depleted or exterminated by wetland drainage worldwide include, besides the medicinal leech over much of Europe, the historic loss of the native British race of the large copper butterfly, finally finished off in the Fens by collectors in the late 1840s; many other insects, such as the wainscot moth *Arenostola extrema*, were made locally extinct at the same time. As recently as 1977 the only known site in Britain for the damselfly *Coenagrion scitulum*, 195 acres of grazing marsh in Essex, were drained and ploughed.

Two famous plants are endangered by wetland drainage in Egypt: papyrus, the largest of the sedges, which was used in ancient times as a precursor of paper, and lotus, an attractive water-lily. Both were once widespread in the freshwater marshes of the Nile Valley and Delta, but are now much scarcer, papyrus being confined to marshes around three small soda lakes. Since the completion of the Aswan High Dam, and the consequent change in the method of irrigation, the marshes have become increasingly saline (as many experts warned) and the habitat for these two plants is becoming extinct. Fortunately papyrus is still common, as a different subspecies, in parts of tropical Africa. Many plants were also lost when the English Fens were drained, including two ragworts: *Senecio paludosus*, which recently reappeared by a fen dyke in the Isle of Ely, and *S.congestus*, which remains locally extinct.

4. Dam Building and Aquifer Depletion

The water supply industry changes or destroys natural ecosystems in two main ways: by building dams and depleting aquifers. As soon as men began to live in large settlements, they needed a good natural supply of fresh water nearby, such as a river, lake or group of springs. Otherwise they had to bring water from a distance by aqueduct, which happened as early as the sixth century BC on Samos in the Aegean, 312 BC in ancient Rome and 1285 AD in medieval London, when the Great Conduit was constructed in Westcheap. By the late eighteenth century, when industry added its demands, very much more water was needed than could be obtained from nearby natural sources; so reservoirs with their accompanying dams had to be built, first just for water supply and later also for hydroelectricity. These provided much new aquatic habitat for waterfowl and fish, but also submerged many terrestrial ecosystems and changed the aquatic ones both upstream and downstream. This led to many species becoming depleted, locally exterminated or even completely extinct.

In the late 1950s, the filling of the great Lake Kariba behind a dam on the Zambezi River on the borders of Zambia and Zimbabwe ushered in the modern concern for wildlife conservation, when the Fauna Preservation Society organised Operation Noah to rescue animals that had been trapped on islands in the rising waters. This was soon recognised to be a humanitarian rather than a conservation matter, since most of the displaced animals are likely to be common or frequent in the surrounding country-side. So it is now the animal welfare societies which organise rescue operations, as at Itaipu, the largest hydroelectric dam in the world, on the Parana River between Brazil and Paraguay. Such rescues provide dramatic stories and serve to interest the public in wildlife, but only concern threatened individuals rather than threatened species.

Nevertheless dams can lead to substantial losses of animals. The proposed Mupata scheme would inundate another stretch of the Zambezi, below the Kariba Dam. A large proportion of the remaining sand banks in Zimbabwe are on this stretch, so that the breeding areas of the African skimmer and two species of pratincole would be lost. In Brazil there is

Southern bearded saki

African skimmer

concern about the eight primate species, including the endangered southern bearded saki, which occupy the 3000 km² of more or less virgin rainforest that will be flooded when the Tucurui Dam on the Tocantins River is completed. In southern India another monkey, the lion-tailed macaque, was one of several endemic species that would have been severely threatened if the Silent Valley Hydroelectric Project had not been stopped, while at the other end of India a unique flora will be submerged if a similar project goes ahead at Garwhal, Uttar Pradesh.

If a lake is enlarged by a dam, the invertebrates adapted to living along its margins are likely to be severely affected. A prime instance of this was Lake Pedder in Tasmania, where the Government went ahead with a dam despite the warning by scientists that fourteen endemic invertebrate species would become extinct, which they duly did. In 1983 it took both international pressure and fierce Australian in-fighting to stop another controversial Tasmanian project, the Gordon below Franklin Dam, which would have destroyed a World Heritage site. Reduction in the shallow areas at the margin of a lake, where young fish spend their first few months, may restrict the carrying capacity of the whole lake, as has been shown at Lake Waikaremoana in New Zealand.

The most famous example of a rare animal threatened by a dam submerging its habitat was the snail darter, a small fish known only in the tributaries of the Tennessee River. The threat of its extinction held up the completion of the Tellico Dam for several years. The legal battle to stop the dam reached the Supreme Court and was won. However, the political battle to overturn this decision, which the conservationists lost, at one time threatened the whole future of the US Endangered Species Act. Fortunately another small population of the fish was discovered nearby, so that in the event it did not become extinct. Nevertheless, the threat of extinction to a scheduled endangered species proved more effective in delaying the dam than either the inundation of sacred ancestral Cherokee Indian lands, or even the report by the US Government Accounting Office that 'neither the current project nor alternatives are supported by cost-benefit analyses'. In West Malaysia too the Kenyir Dam has put at risk some three-quarters of the fish species of the Trengganu River, most of which are endemic to the peninsula.

Water hyacinth

Dams built in forested areas drown large numbers of trees, whose decay releases nutrients that may lead to a great explosion of aquatic vegetation, as happened in Lake Brakopondo, Surinam. Within two years half the surface was covered by a carpet of water hyacinth and a floating fern *Ceratopteris* occupied another large area. When the Curua Una Dam near Santarem, Brazil, was filled in 1977, the floating mats of water hyacinth killed many of the fish.

Siltation above a dam destroys the ecological niches of a great many species that are adapted to fast-moving water. This happened to two small minnow-like fishes: the asprete *Romanichthys valsanicola* in one of the three Danube tributaries in Romania to which it is confined, and the maluti *Oreodaimon quathlambae* on one of the three high-altitude rivers in the Orange River system in Lesotho, where it lives, despite the fact that this watershed has been set aside as a wildlife refuge and the actual habitat of the fish is within a national park. The harelip sucker *Lagochila lacera*, a small fish of eastern North America, the only member of its genus, became extinct around 1900 largely, it is believed, because siltation made its preferred clearwater streams turbid. The giant salamander of Japan, threatened by diverse pressures, has also had its preferred water speed slowed by dams and its river-bank habitat concreted.

Freshwater clams require flowing water with little or no silt, and so can survive only where the current is fast enough to carry both food to them and silt and mud away from them. Some 60 per cent of the unionid clams of the world, a group which includes the pearl mussels, occur in North America; largely due to silting above the many dams throughout the continent, an estimated 90 per cent of these are now either extinct, endangered or at least under threat. Silting due to strip-mining has also reduced the number of mayflies, food of the gray bat, and so further endangers an officially endangered US species.

Stocks of both aquatic and terrestrial mammals can be severely depleted by dam construction. The susu or Indus dolphin is endemic to the Indus River in Pakistan, but fourteen barrages have split the population into separate groups, frustrating its major annual migrations, including one to the estuary and the sea in winter, so that by 1974 its numbers were down to 450-500.

The Mahaweli Ganga Dam and diversion project in Sri Lanka threatens some of the best habitat, outside national parks, of the island's endemic race of elephant. In Zambia the completion of the Kafue Dam has fulfilled Richard Schuster's forecast that it would reduce the population of the Kafue lechwe, an antelope which is both confined to and adapted to the swampy flats below the dam. By disrupting the river's flooding cycle, the dam has not only reduced the grazing area (the area uncovered annually by the falling flood level is crucial to the lechwe's ecology) but has disturbed the lekking routine which is equally crucial to its mating and breeding pattern.

Kafue lechwe

On the other side of the Atlantic, the wood stork is decreasing because the water management policies in South Florida north of the Everglades National Park have struck at the basis of its ecology by controlling the periodic floods. The storks feed on fish which breed in the flooded wetlands; when the water level drops, the fish congregate in pools where the storks can catch them: so the less flooding, the fewer fish, and the fewer storks.

Dams can also influence ecosystems right into the sea; silt can kill coral reefs. The Aswan High Dam has both benefited Egyptian farmers along the banks of the Nile by providing year-round irrigation water, and harmed them by causing a plague of field rats. It has also destroyed a productive shrimp fishery in the delta, by changing the salinity of the water. Moreover, the lack of silt coming down the Nile (it fills up the dam instead) has made the sea-bed off the Levant coast northwards as far as Lebanon less muddy and more rocky; this has changed not only the kinds of fish but also the fishing techniques needed to catch them. Again, when the Suez Canal was closed for six years after 1956, with no ships to churn its bottom sediments, the water became clear and allowed several Red Sea fishes to reach the Mediterranean. As a result, more than half the economically most valuable fish species in the eastern Mediterranean today are immigrants from the Red Sea. Parts of the Bight of Sofala, off Mozambique, have also become a 'dead sea', carpeted with sediments washed down the Zambezi.

Yet another devastating impact of dams on a river system is to disrupt the migrations of such valuable anadromous fish as salmon and trout. This can to some extent be offset by fish-passes or ladders, but these are often not installed. The Columbia River in the north-western United States once boasted the world's largest salmon runs. Today it produces more power than any other river, but many fewer fish. Some 80 per cent of the spawning grounds in its drainage system have been inundated or obstructed by dams and other development, and dams claim as many as 90 per cent of the Columbia salmon as they migrate to the sea. The Grand Coulee Dam in Washington alone wiped out a whole race of Chinook salmon known as 'June hogs', huge rich-tasting fish that spawned in Canada and migrated more than 1000 miles down to the Pacific. The Caniapiscau River in northern Quebec likewise had one of the continent's best Atlantic salmon runs until dams virtually put an end to it. As a result, the possibility of restoring fish stocks by blowing up outdated and uneconomic dams is now

Atlantic salmon

Devil's Hole pupfish

being actively discussed, for instance with the Savage Rapids Dam on the Rogue River in Oregon.

In Europe there are similar problems. Hydroelectric schemes have caused the extinction of two landlocked salmon and six landlocked brown trout populations in Lake Vänern, Sweden, during the past 50 years, all of which had spawned in rivers that flow into the lake and are now obstructed by dams. Four remaining salmon and trout stocks are similarly at risk, victims of a system that disregards the disbenefits of its economic developments.

The lowering of the water table when water is drawn from underground aquifers often has a severe impact on fishes, amphibians, aquatic plants and invertebrates. The classic example is the Devil's Hole pupfish *Cyprinodon diabolis*, a tiny fish whose Latin name is longer than itself. Confined to a single spring in California, it probably has the smallest range of any vertebrate species in the world. Virtually the whole population, no more than 400, can be seen at once in the Devil's Hole, one of 30 cave-like pools in the Amargosa Desert, 15 metres below the land surface of a barren hill and appearing from the air like a black chasm. The water, which is warm (33°C) and crystal clear, arises from an aquifer more than 100 metres deep with no outlet. The surface, 6.5 metres long and 3-5 metres wide, is flanked by nearly vertical walls on both sides, and a rough ramp of loose boulders leads down to a rock-bottomed ledge about 1.5 metres long. Here, in water varying in depth from a few centimetres to one metre, all the pupfish spawn and spend their nursery period. In spring and summer sunlight reaches the ledge for long enough to produce a crop of algae, on which the fish feed. When the sunlight fails to reach the pool, algal growth slows and pupfish numbers crash. Most of them probably live for only one year.

In 1952 Devil's Hole and its surroundings were included in the Death Valley National Monument, and it was hoped that this unique fish was saved. But in 1967 a ranching operation moved into the area, cleared the land, drilled wells and pumped out much more water than the aquifer could sustain indefinitely. The water level in Devil's Hole began to fall, pupfish numbers were down to 150-200, and scientists feared it might not be able to maintain itself. After a prolonged legal battle, the US Supreme Court eventually ruled unanimously that when the Federal Government sets aside land for public use, it acquires rights to both the surface water and the ground water needed to preserve the character of the land, including the wildlife. The Court thus saved the pupfish, for water level and fish population are now both rising again, and no political hassle has so far circumvented the decision. More recently a developer has proposed to drain the whole area to build luxury homes, leading the Nature Conservancy (a private body) to seek to buy the whole site for inclusion in the national monument.

Another small fish, the pygmy sculpin *Cottus pygmaeus*, came near to disaster when the outflow from its sole habitat, Coldwater Spring near Anniston, Alabama, collapsed. If immediate steps had not been taken to repair it, the entire world population might have been swept downstream. The Texan endemic *Gambusia amistadensis*, a relative of the mosquito fish, was actually lost in the wild when its sole natural habitat, the Goodenough Springs, were flooded by the Amistad Reservoir. Ironically, the captive stock that had prudently been set aside was later lost due to a mix-up in the breeding pools.

The Texas blind salamander *Typhlomolge rathbuni* depends on an underground water supply that was being drained for agriculture. When several private conservation bodies bought a cave that held one of its key populations, they installed a warden, stopped the heavy collection by

Socorro isopod

scientists and animal dealers, and replenished the bat guano that is the base of the cave's food chain. Nevertheless, the water level in this cave is projected to fall below the level of the pools by 2000-2020 AD.

The Socorro isopod *Thermosphaeroma thermophilium*, endemic to three warm springs in New Mexico, is now confined to a single water system of an abandoned bath-house, because municipal and private water developments have completely changed the habitats by capping the original spring sources and piping water away.

5. Pollution of the Environment

During the past 200 years, pollution due to human social and economic activity has irreversibly changed the ecosystems of the world. Most of the damage has in fact been done in the past 40-50 years, but the nineteenth century saw a massive contribution to habitat pollution in both Europe and North America. Now even the Antarctic environment contains chemical pollutants that have somehow made their way south from the developed world, perhaps in aerial currents or the bodies of migrant birds and whales, but doubtless also from human, scientific operations on the fringes of the continent.

Every part of the world environment is polluted: the air, the sea, fresh water, the soil, polar ice, the tissues both of plants and of man and other animals. Pollutants include industrial wastes, such as sulphur dioxide and polychlorinated biphenyls (PCBs); pesticide residues, such as DDT and other chlorinated hydrocarbons; raw human sewage; excess fertiliser carried off the land by rainfall; and, increasingly, nuclear waste, which the United Kingdom, for instance, has been dumping in the Atlantic Ocean. Most, probably all human foodstuffs are also affected in some way. Since many of both the direct and indirect effects of pollution, especially nuclear pollution, take years to manifest themselves clearly, and since much of the more insidious chemical pollution only dates from the past 30-40 years, we cannot yet assess the full impact of all this on resource conservation. We can only be sure that it is more likely to be adverse than benign.

Extreme pollution, when chemicals pumped into the water use up all its oxygen, may make a habitat completely sterile, as the lower reaches of the River Thames virtually were in the mid-twentieth century, and as many rivers and streams in industrial areas still are. Or it may reduce the components of the ecosystem to those species able to cope with the prevalent level of the various pollutants. Before it becomes so toxic that it actually kills animals and plants, the level of pollution may both impair health and inhibit breeding, as chlorinated hydrocarbons have done with the peregrine and osprey on both sides of the Atlantic (see p. 120). So far pollution has caused a great deal more depletion of stocks than actual extinction, partly because some attempts have been made to reduce its levels.

Environmental pollution can conveniently be divided into terrestrial and aquatic, water pollution being at present the more serious in its impact on genetic resources. Aquatic food chains, both freshwater and marine, concentrate poisons more rapidly than terrestrial ones, and the fishes which occupy much of the top of the chain are widely preyed on by otherwise terrestrial mammals. The Baltic Sea and the Great Lakes of North America are two regions where many, sometimes all the fish have been pronounced unfit for human consumption because their tissues are so full of poisonous pesticide or industrial residues. In the Baltic these poisons have produced gross pathological changes in some fishes.

Peregrine

Eventually the fishes themselves are depleted or even exterminated. This happened in Chesapeake Bay in the eastern United States, where the once significant fisheries are rapidly declining and the shellfish industry is actually finished. The catch of striped bass fell by 90 per cent to only 600,000 lb in the twenty years up to 1982. Indeed the entire bay now seems to be dying from multiple pollution: eutrophication from agriculture and sewage disposal, kepone and other pesticide residues and spills, and deoxygenation, with much of the deep trench below the Bay Bridge essentially dead from May to September.

Anglers returning to Lake Ontario after World War II found that the blue and yellow pike, black bass and muskie they were able to catch in plenty before the war, were greatly reduced or even extinct as a result of unrestricted pollution by war industries. The Sea of Azov, behind the Crimean peninsula, now yields only one per cent of the fish harvest it had 40 years ago, thanks to pollution, and much the same applies to other large lakes in the Soviet Union: Baikal in Siberia, with over a thousand endemics, Ladoga near Leningrad and Issyk-Kul, the pearl of Kirghizia. In 1983 a major disaster in the Ukraine, spilling more than a billion gallons of waste salts into the River Dniester, killed 920 tons of marketable fish, 1300 tons of fingerlings and so much of the aquatic vegetation that the river is unlikely to recover for many years. The Finnish wood processing industry has destroyed both commercial and recreational fisheries in Lake Paijanne over the past 30 years.

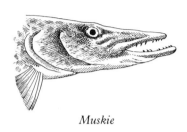

Muskie

In the Riau archipelago in Indonesia the sea has turned yellow from a mixture of the water used for washing bauxite dirt, and yellow mud containing aluminium toxics. This means that local fishermen can no longer catch their 3-4 kg of fish daily from the sea around the village. Instead they must row for 3-4 hours to unpolluted waters. This kind of disbenefit is rarely if ever taken into account in industrial calculations. That polluted waters can be cleaned again, however, is shown by the Thames in London, where fishes have returned even to the inner reaches.

After fishes, birds are the vertebrates most severely affected by water pollution, especially raptors that feed on fish. In Sweden, for instance, the white-tailed sea eagles of the Baltic have the highest concentration of poisons of any birds in the region, an average of 25 mg per kg of fat; so they have recently almost completely failed to rear any young, ensuring that their numbers have fallen dangerously low. In the US the bald eagle and osprey have been similarly affected, and the brown pelican has been pushed to the brink over large parts of its range in California and the Gulf of Mexico, becoming extinct in Louisiana and reduced to 100 pairs in Texas. Gross pathological changes have been reported in young terns reared on fish with high levels of mercury, DDT and PCBs. More than one per cent of common and roseate tern chicks on Great Gull Island, New York, had defects such as feather loss or deformities of eye, bill or foot.

How pesticide residues act on birds is suggested by study of one of the largest recorded kills of seabirds off the coast of Scotland, in September 1969, when no fewer than 200,000 fish-eating birds may have died: guillemots (murres), razorbills, puffins, gannets, cormorants and shags. Birds were washed up dead and dying over a period of two months, but, though some were oiled, the majority were apparently not killed by oil pollution. Some also revealed fairly high levels of DDE and PCBs, but their general emaciated condition suggested that they had in fact died of starvation. If their normal food supply had for some reason failed (as we know has happened to the puffin in northern Norway), the birds would absorb their accumulated fat reserves, and with them the toxic chemicals stored as a result of feeding on poisoned fish.

A hazard peculiar to waterfowl is lead poisoning, from ingesting either pellets of shot that have been scattered about by sport hunters, or weights lost or discarded by anglers. As many as a quarter of all mallards in the United States in any one year ingest lead shot, and four per cent die from lead poisoning, with an additional one per cent being shot. Mute swans on the River Thames, whose numbers have been monitored since the Middle Ages, seem to be steadily dying out, because they pick up so many anglers' discarded lead weights. Their numbers fell from well over 1000 thirty years ago to an all-time low of around 200 in the early 1980s; more than half the swans found dead by the Thames have been shown to have died of lead poisoning. These needless erosions of genetic resources could be avoided if hunters could be persuaded to use steel shot, and anglers to switch to weights made of non-toxic material.

In general, mammals seem to be less affected than other animals by chemical pollution, but this may well be because the pollutants have not yet built up to harmful levels in their bodies. Indeed, the dominant mammal, man, has devised a set of social and economic institutions which seems to be ensuring that the bulk of the food he eats at the end of the twentieth century is well laced with chemicals either known to be toxic, or whose impact on the human body is still unknown. This has led to the black joke that the modern North American is no longer fit for human consumption. Indeed, man may be the mammal most severely affected by marine industrial pollution. The worst case so far reported was at Minamata in Japan, where long-term discharge of methyl mercury into the sea contaminated the fish. Nearly 2000 of the people who ate these fish contracted severe neurological disorders, and some 400 actually died.

Certainly marine fish-eating mammals have so far been more seriously affected than freshwater ones, for instance the two seal species in the Baltic. Eighty years ago there were 100,000 grey seals there; the key reason why there are now only 2000 seems to be the high levels of PCBs in the water. Otters are the freshwater mammals most likely to be severely affected by chemical pollution, and the sharp decline of the common or river otter all over Europe has coincided with increasing pollution of European rivers by pesticide and industrial residues. Combined chemical and radioactive pollution is also blamed for the much lower stocks of muskrats, a valuable fur resource, along the shores of Lake Ontario.

Aquatic invertebrates also have varying capacities for resisting pollutants. Though a number of freshwater annelids, such as burrowing tubificids, can tolerate fairly high levels of organic pollution and loss of oxygen, and some leeches, such as the Nearctic *Helobdella stagnalis*, also thrive in polluted waters, bivalve molluscs need clear clean water, and their presence or absence is often used as a pollution indicator. Sawmill pollution is currently endangering a brackish-water snail in California; the largest population, in Humboldt Bay, was more or less extirpated by half-burnt sawdust blanketing the habitat. The cave shrimp *Palaemonias ganteri*, confined to one cave system in Kentucky, is threatened by contamination of the groundwater by sewage. Heavy metals are unfavourable to almost all life; thus there were no molluscs in the Ystwyth River in mid-Wales for 35 years after the end of lead mining.

Plants are especially affected by eutrophication, the presence of too many nutrients in water, largely due to excess fertiliser draining off farmland. Often a thick growth of algae, such as the appropriately named blanketweed *Enteromorpha*, blankets out other plants by depriving them of light. Untreated sewage can have a similar effect; at Wynbunbury Moss, a national nature reserve in Cheshire, it is changing bog vegetation into fen vegetation. Loch Leven, the most important waterfowl lake in Scotland,

Common guillemot or murre

also suffers from an inflow of nutrient chemicals from both fertilisers and domestic sewage. This results in a build-up of nitrogen, phosphorus and other nutrients in the bottom sediments, a loss of species, especially of aquatic plants adapted to a low-nutrient regime, and the erosion of the shore-line. In Central Europe bladder watertrap *Aldrovanda vesiculosa*, an insectivorous plant related to the sundews, is at some risk from eutrophication, being already extinct in Austria and Bulgaria, and now endangered in West Germany, Hungary, Italy, Yugoslavia, and even to some extent in Russia, where it is more widespread.

Oil spilt in the sea is another specialised form of pollution that has proved especially damaging to seabirds and to some extent to marine mammals. It has certainly caused local depletions, if not extinctions, of some auks, even apart from such major incidents as the loss of the tanker *Torrey Canyon* off the Scilly Isles in 1967, and the platform blow-out and fire in 1979, which allowed 3.2 billion barrels of crude oil to escape into the Gulf of Mexico. Such oil spills have increased steadily over the past 50 years, despite serious international efforts to control them, and are bound to have an impact on vulnerable endemics, such as Kemp's ridley turtle in the Gulf of Mexico.

Oil slicks are particularly lethal to sea ducks and auks, for they provide areas of relative calm in an otherwise turbulent sea, where migrating ducks and auks have been seen to pause for rest or dive for food. Their plumage sops up the sticky oil, so that they can neither fly nor dive. The cold water then penetrates their feathers and they either drown or struggle ashore to die of cold or hunger. Every year thousands of ducks and auks perish in the Baltic and North Seas alone; indeed, bird mortality from oiling in the Baltic may well be the worst in the world. Some 30,000 ducks, mainly long-tailed ducks, once died in a single incident off Gotland, and when a German ship grounded off the Elbe estuary in 1955, the release of some 6000 tons of oil killed 100,000 seabirds. Annual counts of beached birds, mainly oil victims, are made in Britain; nearly three-fifths of the beached auks prove to have been oiled. Many shore birds and waders also suffer when oil is driven in over shallow coastal waters.

Oil on the sea has caused fewer proven mass deaths of mammals, but in California there are fears for the sea otter, the most vulnerable of the marine mammals, if there is ever large-scale drilling offshore. In 1964 more than 100 sea otters perished on the shores of Paramushir Island in the Kuriles after a Russian tanker spill. There can be disastrous oil spills in fresh water too. In the Detroit River, Michigan, oil once killed 12,000 ducks, mainly the decreasing canvasback.

Acid rain or snow is a form of pollution, recently brought into sharp focus, that is both aquatic and terrestrial in its impact. Burning coal, oil and other fossil fuels in power plants, factories and motor vehicles produces two waste by-products, sulphur dioxide SO_2 and nitrogen oxides NO_x, which are soluble in water, so that they are absorbed by rain and snow. Since huge quantities of these two chemicals are now poured into the atmosphere in industrial regions, such as western Europe and North America, the rain falling to the leeward of these areas, for example in Scandinavia and Quebec, may be anything up to 100 times as acid as natural rain, often as acid as lemon juice or even vinegar. This acid precipitation has had catastrophic effects on two habitats and their associated species: the water of rivers and lakes, and apparently also the soil in coniferous forests, though the exact mechanism of the damage to trees has yet to be worked out scientifically.

Sweden was the first to sound the alarm, at the 1972 Stockholm Environment Conference, but the phenomenon is now widely recognised elsewhere, in Germany, eastern Europe, Switzerland, northern Britain,

Long-tailed duck

eastern Canada, New England and even California. In all these areas fish and the invertebrates on which they feed have already become extinct in many lakes and rivers and are in danger in a great many others, to the detriment of many once valuable fisheries. In Sweden, acid rain has certainly killed all the fishes in 2500 lakes and has damaged the ecology of at least 18,500. More than half the mountain lakes in the Adirondacks in New York State have already lost their fishes, and some 2600 lakes in Wisconsin and 2000 in north-eastern Minnesota are also thought to be at risk. Within twenty years, it has been forecast, 48,000 out of 81,000 lakes in Ontario, and more than half of those in West Virginia will be too acidic to support fishes.

In Europe, the first species to go as the acid levels rise are Atlantic salmon, the introduced rainbow trout, minnow and roach, followed by pike and brown trout. The last to disappear are perch, carp, and eels. In Norway there is no more fishing for salmon and trout, once an important economic resource, in an area equal to Switzerland: nine reservoirs and one-third of the lakes in southern Norway are fishless. Several good trout lochs in Galloway are also now completely fishless, including two of the four lochs in southern Scotland that contained char. In both Scotland and Wales dipper populations too have fallen when stream water becomes more acid. Similarly, across the Atlantic the salmon has already disappeared from eleven rivers in Nova Scotia and is expected to vanish from six more in the next five years.

Acid rain may kill fishes in several ways: direct poisoning; indirect poisoning when the acid combines with and releases other poisons, such as aluminium, into the water; suffocation from lack of oxygen; and deprivation of food. Acidification also has a marked impact on invertebrate populations; in Scotland, for instance, it first replaces mayflies and stoneflies with caddisflies and chironomid midges, and eventually eliminates even these to produce as sterile an environment as old-fashioned industrial pollution did in such lowland rivers as the Tame, north of Birmingham. Sparklingly clear water in the hills can be just as lifeless as turbid, polluted water in the lowlands.

The main terrestrial effect of acid rain so far has been on coniferous forests, especially in West Germany, Czechoslovakia, Switzerland and New England. More than half West Germany's trees have now been damaged; a recent survey reveals 17.5 per cent of the total forest area with medium or severe damage, i.e. having lost more than 20 per cent of their needles, and another 33 per cent with slight damage. Altogether 87 per cent of silver fir, 59 per cent of Scots pine and 51 per cent of Norway spruce are affected in some degree, together with 50 per cent of beech and 43 per cent

1. Silver fir
2. Norway spruce
3. Scots pine

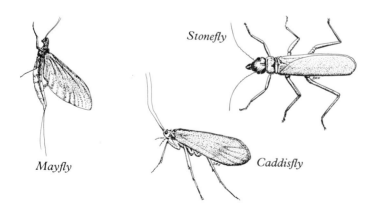

Mayfly

Stonefly

Caddisfly

of oak. In Baden-Württemberg, including the Black Forest, all the spruces and firs are likely to be dead by the end of the century. In one area of Switzerland up to 80 per cent of the firs died during 1983. In Sweden 244 forest stands, mainly of Norway spruce, have been reported as damaged, of which 137 are seriously damaged with one-tenth per cent of the trees affected. Beech damage has also been reported in Sweden, the Netherlands and elsewhere in Europe. In consequence, politicians and administrators in both West Germany and Scandinavia are a great deal more concerned about acid rain than their counterparts in Britain and most of the United States, whose actions suggest they do not really believe that the problem exists, and that if it does it will go away before it forces them to impose what they regard as unacceptable burdens on their industries. Thus the British Central Electricity Generating Board has suggested that it would be cheaper to save the Norwegian salmon fisheries by seeding Norway's rivers with calcium than to fit effective scrubbers on its own power stations. However, the CEGB does not seem to have offered to pay even for this palliative. On the other hand, two British foresters who visited Germany in 1982 and saw the extensive dieback of silver fir and Norway spruce in the Harz Mountains, the Bayerische Wald and the Black Forest, felt that there was 'an element of neurosis' involved in the readiness of many European foresters to attribute any die-back in forest trees to the combined effects of acid rain and atmospheric pollution, mainly from motor-car exhausts, without adequate critical investigation.

More recently various countries south of the Equator are beginning to wonder if their belated industrialisation may not lead to similar acidification problems. Dangerous levels of soil acidity in Brazil and air pollution in South Africa have already been recorded. Australia and Thailand may also be affected.

Although birds are the most spectacular victims of the terrestrial pollution due to pesticide and industrial residues and waste disposal, mammals can also be affected. Indeed, man himself can be a principal victim, as happened at Love Canal, New York State, where houses were built on a former pesticide dump. Voles living close to this site show many physical abnormalities and are shorter-lived than elsewhere.

In both Europe and North America very high levels of organochlorine residues, such as DDT, DDE, endrin, dieldrin and aldrin, and of other pesticides, such as mercury, chlordane and parathion, have been found in the fat and flesh of predatory birds, especially raptors and owls. Since these birds feed selectively, and moreover are at the end of food chains, they quickly accumulate dangerously high quantities of the poisons used to kill insect and other pests.

In Sweden, raptors and owls have greatly decreased due to this secondary poisoning, the worst affected species being the peregrine, kestrel, goshawk, sparrowhawk and eagle owl. High mercury levels have been found in both their fat and their eggs. In Britain a disastrous fall in peregrine numbers was reversed after a voluntary restriction on organochlorines entering the environment. In 1939 there were some 825 breeding pairs in the United Kingdom; by 1963 numbers had fallen by 84 per cent, but are now back to within 8 per cent of the pre-war level. Sparrowhawks have also made a substantial recovery in this period. In North America, before the raptors were subjected to DDT pollution, some 11,000 hawks, mostly accipiters and buteos, could be seen in a single day migrating over the famous watchpoint of Hawk Mountain, Pennsylvania, at peak periods in the fall. Now the number has dropped to less than half. The disastrous effects of rodenticides on birds of prey in Israel were mentioned on p. 89. A similar problem has recently arisen in Malaysia with the rodenticide brodifacoum.

Barn owl

Since this has been killing barn owls, which the oil-palm plantation managers had been relying on to help kill rats, some of the managers have already reverted to warfarin.

These poisons can reach birds by quite roundabout routes. In Britain, kestrels and tawny owls have been shown to ingest dieldrin from the dressed wheat eaten by their favoured prey, bank voles and wood mice; they thus perish for performing a service for farmers. Some pesticides also cause eggshells to become thin and fragile. This, combined with direct poisoning and some illegal killing by game preservers and others, led in the 1950s to the unprecedented breeding failure of the golden eagle and other raptors just mentioned, from which they all took some twenty years to recover. Ominously, eggshell thinning has now been demonstrated in the African fish eagle in Zimbabwe, where so much DDT has been pumped into the environment that the human population now carries a DDT burden in its fat exceeded by only four other countries in the world.

Mass deaths of songbirds have occurred from time to time ever since modern pesticides became available in the late 1940s. At one time spraying of elms against Dutch elm disease caused massive kills of robins in parts of the north-eastern United States and the Middle West; even so common a bird as this might have been eliminated if uncontrolled spraying had continued. Songbirds have often suffered from farmers using too much pesticide, far beyond what was either necessary or cost-effective, due to hard salesmanship by the chemical companies, who played on the folk belief that a double dose must be twice as good. Thus in Sweden, thousands of rooks were poisoned by mercury seed-dressings and 10,000 starlings were killed in one area alone from eating DDT-contaminated insects. Fortunately these are common birds, which can withstand the occasional local catastrophe, but smaller birds, such as the ortolan (once considered a culinary delicacy) and yellowhammer were locally extinct over a large part of central and southern Sweden, while in the north, where agriculture is less developed, they maintained their numbers. And there is still the occasional law-breaking farmer; in 1982 a Bethlehem, New York, farmer deliberately put down poisoned rye grain which killed more than 3000 red-winged blackbirds, grackles and other birds.

The largely unknown effects on birds and other wildlife of tsetse control operations in Africa were mentioned on p. 90. The effects of other African pesticide campaigns are, however, on record. Locust control in Mali and elsewhere has been shown to harm a wide range of birds: raptors, herons, shrikes, rollers, bee-eaters and small Palaearctic migrants, such as the European whitethroat. So has control, with parathion or fenthion, of the red-billed quelea and other grain-eaters at their roosts. This also destroys many other birds that roost in the same reedbeds, and in one case is known to have killed almost all the other birds on the site except the queleas. Moreover, the resulting corpses attract raptors, which thus die of secondary poisoning. A curious side effect has been the decline of yellow-billed oxpeckers in Nigeria, due to improved cattle-dipping, which kills off the ectoparasites on which they feed.

A more indirect effect of pesticides has hit the grey or Hungarian partridge in western Europe, especially in England. Here the pesticides have killed off the insects which the partridge chicks eat, so that the bird has become quite uncommon in many parts of England, its place often being taken by the introduced red-legged partridge from southern Europe.

Invertebrates and plants are the main victims of the increasing problems of spraydrift, when pesticides are carried on the wind; and of vapour drift, when under hot, humid conditions they vaporise and lift off the target crops like an invisible cloud. Honeybees also suffer from this as well as from

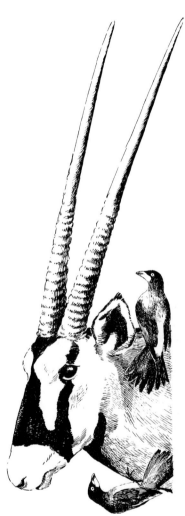

Yellow-billed oxpeckers on oryx

Dog rose

Wolf spider

legitimate uses of pesticides, and the decline of the wild dog rose in England has been attributed to spraydrift.

The use of defoliants in modern warfare can have a quite devastating effect on the wildlife of the forest sprayed. Since the Vietnam War, for instance, as a recent study by Dr John Mackinnon for IUCN shows, the combination of bombing and defoliants has permanently reduced the population levels of many species in Vietnam, and doubtless in Laos and Cambodia too. Thanks to the existence of 25 million bomb craters and the spraying of 19 million gallons of herbicides on the forests and croplands, one-third of Vietnam is now considered as waste land and the proportion covered by forests has fallen from 44 to 23 per cent. Even twelve or more years after the end of the war, the forests have not recovered, wildlife has not returned, and fisheries are severely affected, even in coastal waters.

6. Multiple Threats: Caves, Coral Reefs and Mangroves

Habitats whose ecosystems and numerous specialised plants and animals are especially subject to multiple threats include caves, coral reefs and mangroves. Caves are very fragile ecosystems, with a unique array of often endemic animals adapted to life underground in constant darkness, temperature and humidity. They are threatened directly by human disturbance and indirectly by mining, water supply and other development. The threats to the Kentucky cave shrimp were mentioned earlier. Elsewhere the Melones cave harvestman *Banksula melones*, a spider relative, is currently threatened by quarrying, a rising reservoir and human visitation. The wolf spider *Adelocosa anops* and the amphipod crustacean *Spalaeorchestia koloana*, confined to two lava tubes and a small cave on Kauai, Hawaii, are in serious danger from a diminishing water supply, nearby commercial development, pollution and human visitation. Ice caves are also vulnerable to environmental disturbance from human visitation. Frequent use of such caves along the Snake River, Idaho, causing significant ice-melt, is a potential threat to the beetle *Glacicavola bathyscoides* and to diplurans, collembolans, millipedes, phalangids and other invertebrates endemic to these caves.

Many bats roost in caves and some species are seriously at risk from disturbance of their roosts at the critical times, in the winter and early spring, when they may not survive if awakened before the temperature is right. Metal grilles are sometimes fitted over the entrances of bat caves, so that the bats can get out but people cannot get in. Grilling is especially used to protect the endangered endemic British race of the greater horseshoe bat, now confined to a few caves in the south-west. Two North American bats have been greatly endangered by disturbance of their roosting caves. The Indiana bat , whose total total population fell in fifteen years by 28 per cent to 46,000 in 1975, depends on a limited number of caves where the right temperature, between 4°C and 8°C, remains stable throughout the winter. Some 87 per cent of them live in only seven caves or mines. At one cave excessive disturbance, causing repeated arousal, killed 60,000 bats, and at least 80,000 more were lost when the entrances to three other caves were intentionally blocked, so that they warmed up. The gray bat, restricted to limestone caves in the south-east, still numbers just over one million, but this represents an estimated 80 per cent decline from the recent past. The main and continuing causes appear to be disturbance by spelunkers (potholers) and direct killing by vandals. Several of the largest colonies were destroyed when their caves were commercialised or dams were built nearby, and these threats continue. Water pollution and siltation, with consequent decline of mayflies, the bats' major food, may aggravate the situation.

In Thailand some caves used to hold hundreds of thousands or even millions of bats; today only those protected as bat guano mines by private owners survive. Even at one of these, however, guano output has fallen by half over five years, due to poaching for human food and folk medicines, and another has been almost destroyed by limestone quarrying. This also threatens the now rare ghost bat *Macroderma gigas* in northern Australia, the famous Batu Caves in West Malaysia, and the thousands of bats of nine species that roost in the St Pietersberg tunnels in South Limburg in the Netherlands. A similar story comes from the unique coastal bat caves south of Mombasa, Kenya, some of which are already lost to bats by disturbance, rubbish dumping and loss of the surrounding forest, which helps to keep the tunnels cool.

Coral reefs are genetically rich and diverse communities, occurring in warm shallow oceanic water in some 85 tropical countries. Formed mainly by the asexual budding of coral colonies, they may extend over large areas, most notably along the Great Barrier Reef off the coast of Queensland. Corals grow slowly, so that reefs may represent thousands of years of continuous growth, which can easily be broken off by a careless tourist. The physiology of corals is closely associated with symbiotic zooxanthellae, which are microscopic algae, flagellates which speed up coral growth by producing oxygen. Corals are thus generally limited to depths where there is enough light for photosynthesis. The encrusting and branch-like growth pattern of corals creates microhabitats for many forms of marine life, including fishes. Nutrients flow into the reefs both from oceanic currents and from land run-off, and have created one of the most productive, and at the same time most fragile, known ecosystems. Reefs are crucial to many local fisheries.

Unfortunately man subjects coral reefs and their animals to multiple destructive uses throughout their range, including the direct predation mentioned on p. 76. Dredging of dead coral for construction, lime and other industrial uses causes extensive destruction of living corals, notably in south-east Asia and Brazil. In Sri Lanka a recent exponential increase in the demand for lime threatens live coral reefs along the south-west coast with extinction. The massive slow-growing corals, such as *Goniopora* and *Porites*, which are basic to the structure of the reefs, are still often used in the construction of airports, hotels and other public buildings, especially in the Philippines. Tourists' feet can do comparable damage; on Pigeon Island, off Trincomalee, they have almost destroyed the fringing reef, so that every storm now throws up mounds of dead coral.

Pollution and sedimentation from terrestrial run-off also seriously disturbs the food supply and destroys the habitat for the reef fauna. The soil washed on to the reefs from eroded hillsides is, however, less harmful than the massive damage done by the dredgers, which fill their excavations several metres deep with fine white silt, blanketing almost all marine life. Certain fishing methods, usually illegal, involve dynamiting near the reefs, a catastrophic practice especially prevalent in the remoter parts of Indonesia, Malaysia and the Philippines. The damage done by fishermen with their anchors designed to hook corals is also very noticeable in Philippine coastal waters. In Kaneohe Bay, Hawaii, dredging, combined with freshwater run-off and sewage, has killed corals over wide areas. Some patch reefs off Venezuela too are dead or dying due to industrial waste or sewage, with their once plentiful stocks of fish and lobsters now almost gone; in Panama many of the corals on reefs bordering heavily cultivated land have herbicide residues in their tissues, and more than half are dead. In

Porites *coral*

French Polynesia traumas to the reefs, both natural and man-made, apparently encourage a dinoflagellate which produces outbreaks of human seafood poisoning called ciguatera.

Mangroves are another very productive tropical coastal ecosystem that is subject to multiple destructive uses, both to overexploitation by traditional users, such as charcoal burners, and to outright destruction. Mangrove is a term applied both to the habitat and to its characteristic woody plants, especially species of *Avicennia* and *Rhizophora*. Mining for sand or shale, and conversion to agriculture or aquaculture destroy the ecosystem completely, but development outside the ecosystem, such as dam building or mining nearby, can be almost as fatal. Sand mining, for instance, destroyed a mangrove tract in Puerto Rico by removing most of a coastal dune, and shale mining in Queensland is expected to destroy adjacent mangroves by diverting fresh water into them. The Sundarbans in West Bengal and Bangladesh, perhaps the greatest mangrove forest in the world, and an important tiger habitat, are threatened by a reduced flow of fresh water, due to dams, barrages and irrigation along the Ganges. Mangroves in Senegal, the Gambia and Sierra Leone have been converted to ricefields, and mangroves in Ecuador, Costa Rica and the Philippines have had to make way for ponds for farming fish and shrimps, to mention only a few. In Venezuela and the Guianas drainage and development of mangroves are an important factor in the severe decline of the scarlet ibis, which is now down to four main colonies.

7. Recreational Pressures

Tourism, local, national and international, can have a serious impact on ecosystems and their genetic resources, both by physical destruction and by disturbance. Indeed it often competes directly with wildlife for habitat, especially on the coast. In Sri Lanka, for instance, the beaches with smooth slopes and large beach platforms that are ideal for sea turtles are also ideal for the expanding tourist industry. In Greece, conservationists' attempts to preserve the coastal habitat of the land tortoise *Testudo hermanni*, which local people wished to develop for holiday homes, recently led the villagers to set fire to it in an attempt to destroy the tortoise population; it has, however, recovered. In California several winter roosts of the migratory monarch butterfly have been lost when their trees at Pacific Grove have been felled to make way for apartments and condominiums.

Vehicle tracks are most destructive in sand dunes, where they may cause blow-outs, and in the Arctic tundra, where they may last for many years. Damage by army manoeuvres in the Death Valley area of California in the 1940s is still evident. Larger blow-outs lead to sandstorms, which are capable of overwhelming whole villages, as happened at Culbin on the Moray Firth in Scotland in the seventeenth century. In northern France, where motorcycle scrambling has in the past ten years been steadily destroying the dunes at Le Touquet, some dunes are already beginning to smother the vegetation behind them.

In North America driving across wild habitat of all kinds by ORVs (off-road vehicles) has become a serious problem, especially in winter, when chasing a deer in the snow may easily kill it by exhaustion. ORVs are destroying many areas of desert and semi-desert habitat in the south-western United States: even a few passes will harm slow-growing desert shrubs, and 20-30 passes will lay their upper roots bare. Great damage was done to Eureka Dunes, California, by often illegal ORV activity in the 1970s. At Cadden Beach, the most important breeding site in Nova Scotia of the piping plover, trail bikes have reduced the number of nesting pairs by

Piping plover

one-third. In California heavy ORV and camping use are said to be the primary threat to the San Benito evening primrose *Camissonia benitensis*. In Crete vehicle pressure combined with beach fires almost eliminated the island's most famous endemic, the Cretan date palm, until it was fenced in to allow regeneration.

Similar problems arise with motor-boats, which are, for instance, blamed for significantly reducing the numbers of wintering wildfowl on Llangorse Lake in Wales.

Even walkers can do great harm to plants. The bare ground under the trees of Highgate Wood, North London, gives no clue that when it was first opened to the public at the end of the last century it was a fine bluebell wood. The bluebells were trampled away by the people who came to enjoy them. So many hikers were trampling the habitat of the rare alpine cinquefoil *Potentilla robbinsiana* on Mount Washington, New Hampshire, that $7000 had to be spent on a wall to keep them out and a $500 penalty imposed on those who did not. The single remaining British site of the lady's slipper orchid has also had to be fenced off to prevent erosion by the footsteps of its many admirers. Other rare orchids in Britain are having to be wardened against photographers. It is all too often possible to pinpoint the exact site of a rare plant by the flattened grass all round it, where photographers have lain down to get a better picture, oblivious of the young plants they are crushing.

Walkers are, of course, disastrous anywhere near colonies of breeding birds, while disturbance by skiers has probably led to the decline of the capercaillie in parts of West Germany and of the ptarmigan in parts of the Scottish Highlands. Fishes too can suffer from recreational pressures: contamination of mountain streams by tourists is blamed for endangering 70 per cent of the fishes of lower Bavaria.

Grizzly bears tend to avoid areas within half a mile of a road, so that any new road, let alone ORVs patrolling their habitat, will drive them further into the wilderness. On the other hand, some grizzlies do become habituated to human presence, especially if attracted by waste food in refuse bins, and these not only lose their fear of man, but may actually attack and kill sleeping campers.

The very act of watching wildlife may have a harmful effect, as when boatloads of tourists harass breeding gray whales in Scammon's Lagoon on the west coast of Mexico, southern right whales in the Golfo Nuevo, Argentina, and humpbacks in the Hawaiian archipelago. In Africa similar boatloads have threatened Nile crocodiles by allowing photographers to approach close enough to drive the females from their nests and enable monitor lizards and other predators to take their eggs. Motorised tourists have chased such rare species as cheetahs in East Africa and addax in Niger, both to photograph them and for the fun of clocking them against the speedometer. For the addax at least the chase may end in the exhausted animal being run over and killed.

Lady's slipper orchid

Grizzly bear

8. Introduced Species

Destruction or degradation of their habitat is one of the most important adverse effects on native animals and plants of alien species introduced, either deliberately or accidentally, to new territory. Introduced species, as discussed on p. 90, may also compete with native ones for space or food, prey on them, or transmit to them various parasites or diseases.

Large herbivore mammals are the most likely to degrade or destroy the habitat, and many of these are escaped domestic stock, although pigs, goats and rabbits are sometimes deliberately released on islands to provide a food supply for fishermen and mariners. In the absence of predator control all three are efficient destroyers of habitat, but because goats have been released or have escaped more widely, they have probably done the most damage globally. Goats do most harm on oceanic islands, whose vegetation is not adapted to being grazed or browsed. On St Helena in the South Atlantic, for instance, goats were released in 1513 and by the end of the century had formed herds nearly two kilometres long. They so devastated the original continuous forest of endemic trees that by the time the first botanist arrived in 1805 these were reduced to a few areas on the central ridge. He found some 30 endemic species, of which ten are now extinct and fifteen endangered, but the great Victorian botanist Sir Joseph Hooker estimated that there must originally have been about 100 endemic plants in this 'wonderfully curious little flora'. Most of these plants can now never be known to science. Similar threats from goats and other domestic stock still threaten such important island centres of endemism as Socotra in the Arabian Sea south of Aden, with 216 endemics, and Juan Fernandez off Chile, with 115: 98 flowering plants and 17 ferns.

Galapagos land iguana

Goats have also done untold damage in the Galapagos Islands, 600 miles into the Pacific off Ecuador. By grossly overgrazing the vegetation, they appear to have exterminated at least four of the island races of the giant tortoise and have also seriously endangered many of the land iguana colonies, both by depriving them of food and by removing the cover that protected the young ones from attacks by the Galapagos hawk. The distinct species of land iguana which inhabits Santa Fé (Barrington) Island has now been saved by killing off all the goats. Round Island off Mauritius is another classic instance of the harm that can be done by goats and also by rabbits, which were both released there in 1850. This small island was a positive zoo and botanic garden of endemic reptiles and palms, all of which are now endangered and some actually extinct, overgrazing having almost completely removed the vegetation. The endemic palms, including *Latania loddegisii* and *Pandanus vandermeeschii*, survive as fully grown trees, but cannot reproduce themselves as the rabbits eat all the seedlings. The reptiles are two geckos *Cyrtodactyla serpensinsula* and *Phelsuma guentheri*, a skink *Leiolopisma telfairii* and two snakes, both boas: *Bolyeria multocarinata* which may already be extinct, and *Casarea dussumieri*, of which about 75 survived in 1974. The goats have now been shot out, but that merely leaves more food for the rabbits, which are still breeding apace, despite numerous attempts at control or extermination. Rabbits too killed off three endemic birds, and nearly a fourth, the duck *Anas laysanensis*, when they overgrazed Laysan in the Hawaiian chain before themselves dying out in 1923.

Burros or feral donkeys and mustangs or feral horses can also destroy habitat and compete with other animals, especially in the western United States. In Death Valley, California, the 2000 or more burros eat 2650 tonnes of vegetation each year, to the disadvantage of the bighorn sheep, now reduced to barely four per cent of their former numbers. The burros also destroy vegetation with their hooves, as they gather around the sparse water-holes. The 29 reindeer released on St Matthew Island in the Bering Sea in 1944 provide an even more striking example. Within twenty years their grazing of the abundant supplies of reindeer moss had brought the population up to 6000, at a density of 3.6 times the estimated carrying capacity, so that both animals and habitat were in poor condition. As a result the heavy snows of the ensuing winter virtually exterminated them. Three years later only 42 could be found.

Bighorn sheep

Plants can destroy habitat as well. On St Helena the remnant native forests, originally devastated by goats, are now under attack from New Zealand flax *Phormium tenax*, which was cultivated and has now gone wild. As the industry dwindled, the plants were not cut and so seeded abundantly. The paths separating the plantations from the indigenous forests became overgrown, allowing the flax to spread uphill into the remaining fragments of native forest. Once there, it is almost impossible to remove. On Juan Fernandez *Aristotelia* and the Old World bramble are both steadily invading and suppressing the native vegetation. So, in the Galapagos, are the guava and the avocado. In Hawaii numerous exotic species are invading the native forests, among them banana poke *Passiflora mollissima* and strawberry guava *Psidium cattleianum*, whose seeds are distributed by feral pigs. They are one of the factors which have dramatically changed the physiognomy and species composition of these forests. Even in Britain two woody plants introduced from Europe, sycamore and *Rhododendron ponticum*, are invading some native woodlands, the rhododendron's thick leathery foliage shading out everything beneath it.

The problem exists on continents too. The endemic Fynbos flora of South Africa is threatened by numerous aliens, chiefly wattles and hakea from Australia and pines from Europe, which badly infest a quarter of its remaining territory. A single wattle tree can shed 10,000 seeds per square metre beneath it. In southern Florida too, such introduced trees as punk tree *Melaleuca leucodendron* (which produces both cajuput oil and timber), Brazilian pepper tree *Schinus terebintha* (which yields a resin) and Australian she oak *Casuarina equisetifolia* (also a timber tree) are causing major habitat problems. In Alabama the Japanese honeysuckle has been blamed for the actual extinction of the endemic pitcher plant *Sarracenia alabamensis*.

Two introduced aquatic plants, water hyacinth and the water fern *Salvinia molesta*, have brought widespread changes to fresh waters throughout the tropics, many of which they now completely dominate. The salvinia, for instance, has changed the whole ecology of Lake Naivasha in Kenya, and is blamed for the depletion of fish stocks in the River Sepik in Papua New Guinea, where it was introduced by missionaries as shading for the pools of their commercial crocodile farm. Water hyacinth is actually toxic to fish, so that many of the fish in the Curua Una Reservoir in Brazil died soon after the plant appeared there.

Important habitat changes have occurred as a result of alien disease organisms entering the environment and affecting prey species or food plants. The introduction, probably deliberate, of the rabbit disease myxomatosis into Britain in 1953-54 not only reduced the number of rabbits by more than 90 per cent at first, but caused buzzards, which had been feeding heavily on them, not to breed at all for a season or two, and diverted many other predators, such as foxes, stoats and raptors, to mice, voles and other prey, thus causing temporary fluctuations in both predators and prey. As already mentioned, resultant relaxation of rabbit grazing pressure also led to the scrubbing up of a great many grasslands, notably chalk grasslands with hawthorn, and so radically changed the habitat of many plants and insects. Dutch elm disease not only devastated British elms during the recent severe epidemic due to a new and more virulent American strain of the fungus *Ceratostomella ulmi*, but has also threatened the already uncommon white-letter hairstreak butterfly, whose larvae feed on elm, and may have played a part in the recent severe decline of the elm-loving cirl bunting. The almost total loss of the American chestnut from the climax forests of eastern North America between 1904 and 1940, due to an epidemic of chestnut blight *Endothia parasitica* from Asia, also destroyed

Water hyacinth

White-letter hairstreak butterfly

the habitat and caused the disappearance of at least five species of Microlepidoptera.

So far we have considered the problems of species conservation, mainly arising from the two great threats of overexploitation and habitat destruction. Now we turn to the practical details of how species can actually be conserved.

The Future of Genetic Resources

Part II

Greater bird of paradise

Badger

Maintaining Ecosystems　　　7

To Aristotle, the world appeared to be composed of four elements: earth, air, fire and water. E. B. Worthington found these to be appropriate headings under which to consider the physical background of conservation. They are equally convenient for considering how to maintain ecosystems, for the animal and plant species which are the essential components of all ecosystems exist in a matrix of soil, water and air, with fire as a dynamic factor in many terrestrial ecosystems. Fire came first in the development of the world, but for the evolution of life in its manifold forms, first air, then water and finally dry land were necessary.

1. Air

No life could exist without oxygen – apart from a few anaerobic bacteria – and most animals and plants get their oxygen either direct from the atmosphere or, if they are aquatic, indirectly from air dissolved in water. Pure air is thus one of the most basic requirements for species conservation, and we have seen earlier how disastrous atmospheric pollution, especially in the form of acid rain, can be to vegetation, notably coniferous trees, and to aquatic life, such as salmonid fish. Hence all advanced countries, invariably against stiff resistance from the polluting industries, which chorus that jobs are at risk, now have laws to control what industry, or even householders may put into the atmosphere from their smoking chimneys. After a slow start, the worst excesses of the industrial revolution, which led to part of the English Midlands being called the Black Country, and had similar effects elsewhere in Europe and North America, have now been checked. However, the widespread incidence of acid rain shows that either these laws are not strict enough or they are not adequately enforced. Third World countries have been equally slow to initiate controls; in due course, after much needless damage, all will doubtless do so. The international instrument designed to combat atmospheric pollution and acid rain in particular, the Convention on Long-range Transboundary Air Pollution, came into force in March 1983. So far only 24 of the 35 signatory nations have ratified.

Climate is a vital factor in any ecosystem, and microclimates determine the distribution of many animals and plants, but deliberate major alterations of climate are part of the agenda for the twenty-first century rather than for the next twenty years. Yet there are already indications of local climatic effects of the removal of forest cover in some areas. It certainly should be part of the agenda for the rest of this century to check such unwanted climatic changes, which by reducing rainfall could seriously affect agriculture. There appears indeed to be a link between the worldwide destruction of rainforest and both the southward advance of the Sahara Desert and the increase of carbon dioxide in the atmosphere. This is due to substantial recent increases in the burning of fossil fuels, and also in forest clearance, with consequent oxidation of leaf-litter and humus. Atmospheric carbon dioxide has been increasing for more than a century, and this is bound to warm the atmosphere because it absorbs specific wavebands of infra-red radiation. This is the so-called 'greenhouse effect'. Recent small increases in atmospheric temperature may or may not be a direct consequence of this increase in carbon dioxide. How soon and to what degree the greenhouse effect is likely to change the climate of the world is currently the subject of much scientific controversy. If the greenhouse effect develops as has been forecast, entire ecosystems, such as the tundra, along with all their species, will be at risk and could even disappear during the twenty-first century. As Norman Myers has pointed out, this could nullify all our present plans for conserving genetic resources through networks of protected areas.

2. Water

Life began in the water, and a great many species, both animal and plant, some of them of vital importance for human welfare, still inhabit water as their principal medium. Hence the maintenance of pure water is a top priority if ecological processes and life-support systems are to be maintained. Chapter 6 gave examples of the extremely harmful effect that water pollution can have on genetic resources.

As with atmospheric pollution, most advanced countries have reasonably effective control over the grosser forms of freshwater pollution, but many Third World countries have hardly begun to enter this field. The World Conservation Strategy calls not only for control of the discharge of pollutants and poisons into the environment, but for special care to avoid contaminating the habitats of threatened, unique or economically important species. Fish stocks have on the whole suffered more from overfishing than from pollution, but many streams in the industrialised world have become too polluted to support fish. A good instance of a fish stock being restored by cleaning up a river comes from Maine, where a quarter of a million Atlantic salmon used to be taken in the Penobscot each year until 80-90 years ago. By 1957 pollution had completely eliminated the salmon run, but after the clean-up began in 1960 the fish came back, and 914 salmon were caught in 1982. The effects of acid rain can sometimes be directly combated by adding lime to the water; Sweden has limed some 1500 lakes since 1976. In Britain acid water has been seeded with granular chalk in East Anglia, both to restore the fish and submerged vegetation in Calthorpe Broad and to enable natterjack toads to breed again in coastal pools.

Marine pollution, especially by oil, has proved extremely hard to control, despite several international conventions and the efforts of the International Maritime Conservation Organisation to persuade nations to sign, ratify and enforce them. In one recent year 76.6 million barrels of oil were released, accidentally or otherwise, from offshore oil rigs in the Caribbean and the Gulf of Mexico. Sweden, with its 7400km Baltic coastline, has had a special interest in combating oil pollution, and Swedish scientists have built up a body of expertise that has helped to deal with the worst effects of oil pollution in many parts of the world. However, as with all pollution, remedial measures are always second best to prevention. Many sea captains still flout international law and opinion by discharging oil directly into the

Atlantic salmon

sea; one Greek tanker captain recently killed half a million seabirds in the North Sea by pumping out 40 tons of bunker oil while routinely cleaning his tanks.

The most important Antarctic ecosystems are primarily marine and freshwater, although some species breed on land. These are the ecosystems which the Convention on the Conservation of Antarctic Marine Living Resources (1980) aims to protect and conserve. This was the first international conservation convention to be soundly based on scientifically managed sustainable utilisation. Difficulties are still being experienced in launching the environmental safeguards envisaged in the Convention, but at the very least it is hoped that the future regime for the Antarctic will include measures for checking on the likely environmental impact of any mining or other development projects, regulations to reduce or avert such impact, and arrangements for monitoring the actual impact. Many conservationists go further, and urge that the whole of Antarctica be set aside as an international park or reserve, where no exploitation of minerals would be allowed. IUCN has adopted a middle way by calling on the Antarctic Treaty Consultative Parties to maintain for all time the intrinsic value of the Antarctic environment for mankind and the biosphere; to ensure that all human activities there are compatible with the maintenance of these values; and to give the whole Antarctic ecosystem a designation which connotes, worldwide, its unique character and values and the special measures accorded to its planning, management and conservation. The problems of Antarctic conservation are well illustrated by the decision of France, one of the Convention's signatories, to build an airstrip in the Pointe Géologie archipelago in Adélie Land; quarrying for it has already destroyed the nesting places of several hundred birds.

More limited international agreements to control marine pollution have recently been agreed by nations surrounding both the Caribbean and the Mediterranean, as part of UNEP's Regional Seas Programme. The Caribbean convention, which thirteen countries signed in March 1983, seeks to control six sources of marine pollution, including discharges from rivers and estuaries and exploration and exploitation of the sea bed. It is too soon, of course, to know whether these agreements will actually stem the increasingly serious pollution of both seas.

Maintaining aquatic ecosystems, however, entails more than just preventing pollution. Many fish, both freshwater and marine, come inshore to spawn in shallow water, where oyster beds and other important marine mollusc resources are also found. To maintain fisheries, it is therefore vital to minimise disturbance in estuaries, mangrove swamps and other suitable spawning areas. Thus IUCN's Ecology Commission recommends that to minimise the impact of aquaculture on mangrove ecosystems, not more than one hectare of fishponds should be allowed for every four hectares of mangroves left untouched. Coral reefs and active floodplains are other fishery support ecosystems where management must take the impact on fisheries into account. Economists are very ready to estimate the potential benefits of new developments, but often seem to regard the likely losses, such as the disappearance of a thriving fishery, as so problematical as not to be calculable. And in this context management includes no management. Lack of management may not matter if an ecosystem is functioning smoothly, but once it is affected by pollution (now almost universal) or siltation from a distant dam, lack of management is in fact a regressive management policy that will eventually destroy the ecosystem or transform it into something quite different. As indicated on p. 136, it only needs one key species to disappear or be heavily reduced to change the whole ecosystem in many subtle ways.

At the interface between water and land, good conservation management calls for some knowledge of the hydrological equation in each area: precipitation (rain + snow) = evaporation + percolation + run-off. Adequate percolation, so that plant roots can absorb enough moisture, thus requires that too much rainfall must not either evaporate or run off into rivers. Deforestation increases both forms of water loss; by exposing soil to the sun it increases both evaporation and water run-off, and the soil runs off in the water as well. Destruction of mountain forests which protect watershed catchment areas, as in the Andes and Himalayas, not only produces harmful floods and removes the topsoil from the mountains, but adversely changes the ecosystems of the lower reaches of rivers and inshore seas, as in the Bay of Bengal, by depositing that soil in the form of silt. In Uttar Pradesh, northern India, flood-prone areas have doubled to 40 million hectares at the same time as 2300 out of 2700 government water projects have failed as water sources dried up. Yet in many Third World countries the situation is much worse, for few governments are taking any effective steps to reverse or even stem the destruction of what remains of their mountain forests.

3. Earth

Once life emerged from the water, the soil became its primary resource, so maintaining soil fertility is essential to maintaining terrestrial ecosystems. Soil may be degraded in three ways: its plant nutrients, such as nitrogen, calcium and phosphorus, may be exhausted by cropping or grazing, and not replaced; it may be polluted or impoverished by acid rain, industrial wastes, excessive use of fertilisers, especially nitrogen, or overuse of long-lasting pesticides; or it may simply be removed, either semi-naturally after deforestation or deliberately in the course of industrial development. The construction of a major road leaves a scar that may take thousands of years to refill with soil, if indeed it ever does. The devastating impact on the tundra of the passage of just one wheeled or tracked vehicle was mentioned on p. 124.

Most countries try to maintain the fertility of their soil by subsidising agricultural products. This, however, often leads to needless and uneconomic cultivation of marginal land, thanks to overproduction of food for which there is no market at the artificially high prices often imposed for political reasons, for example by the European Economic Community. Ecologically, it would be sounder to aim such subsidies directly at the maintenance of fertility. If the subsidy system used in the Scottish Highlands had rewarded measures to reduce the long-term loss of nutrients, instead of encouraging high sheep-stocking rates, the Highland hills and moors would not have become a wet desert. And if the ancient Greeks and Romans had had a similar policy with regard to goats, Mediterranean landscapes would today be grassy and fertile rather than rocky and barren.

Good management of farmland and forests requires first that the most fertile land be reserved for cultivation, and not built over, as happened when suburbs such as Fulham and Chelsea were allowed to grow up on the fertile brickearth soils of London, once noted for their market gardens. Many communities began as a cluster of farmhouses near the fields they cultivated, chosen for their high fertility, so that as populations grew and the hamlet became a village and the village a town, urban sprawl covered the most fertile farmlands first. At present industry is allowed to destroy good farmland, and agriculture good forestry land, because both bring in higher short-term profits. Yet in all countries the public interest to maintain the most fertile cropland under crops should be the overriding factor.

The proper management of fertile land, as the World Conservation Strategy points out, calls for soil and water conservation, recycling nutrients by returning crop residues and livestock wastes to the land (not burning them, as happens with straw in Britain and cow dung in India), and retaining the habitats or organisms especially beneficial to agriculture, such as earthworms (for soil recycling), honeybees (for pollination) and the small predators, such as raptors and mustelids, that control such pests as rats, mice and rabbits. It also requires the control of stock numbers to prevent the overgrazing which is almost as universal among stock-rearers as overfishing is among fishermen. The political and social resistances to such sound policies were well illustrated on St Helena in 1745, when the East India Company actually forced the island council to repay to two offenders the £10 fines imposed for illegal grazing in an area where the goats were barking the already endangered endemic ebony *Trochetiopsis melanoxylon*. Two of many examples of how overgrazing can be controlled, even if sometimes inefficiently, are the system of grazing permits operated by the Forest Department of Himachal Pradesh in northern India and the control of pony grazing by the Verderers of the New Forest in southern England. The public grazing lands of the western United States are also controlled, but politically and in such a way as in fact to ensure overgrazing.

Honeybee

Tropical rainforests have so far been harvested almost entirely on exploitative rather than conservation principles. How different much of Latin America would look today if governments had only heeded Simon Bolivar's far-sighted ruling more than 150 years ago that destruction of the forests should cease and millions of trees be planted. In its recommendations to the UN Conference on Tropical Timber at Geneva in 1983, IUCN showed what is needed for the sustainable harvesting of tropical timber: harvesting timber only from forests that can be exploited sustainably; developing and implementing more efficient, less destructive methods of extraction; and reforesting logged lands, preferably with native species. China is a pioneer in reforesting land devastated by exploitative forestry, and has planted, over the past 25 years or so, some 30-60 million hectares for fuelwood, amenity and timber. In 1980 alone 12-14 billion trees were planted; the percentage of China's surface area under forest has risen from 8 in 1949 to 12.5 in 1982 and is intended to reach 20 by the end of the century. A second Great Wall, some 7000 km long, is planned: a wall of trees to stem the advance of the desert. A similar broad ribbon of planted trees has been proposed to combat the southward spread of the Sahara. Indeed, there is now widespread interest in reforestation, especially for fuelwood on urban fringes, which is being grant-aided by the World Bank, UNDP and other agencies.

The measures to control various kinds of environmental pollutants, mentioned on p. 132, serve also to safeguard the fertility of the soil.

4. Fire

Fire, so important an element in the early stages of the earth's history, is now, as a natural occurrence, of comparatively minor importance. However, many existing ecosystems, from the African savanna to the North American taiga, depend on fire from lightning or from volcanic activity if they are not to change into quite different ecosystems, and also to provide the diversity of habitat that their animals and plants need. Thus in Etosha National Park in Namibia fires, more than half of them caused by lightning, are so frequent that virtually all the vegetated areas of the park burned at least once in the 1970s, and fire does not need to be used in management. The species inhabiting taiga also greatly benefit from forest

Sitatunga

Marsh rose protea

fires, as illustrated on Isle Royale, Minnesota (p. 137). Volcanic soils too are extremely fertile, so that the devastation caused by eruptions has long-term advantages.

In most habitats, however, man-made fires make a greater impact, if only because species have become adapted to the natural fire frequency and are likely to suffer if man increases the rate of burning. Since man emerged as a hunter, he has burned vegetation, sometimes to clear thick cover, sometimes to drive quarry towards a steep cliff or other trap, sometimes to improve the food supply for his prey. Even today local antelope hunters regularly burn the swamps along the Uganda shore of Lake Victoria to enable them to catch the swamp-dwelling sitatunga. In the Scottish Highlands the heather is burned to increase the food supply of young shoots for the red grouse. The moors have lost much fertility because the game preservers no longer have the abundant cheap labour that once enabled them to carry out the muirburn in small blocks, to ensure that no section of the hill was burned too often.

Some man-made fires will always occur, but the soundest conservation policy is either to forbid deliberate burning altogether, as in Etosha, or to minimise its use, while not preventing natural fires. The US National Park Service, for instance, now suppresses fires due to man, but lets natural fires burn themselves out.

In Britain, straw-burning has increased greatly in recent years as an economical method of disposing of unwanted straw after harvest, relying on the farmers' own voluntary code of practice. Unfortunately, especially in some recent hot dry summers, many fires have got out of hand and have destroyed hedges, small woodlands and even crops and gardens, so now there are increasing calls for legislation. Straw is a valuable resource in its own right, used as such in Europe, and it is remarkable tribute to the perversity of modern economic motivation that the British farming community has so far been unable to follow suit.

Fire plays an important part in the ecology of certain plants. Some conifers, for instance, depend on fire to open their cones and scatter their seed. In South Africa the marsh rose protea *Orothamnus zeyheri* of the Cape Province increased from 90 to over 2000 specimens in a dozen years, partly due to fire stimulating dormant seed in the soil. Further research is under way to find out how often the vegetation needs to burn for the sake of this and other rare plants in the area.

5. Species with a Key Role in their Ecosystem

All ecosystems are an extremely complex web of animal and plant species, but some individual species play such a key role in their ecosystem that it changes completely if they are removed. Oaks in temperate forests, brachystegias in tropical Africa and dipterocarps in South-east Asia are all dominant trees in their ecosystem; their destruction or overharvesting will change those ecosystems, often irreversibly. On temperate sand dunes, marram or beachgrass plays a vital part in holding the sand together with its tough and extensive root system. If it is removed, for instance by military tank practice in the dunes, blow-outs occur; if the disturbance is on a large enough scale, the sand may engulf farmland or even villages. The Culbin Sands on the Moray Firth in Scotland, now largely planted up to conifers, are the end result of a series of gigantic blow-outs that overwhelmed a prosperous village with fertile farmland in the centuries up to about 1700.

Predators, which are often among the first species in an ecosystem to be removed by man, play a key role in maintaining ecosystems in balance. There are many well attested examples of deer undergoing population explosions and destroying their own food supply, due to the absence or removal of predators. The moose of Isle Royale, Minnesota, an island in Lake Superior, are one such example and also illustrate the importance of fire in the taiga, mentioned on p. 135. Moose colonised the island about 1910, probably crossing the ice from Ontario, eighteen miles away. Numbers increased rapidly, to some 2000-3000 by the late 1920s, when they had destroyed almost all the browse of the forest understory. This led to a big die-off in the early 1930s, which was fortuitously followed by a major fire in 1936, the drought year that created the dust bowl further south. The greening that followed the fire led to an increase in moose, and the cycle seemed set for another explosion and crash. But in the winter of 1949 a pack of wolves also crossed the ice and began to prey on the moose. This has led to a balanced environment for both predators and prey, rescuing the vegetation from its overexploitation by the moose. The wolves feed on beavers in the summer and moose in the winter, and both predator and prey populations fluctuate within fairly narrow limits, the moose between 800 and 1000, largely determined by snowfall and other climatic conditions. By now the trees resulting from the 1936 burn are reaching maturity, and soon a fresh burn is likely.

The status of cougars in some districts may also be linked with the presence or absence of moose. The fact that wolf and cougar populations fluctuate with their prey illustrates the truism that predator populations are controlled by the size of their prey populations, i.e. by their food supply, and not vice versa, which is what game preservers almost universally believe. The problem here is that game preservers try to maintain population levels that are artificially high in relation to the carrying capacity of any habitat, and these are just the conditions in which a predator is needed to carry off the surplus. Thus game preservers are also inevitably preservers of predators, much as they kick against the pricks.

In some aquatic ecosystems crocodiles play a major balancing role, often keeping under control predatory fish that would otherwise reduce the stocks of the fish needed by man.

Marram grass

Certain small prey species can play as vital a part in maintaining ecosystem balance as the top predators. Voles act as a kind of universal provider for a wide range of mammal and bird predators; a population explosion of field voles in upland areas in Britain attracts local concentrations of short-eared owls and hen harriers to take advantage of the temporarily abundant food supply. But it is not, as used to be assumed, the raptors that bring about the eventual collapse of the vole plague, but high-density stresses within the vole community structure itself.

In the southern ocean the abundant and highly nutritious crustacean krill is a similar direct or indirect food basis for many animals. Of the total annual production of some 650 million tonnes of krill, penguins and seals are each estimated to account for 130 million with the baleen whales taking a further 40 million.

In the north-east Atlantic the equally nutritious sand eel plays a similar part in the diet of auks, terns and other seabirds, and also, recent research has shown, in that of grey seals. Human overfishing of sand eels is now believed to be one of the main causes of the recent sharp fall in the numbers of breeding puffins in northern Norway. On the extensive mudflats of the Bay of Fundy in eastern Canada, the mud shrimp *Corophium volutator* is a universal provider for the semi-palmated sandpipers and millions of other shorebirds, fattening them up before and after their long migration 2600 miles across the ocean to and from South America. There are between 1000 and 2000 mud shrimps per square foot over much of the nearly 400 square miles of the intertidal zone; each day

Wolves

Bush-baby

each bird eats between 10,000 and 20,000 shrimps, and gains one gram in weight.

Flower pollination gives many insects and other species key roles in various ecosystems. The honeybee is by far the best known pollinating insect, but many other Hymenoptera, other flying insects and, in the tropics, hummingbirds and bats can also be important. In Britain alone there are 240 bee species; without cross-pollination by some of them, orchard fruit trees, brassicas and legumes would never produce a crop. Fruit growers are well aware of the disastrous effect excessive pesticide spraying by farming neighbours at blossom time, which kills all the pollinators, can have on their output for the year. On the other hand, the honeybee, introduced into Hawaii, is accused of disrupting the natural reproductive patterns of many native plants. In the tropics many plants of economic importance depend on bat pollination, such as durian in Malaysia and iroko timber in West Africa, or even on pollination by other mammals, such as the baobab by the bush-baby.

There are many other ways in which the interdependence of species gives apparently insignificant animals and plants a key role in the survival of species and ecosystems. Earthworms maintain many terrestrial ecosystems by circulating nutrients in the soil. The example of the European large blue butterfly, which relies on the ant *Myrmica sabuleti* to care for its larvae, was cited on p. 108. Less widely known is the fact that one-fifth of the proteas and other Fynbos plants in South Africa rely on ants to transport their seeds. The European mistletoe has sticky seeds which germinate on the bark of a tree, where they have been deposited by mistle thrushes and other birds which have wiped their bills after feeding on them. Many plants too have fruits which must pass through a bird's gut in order to germinate.

Many species of fungi form a symbiotic relationship with trees, orchids and other higher plants by developing a remarkable web of whitish threads known as mycorrhiza. Sometimes the presence of the fungi is obligatory for the germination or development of the higher plant, so if a rainforest or other woodland is felled and the ground lies bare long enough for the mycorrhiza to be lost, the original tree species may not be able to re-establish themselves.

6. Protected Areas

The standard method of preserving wildlife is to set aside a protected area, whether a national park, a wildlife refuge, a nature (p)reserve or a sanctuary, in which the maintenance of the habitat, which of course includes all its species, takes priority over all other uses of the land. The original idea was to preserve the habitat of certain species believed to be threatened or endangered, such as a seabird colony, a heronry or a meadow full of orchids. Quite soon, however, it was realised that whole ecosystems, or at least substantial samples of them, need to be included, although this may not be easy when the ecosystem is as large as the Serengeti Plains in Tanzania, with their hundreds of thousands of seasonally migrating wildebeest and other ungulates; or a marsh or estuary that depends on upstream feeder areas for its nutrients. The founders of the national park movement sought the ideal of the *reserve intégrale*, in which absolutely no human activity could take place, but in many protected areas throughout the world this ideal has had to be compromised. Practical exigencies compel the responsible authorities to allow the continuance of major tourist facilities in Yellowstone, Yosemite and many other national parks in the western United States, of fishing villages in the Queen Elizabeth National Park in Uganda, and of traditional hunting, shooting and even livestock grazing in many reserves worldwide. In Britain a motorway, the M 40, was even allowed to cut a national nature reserve in half. However, the view is usually taken that imperfect protection is better than none at all.

The third World National Parks Congress, held on Bali in 1983, produced an action plan designed to establish by 1992 a worldwide network of national parks and other protected areas, to cover all terrestrial ecological regions, with accompanying marine, coastal and freshwater protected areas. Although mention of species in this plan is minimal, speakers at the Congress fully recognised the inescapable importance of species in the ecosystems to be preserved. The most notable instance of a species being used to preserve ecosystems is, of course, Project Tiger in India. As indicated on p. 183, by using the image of the tiger, India's largest carnivore, it has been possible to enlarge the area and enhance the protection given to habitat in fifteen existing national parks and wildlife sanctuaries. In Rwanda, the mountain gorilla is being similarly used to preserve the Parc des Volcans, previously threatened by cultivation round its edges. Another example is provided by the highly successful International Polar Bear Agreement of 1975. The five signatory circumpolar governments have agreed both to protect ecosystems containing polar bears and to control hunting.

Tiger

In 1971 Unesco's Man and the Biosphere Programmme promoted the concept of biosphere reserves, whose main objective is the long-term *in situ* conservation of the representative ecosystems of the world and of their component micro-organisms, plants and animals. Ten years later there were 209 such reserves in 55 countries, the great majority being national parks and strict nature reserves that had already been set up in the countries concerned. The biosphere reserve network, when completed, will form a fine basic framework, ensuring that examples of every major ecosystem are preserved, but it will always need to be supplemented by a much larger network of national reserves. All but the smallest Third World countries now have national parks or nature reserves, and some, such as Costa Rica, Kenya, Sri Lanka and Tanzania set a high standard to the rest. More advanced countries have sophisticated networks, which include many reserves owned or managed by voluntary bodies, such as the Nature Conservancy in the US and the 44 county conservation trusts in England and Wales. Nevertheless, only two per cent of the land surface of the planet and 0.0001 per cent of its waters are covered by protected areas today. Moreover, as just mentioned (p. 132), the greenhouse effect, as it increasingly develops, may destroy the value of many currently protected areas.

To achieve adequate conservation of the world's genetic resources, it will always be necessary to exercise some degree of management outside specially protected areas. Thus the Botswana Minister of Planning has said that three-quarters of his country's land should be set aside for wildlife and its utilisation. In Kenya the planning concept for national parks includes two concentric buffer zones round each park, where wildlife would still be protected, but other activities, such as tourism, cattle grazing and tribal hunting and residence would be allowed. The South Pacific Regional Environment Programme calls, among other objectives, for the balanced management of mangrove ecosystems to maintain their fisheries and many other uses, the management of the land/lagoon/reef ecosystem to maintain its health and condition, and the management of forests so as to safeguard their health and vigour. It is never likely to be possible to include all forests, mangroves or reefs in the South Pacific in formally protected areas, so other means will have to be found to achieve these aims.

Young mountain gorilla

8 Maintaining the Stocks

Populations of animals and plants can be maintained either 'on site' or 'off site'. There can be no doubt that off-site preservation is a second-best device, although the great tide of habitat destruction that is sweeping the world in the late twentieth century makes it increasingly necessary to resort to the second best. On-site conservation is best achieved by conserving ecosystems and setting aside protected areas, as described in Chapter 7. However, as we have also seen, ecosystem conservation is not enough; means to prevent overexploitation and disturbance must also be sought. Active habitat management, removal of (usually introduced) predators and competitors and even translocation will sometimes also be necessary.

If prevailing social customs do not allow us to maintain or create the conditions in which species thrive, legislation must be used. It is always easier to pass a law than to establish a new social custom, but enforcement of laws that go against long-established social customs can be and indeed usually is difficult. After a generation or two, however, reasonable and well enforced laws may lead to new and benign social customs. Thus the nineteenth-century bird protection laws in Britain produced a nation which, instead of being largely indifferent or even malevolent towards birds, has become for the most part actively benevolent and protectionist. Victorian England, where gulls were shot from the Thames bridges in the middle of London, would have marvelled to see how householders now almost universally feed the birds in their gardens or on their windowsills. But our present time-scale is too short. Species are being lost too fast for us to await the growth of benign customs throughout the world. There is nothing for it but legislation and the means to enforce it, until new traditions can be established.

1. Controlling Exploitation

Control of the harvest of certain wild species has a long history. As soon as the great ones of the earth realised that their subjects were overexploiting the animals they themselves liked to hunt, game laws were born, which reserved the right to overexploit to kings and nobles and laid down close seasons even for them. Some countries have still not progressed beyond the point where only game animals, those that people like to hunt, are protected. In others there is no protection for any species outside certain protected areas.

Within a national park or a wildlife reserve the protection of species, endangered or otherwise, requires resources for law enforcement and administration as well as for scientific management of the habitat. Outside these protected areas the same three elements are still needed, but are much harder to achieve. Most larger and more developed countries have reasonably satisfactory laws for the general protection, not only of endangered species but of all birds that are not regarded as pests, and increasingly of other vertebrates, plants and even some invertebrates. Australia, New Zealand, Switzerland and the countries of eastern Europe are particularly well equipped with such legislation, whereas in much of Africa, Asia and Latin America there is little protection of wildlife outside the official protected areas, and in many of these law enforcement is extremely lax or even non-existent.

The problems of controlling the harvesting of species of economic importance are discussed in Chapter 9.

A model law for species conservation is provided by the Agreed Measures under the 1964 Antarctic Treaty. As Brian Roberts, who was largely their author, pointed out, these measures constitute a comprehensive international agreement on the conservation of wildlife in the Antarctic and all islands south of 60°S before man has seriously disturbed the natural ecological balance of this unique region, which covers more than six million square miles around the South Pole. They forbid the killing, wounding, capturing or molesting, except under permit, of any native mammal or bird, or any attempts at such acts. Permits are only to be granted for scientific or educational reasons or to provide 'indispensable foods for men or dogs'. Presumably Edward Wilson would have been granted such a permit for his famous 'worst journey in the world' in 1911, to collect from Cape Crozier the first emperor penguin embryos known to science. Such permits must ensure that 'no more native mammals or birds are killed or taken in any one year than can normally be replaced by natural reproduction in the following breeding season', i.e. that any harvesting must be based on sustainable yield. The variety of species and the balance of the natural ecosystems in the Antarctic must also be maintained. Provision is also made for specially protected species, of which only the Ross seal has so far been scheduled; these permits are extremely strictly controlled. Others of the Agreed Measures deal with disturbance by dogs, men and firearms, to which the seal, penguin and other seabird colonies are especially vulnerable, and forbid the introduction of alien species, parasites and diseases.

Such ideal legislation is only possible because there is no settled human population in the Antarctic; laws elsewhere have to make political and social compromises. Thus the United Kingdom's Wildlife and Countryside Act 1981, while full of such compromises in the direction of farmers and landowners, is a model of species protection in areas where these powerful elements of the body politic are prepared to accept the existence of wild species or their habitat. In many countries of western Europe the compromises are more in the direction of allowing the traditional shooting, which is all too often overshooting, of wild birds. In the United States both hunting and grazing interests make species protection much less effective than it otherwise would be. Almost every country, with however excellent a basic set of laws, has loopholes through which traditional overexploitation – of seals in Canada, kangaroos in Australia, or marine turtles throughout the tropics – or underexploitation, of animals harmful to native vegetation, such as deer and other ungulates in Hawaii and New Zealand, is allowed to continue.

As an example of a conservation plan for a species or group of species, the recommendations of the International Bustard Symposium held in Pakistan in October 1983 may be cited. These call for the initiation or strengthening of legal protection for the houbara bustard, especially in

Emperor penguins

Bengal florican

Egypt, Morocco and Pakistan. Tunisia, which was congratulated on its firm protection of the houbara, was asked to take the initiative in promoting bustard conservation throughout North Africa. Research on status and campaigns of public education were also proposed. India was congratulated on its measures for the conservation of the great Indian bustard and urged to create sanctuaries for it, with comparable recommendations for the highly endangered Bengal florican and the greatly depleted lesser florican. Finally, in Australia, where the native bustard is already fully protected, three states which have not yet begun ecological studies of the species were urged to do so.

Where wildlife protection laws do exist, the main problem is enforcing them, especially as Third World bureaucrats often seem to think they have done the job by putting a law on the statute book. Law enforcement is largely a question of manpower, which means finance, coupled with good staff and intelligence work. The civil police all too often do not take wildlife protection seriously: partly from inability to distinguish between protected and unprotected species, partly from failure to grasp the importance of conserving wildlife, and partly just from pressure of too many other things to do. Some countries fall back on citizen aid. In Western Australia, for instance, the Department of Fisheries and Fauna enrols private citizens as fauna wardens to help enforce the law relating to rare species. In Jordan law enforcement has actually been handed over to the organised sportsmen, who in many countries are the one influential force that can not only perceive the need to conserve stocks but also have an interest in achieving this aim. The Royal Jordanian Society for the Conservation of Nature has been most active in preventing poaching and other breaches of the law, often by indignant soldiers, who are not accustomed to being checked in this way.

The problems involved in enforcing wildlife protection in the Third World are well illustrated by the situation in Himachal Pradesh, in the Himalayan foothills of India. Here most local wildlife killing is unlicensed, and traps and snares are used much more than firearms. Such are the shortages of forest guards and police, and the difficulties of the terrain, that this poaching can only be controlled over limited areas. Especially with the chief quarry, the musk deer, the high market price of its musk far outweighs any threat to the poachers from the Forest Department or the police. Hence musk deer are likely to disappear from most of their local range in the near future, and the most that can be hoped for is to protect them in selected areas.

Much the same applies to the widespread poaching of elephants and rhinos for their ivory and horn in various parts of Africa and Asia. Moreover, as David Western and Lucy Vigne have recently pointed out, when threatened stocks become fragmented as the rhinos have, the logistical difficulties and cost of protecting them against heavily armed and determined gangs of poachers are simply too formidable, even where, as in Ethiopia, the political will exists.

One special set of problems arises when rare or uncommon animals conflict with man's social or economic welfare or when imbalanced predator/prey ratios adversely affect either the prey or the predator. Thus the IUCN/SSC Wolf Specialist Group has recommended that any control measures deemed scientifically justifiable for the wolf should be selective, specific to the problem and highly discriminatory, and should also minimise any adverse effects on the ecosystem. Alternative ecosystem management, including both changes in human attitudes and activities and non-lethal methods of wolf management, should be fully considered before any wolves are actually killed. Wolf management programmes must seek to restore and maintain a healthy balance in all components of the ecosystem, and in particular should never lead to the permanent disappearance of the wolf from any part of its existing natural range.

Another special problem is the banning of wildfowl shooting during spells of severe weather, when ducks, geese and waders, weakened by lack of food, are especially vulnerable. If adequate breeding stocks are to survive, the birds must also be allowed a few days of grace to restore their energy reserves when the thaw arrives. Although sportsmen usually acquiesce in shooting bans during hard weather, they find it less easy to accept the days of grace. After the frost and snow of the 1981-82 winter, pressure from wildfowlers led the UK authorities to lift the ban two days sooner than had been recommended by their scientific advisers. In the rest of Europe sportsmen tend to be even more impatient of these vital bans.

Most of the examples in Chapter 11 of species that have been successfully rescued from severe depletion or impending extinction were largely due to prevention or control of exploitation or incidental killing. To these may be added the goldfinch, a popular cage bird, and the great crested grebe, whose feathers were used to adorn ladies' hats. The population decline of both in Britain was reversed by the early bird protection laws.

Great crested grebe with young

The most important instrument for controlling international trade in wildlife is the Convention on International Trade in Endangered Species of Wild Fauna and Flora (CITES), which came into force in 1974. By 1985, 88 countries had joined it. These countries have agreed not to allow trade across their borders in species threatened with extinction, except as permitted by CITES, which allocates these species to two main groups. Animals and plants in actual danger of extinction are in Appendix I; trade in these may be authorised only in exceptional circumstances and never primarily for commercial use. Species in potential danger from trade may be placed on Appendix II so that their trade can be monitored. CITES will never be fully effective until all the chief trading nations have adhered to it, and at present some are still unwilling to do so. Other loopholes also exist, such as the reservations made by France and Italy to protect their crocodile and sea-turtle leather industries. The difficulties experienced by customs officers in identifying endangered species, which also hamper the full effectiveness of CITES, are being met by identification manuals.

CITES is even harder to enforce for plants. To start with, as many as 90 per cent of all transactions in plants between party states were reported by only one party to the transaction, making the compilation of meaningful statistics extremely difficult. Moreover, most threatened plants, in the form in which they travel, cannot readily be distinguished (outside a laboratory) from their near relatives, which may be common species. Orchids, for instance, are traded as pseudobulbs, and even botanists cannot identify orchids to species level without their flowers. Further, one important method of conserving rare wild plants on site is to encourage trade in artificially propagated specimens, which often cannot be distinguished from plants collected in the wild.

Pseudobulbs

Finally, in many parts of the world it is vital to encourage botanical exploration and research, both for conservation and for science, so that more exemptions are needed for plants than for most animal groups. However each successive meeting of the parties to CITES makes slow progress towards shaping it as an effective workable instrument to protect endangered plants. Thus the International Organisation for Succulent Plant Study has produced a useful code of conduct for collectors and growers of cacti and succulents.

White-tailed tropic bird

2. Habitat Management

To maintain stocks of desired species, it may not suffice to preserve and manage ecosystems to keep them just as they are, as discussed in Chapter 7. Direct intervention on behalf of the species may be necessary, as with the coppicing of its woodland habitat needed to maintain the heath fritillary butterfly in its two remaining sites in south-east England. This may even extend to the creation of new habitat, as in the Keoladeo Ghana National Park at Bharatpur, India, an area of farmland that was originally deliberately flooded to encourage waterfowl for sportsmen to shoot. Over the years the water in the park has become very fertile, largely because cattle and buffaloes were allowed to graze the area and fertilise it with their droppings, so that large numbers of storks, egrets, ibises and spoonbills have been able to nest, and a flock of the rare white Siberian crane has wintered there.

Since the value of much habitat depends on the maintenance of precise water levels, various means, such as sluices, channels and small dams, of controlling this factor are essential wetland management tools throughout the world, and often need to be supplemented by digging ponds or creating islands for nesting or resting birds. Thus, vegetation has been removed to improve water flow in sites in Astrakhan State Nature Reserve in the USSR where dabbling ducks congregate to moult; controlled water-level impoundments and ponds have been constructed in the Tintamarre National Wildlife Area in New Brunswick; breeding islands for flamingoes have been made in the Camargue in southern France; a nesting and loafing island has been made at Hjarbaek Fjord, a shallow brackish lagoon in Denmark; and shallow scrapes for waders have been dug out at the Minsmere reserve on the east coast of England.

Not only nesting places, but actual artificial structures, such as nest-boxes, nest platforms or specially excavated burrows, may have to be provided to encourage birds to nest. These have been widely used to augment wildfowl stocks in the USSR and North America, and to increase the populations of insectivorous birds, such as the pied flycatcher in European forests. They are also often used to help endangered species, as with the white-tailed sea eagle in the Gulf of Bothnia in Finland, the osprey in Connecticut, the Dalmatian pelican in the Volga delta, the cahow petrel in Bermuda and the endemic *Amazona* parrot in Puerto Rico. In the last two instances the artificial sites are designed to exclude larger competitors for nest holes, the white-tailed tropicbird and the pearly-eyed thrasher respectively.

Osprey

Pearly-eyed thrasher

Griffon vulture

To provide nesting places for herons and egrets in the Camargue, whose natural sites were being felled by farmers and oilmen, Heinz Hafner of the nearby Tour du Valat research station went to great lengths. He made an island, planted trees, built 65 nesting platforms, and broke up into suitable lengths several tons of twigs he had collected as nest material. Finally, to provide decoys he built a large aviary to contain ten zoo egrets and in the trees posed fifty white egrets sculpted in polythene. His reward by 1984, seven years after the trees became tall enough, was a new colony of 1500 herons and egrets.

Sometimes direct steps need to be taken to augment food supply. The griffon vulture in the Pyrenees was threatened by the lack of carrion in late winter and early spring, because farmers no longer leave sheep carcases out on their farms. Since the winter of 1969-70 the French National Park Service has established a feeding enclosure in the Ossau valley in Béarn where they put meat out weekly from November until the spring. Lammergeyers, golden eagles and red kites have also benefited.

Some countries take special measures to prevent animals being killed on their major roads. In Britain special tunnels or underpasses have been constructed under motorways on routes known to be used regularly by deer or badgers. Deer can also be dissuaded from crossing at night by special reflectors that shine car headlights off the road. In 1985 during the Fauna and Flora Preservation Society's 'Toads on Roads' campaign, volunteers rescued some 50,000 common toads that were crossing roads during their annual spring migration. Low-flying birds can often be diverted by planting barriers of trees that make them fly above the height of the traffic.

3. Preventing Disturbance

The conservation of some species calls for them to be protected from human disturbance. This is well illustrated by the increase of wildlife in out-of-bounds areas between warring parties, such as the cranes in the demilitarised zone between North and South Korea and the African wild ass in the no-man's-land between the traditionally warring Afar and Issa tribes in Ethiopia.

Seals and nesting birds are especially vulnerable to disturbance. There was a tenfold increase in Hawaiian monk seals hauling out at Tern Island in the Hawaiian chain in the three years after the US Coast Guard's Loran station was decommissioned in 1979. Indeed disturbance of breeding beaches is an effective (if often inhumane) method of controlling seals. Beach-nesting seabird colonies are just as vulnerable. Early in the nesting cycle whole colonies, notably of sandwich terns, may desert after a quite minor disturbance. Colonies of the little tern, with nests more widely scattered on the beach, are in actual physical danger. Even well-intentioned holidaymakers can unknowingly trample on eggs or cryptically hidden young, so that in Britain many colonies have to be wardened.

Feeding flocks of wild geese also react quickly to disturbance; the main causes of this have been analysed for the 16 per cent of the world population of pink-footed geese that winter in Lancashire. The three principal causes prove to be vehicles (36 per cent), aircraft (20 per cent) and pedestrians (20 per cent). Fortunately the actual level of disturbance is low, and the recent great increase in food supply has enabled this goose population to grow from 1500-4500 to more than 16,000 over the past twenty years.

An important method of protecting the extremely endangered Philippine (monkey-eating) eagle has been the establishment of a mini-sanctuary of at least one hectare round each nest, surrounded by a one-kilometre 'red zone', where no logging or road-building is allowed during the critical parts of the breeding season. A similar scheme has been used to protect nests of the endangered bald eagle, America's national bird, in the United States.

The danger of disturbance to hibernating bats (see p. 122) can be dealt with by fitting metal grilles over the entrances to bat caves, so that the bats can get out but people cannot get in. Grilling is especially used in the Netherlands and Britain.

In developed countries rare plants may also need to be wardened, not just to prevent predation by collectors, but to stop photographers and other sightseers from trampling on young plants. Three rare orchid species are now wardened annually in southern England for both these reasons.

The need to protect rare species from disturbance is one of the factors that have given nature reserves a bad name among the general public. In any district, if a new nature reserve is proposed, local residents immediately assume that they are going to be kept out, sometimes from a site which they have been accustomed to visit for many years. It is thus of the utmost importance that offensive sights such as barbed-wire fences should be kept to a minimum, and the period during which the reserve is out of bounds because of a nesting or flowering season should also be as short as possible, if public goodwill is to be maintained. In the long run it is only public goodwill that will preserve the species.

4. Removal of Competing Species or Predators

Philippine or monkey-eating eagle

Some examples of successful conservation by removing species that were either competing for a limited food supply, or overexploiting the stocks by predation, are given in Chapter 11. Such competitors or predators are often introduced but they can also be natives of the area. Thus, red deer, either native as in Europe or introduced as in New Zealand, may overgraze or overbrowse. One reason for the original slow increase of the European bison in the Bialowieza Forest in Poland was that red deer were competing with them each spring for the new and nutritious shoots of trees and shrubs. The Puerto Rico parrot, down to a handful of breeding pairs, not only faces competition from the native but recently increased pearly-eyed thrasher (p. 145), but is preyed on by the native red-tailed hawk. When a species reaches a very low level, such combined competition and predation, which it could withstand separately and when more numerous, become crucial factors in its survival. Few people, except for some sportsmen in Hawaii and New Zealand, object to the removal of introduced species to save an endangered one, but when the species is native, it becomes more controversial. The Royal Society for the Protection of Birds discovered this when it decided to remove the eggs of the black-headed gulls that were preying on the young avocets at the well-known colony on Havergate Island, Suffolk.

If rare and endangered species are to be maintained on site in future, more control of this sort will undoubtedly have to be undertaken, as is already the policy of the New Zealand Wildlife Service, among others. The control of native predators, however, raises a controversy which has split the sporting side of the conservation movement from the rest for many years. Should predators be controlled as a matter of course? There are two aspects of this: the extent to which predators do control prey numbers, and the relation of specific predators to specific prey.

A classic case is gamekeeping in Britain, which, as already indicated, was largely responsible for exterminating such predators as polecat and raven over much of the south. In the nineteenth and early twentieth centuries, very few British game preservers had any doubt that any small carnivore or bird with a hooked beak was harmful to their charges, which were mostly grey partridges, pheasants, and red grouse. The old-fashioned game-keeper's gibbet, only thirty years ago, displayed not only innumerable stoats, weasels and hedgehogs (these last accused of stealing partridge eggs), but also such protected birds as kestrel, barn owl and tawny owl. Where foxhunting was not important, foxes were also strung up. The killing of owls, kestrels and also of sparrowhawks was almost wholly misguided; these predators feed predominantly on small rodents or songbirds, and only the occasional 'rogue' individual becomes sufficiently addicted to gamebird chicks to become a genuine menace. Nowadays gibbets are rarely seen, partly because they are such a clear guide to law-breaking, but the old idea that a bird with a hooked beak must be up to no good dies hard, and keepers still kill many predators.

Just what a waste of time and resources much predator control by keepers is, was demonstrated by Richard Meinertzhagen, who quoted several instances where its relaxation led to a substantial increase in the numbers of game species, and vice versa. On two estates in Easter Ross in the Scottish Highlands, totalling 25,000 acres, the keepers were only allowed to shoot brown rats and lesser black-backed gulls. After fifteen years, despite a great increase in the number of nesting raptors, ravens and magpies, there was a large increase in the bag of partridges, pheasants, red grouse, capercaillie and blue hares, as well as 'a plague' of rabbits. The increase of stoats and weasels was said to have 'completely cleared' the farm of rats that had been 'a scourge'. A similar story came from a 4000-acre estate in Sweden, where the owner did not shoot at all, and the land abounded in predators, game species and small songbirds.

The contrary situation arose on a 4000-acre estate in Hampshire, where for fourteen years the three keepers were only allowed to shoot rats and carrion crows, but the annual bag was 2000 pheasants and 700 partridges, with numerous trout and grayling in the River Test. The next tenants instituted a very different regime, all 'vermin' being destroyed, including a heronry of 40 pairs, four large rookeries and many others right down to moorhens, coots and water voles. In the event the stock of partridges fell by half and the trout had to be augmented from a hatchery, but this may well have been partly due to the new tenants both overshooting and overfishing. What is clear, however, is that the presence of natural levels of predators, i.e. not artificially inflated by some nearby food source such as a rubbish tip that attracts rats and gulls, does not reduce the natural levels of their prey species.

At the root of the problem is the attempt by game preservers to maintain artificially high stocks of their preferred prey, in order to maximise their bags. This is a situation of which predators naturally take full advantage. Over thousands of years the partridge and the red grouse in Britain (the pheasant is not native) have achieved an equilibrium with such predators as raptors and stoats, because if predators were to exterminate their own main prey, they would themselves die out. The levels of predator stocks are in fact largely controlled by the levels of prey stocks, as is nicely demonstrated every time a population explosion of field voles attracts a breeding group of short-eared owls and other predators. By controlling or attempting to control predators, keepers are taking on an open-ended commitment. As long as they maintain the food supply, in the shape of gamebird eggs and chicks, artificially high, they will always attract more predators in from the surrounding area. Only large and relatively slow-breeding predators can be

Capercaillie

actually exterminated, as with the polecat and raven mentioned above. The numbers of such numerous and resourceful animals as stoats and weasels will always fluctuate in response to their prey numbers rather than in response to gamekeeping effort.

The inference of all this for the protection of rare species is that the population level of the offending predator *ex hypothesi* depends not on that of the rarity but on that of some more numerous prey. The rare species is being taken only incidentally, because it happened to be there when some other prey was being sought, or, as with the avocets on Havergate, because an abundant food supply elsewhere has encouraged an abnormally high population of the predator. The bird protectionist is faced with just the same problem as the gamekeeper in trying to keep down a numerous predator with a large food supply. Predator control in fact should only be a last resort for him, but with feral cats and other introduced predators on islands extermination may be essential

Plants present different problems. When fungi attack plants, for instance, we call it disease. However, as mentioned on p. 127 large vigorous alien vascular plants can overwhelm and displace native vegetation and may have to be controlled in the interests of both plants and animals. The Cape flora is especially afflicted by invading aliens; thus *Leucadendron macowanii* (Proteaceae) is threatened at its main locality near Smitswinkel Bay by alien acacias, many of which have already been removed by the staff of the Cape of Good Hope Nature Reserve. On St Helena the endemic gumwood tree *Commidendron robustum* has regenerated freely when New Zealand flax *Phormium tenax* has been cleared. In California more than 400 cubic yards of the introduced iceplant (hottentot fig in British floras) *Carpobrotus*

European avocet

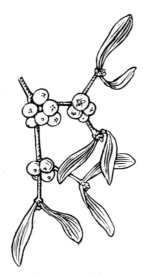

European mistletoe

New Zealand flax

edulis have been removed from the Morro Bay Ecological Reserve in order to restore the habitat of the endangered endemic kangaroo rat.

Some plants, such as the composite *Tagetes*, have developed the capacity to emit from their roots chemicals which reduce competition by deterring other plants from coming too close. So far, however, there do not seem to be any instances of this allelopathy threatening rare plants. Nor are there apparently any such threats from the truer equivalent of animal predation, plant parasites, whether on roots, such as the broomrapes, or on trees, as with the mistletoes.

Iceplant or hottentot fig

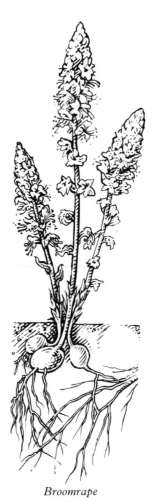

Broomrape

5. Translocation

As the last stage before off-site conservation (captive breeding), translocation has in recent years become an increasingly popular method of preserving species. Translocation means the removal of wild animals or plants taken from the wild to another suitable wild habitat, which may be in a national park or reserve, but is not a fenced enclosure. Since about 1960 increasingly sophisticated immobilising drugs have been used to catch and transport, with minimal psychological disturbance, many large mammals,

such as leopards and black rhinos in East Africa, from farming areas where
they are not wanted to national parks where they are assets. Drug-darting
has also been widely used to increase the range of endangered or threatened
species.

Translocation, and the release of captive-bred animals discussed on p.
154, are both at present often conducted very much on a hit-or-miss basis.
The amount of information needed before reliable scientific advice can be
given on the prospects of successfully translocating a particular species
from one place to another is formidable, and is rarely if ever all available.
The various considerations are discussed in detail on p. 153 and also in
the IUCN position statement on restocking, and in the special case of
primates by Julian Caldecott and Michael Kavanagh in *Oryx* for July 1983.
However, so little is known either about the adaptations of species to their
habitat or indeed about any ecosystem, taking into account the extremely
complex webs of species that most ecosystems represent, that until much
more knowledge is available on computers, any scientific advice on this
subject is unlikely to be more than an informed guess. One such guess is that
translocating a wild species from one locality to another in a similar
ecosystem is more likely to succeed, than releasing species that have been
raised in captivity into an appropriate habitat. However, advance studies,
like the one undertaken by the Jersey Wildlife Preservation Trust to
determine the possibility of re-establishing the skink *Leiolopisma telfairii*
on Gunners Quoin off Mauritius, are fortunately becoming more frequent.
This particular study showed that the island still held too many of the black
rats which had originally eliminated the skink, for a reintroduction attempt
to be likely to succeed. The use of translocation to save endemic New
Zealand birds is described on p. 192.

White rhino

By far the most ambitious series of translocations so far attempted, and
one of the most strikingly successful feats in the whole history of wildlife
conservation, is the continuing effort of the Natal Parks Board to relieve the
overpopulation of the southern white rhino in the Umfolozi and Hluhluwe
reserves. As described on p. 185, protection of this once almost extinct race
of the white rhino in these two reserves increased their numbers to the point
where they would have had to be culled if the far-sighted plan of Jack
Vincent and Ian Player had not been carried out. This plan has led to the
capture and redistribution of more than 2700 animals over the past 23
years, most of them to African national parks and reserves and the rest to
zoos and safari parks all over the world. As a result there are now thriving
white rhino herds in the Kruger National Park, Transvaal, the Kyle Dam
Recreational Park, Zimbabwe, and many others. A similar but ultimately
unsuccessful attempt was made with the northern subspecies in Uganda,
where some were taken in the early 1960s from the Nile Province to
Murchison Falls National Park and did well until they were almost all
poached during the lawlessness of the Amin regime.

Asiatic lion

The considerable hazards accompanying these translocations of rare
animals are also illustrated by the removal, in 1957, of three Asiatic lions
from the last wild stock in the Gir Forest in Gujarat, India, to Chandra-
prabha sanctuary in Uttar Pradesh. Here they increased at first, but later
failed to establish themselves. The removal of 30 hirola or hunter's
hartebeest from their threatened range on the borders of Kenya and
Somalia to the Tsavo East National Park in 1963 appears to have been only
partially successful. A small group continues to be seen from time to time.
A similar enterprise with roan, moved from the Ithanga Hills in central
Kenya to the Shimba Hills reserve near Mombasa in the early 1970s, also
had a chequered history. By 1973 only eight of the original 38 animals could
be found, and even five years later there were only 22. On the other hand,

the attempt to move Grevy's zebra from the Samburu reserve to the Tsavo National Park, both in Kenya, ended in failure.

Nor is there yet any firm evidence as to the ultimate success of all except one of the various attempts to rehabilitate and return to the wild young apes that have been recaptured from poachers and their clients, notably orang-utan in Sabah, Kalimantan and northern Sumatra, and chimpanzees in the Gambia and Senegal. The success story is the release by the Frankfurt Zoological Society of seventeen chimpanzees from European zoos on Rubondo Island in Lake Victoria, Tanzania, in the late 1960s. By the mid-1980s there appeared to be a second generation of animals born in the wild.

The project to restore Kemp's ridley turtle in the Gulf of Mexico involves an element of captivity, the eggs being taken to Texas for hatching and the release of head-started hatchlings at about nine months. There is as yet no real evidence as to whether any of the many turtle release schemes around the world are succeeding. Most schemes for augmenting Atlantic salmon stocks, such as those put into the Baltic from Swedish hatcheries, also involve a substantial element of captive care of the young fish.

Evaluation of the translocation of smaller reptiles, such as lizards, and of amphibians presents different problems, in view of the ease with which many species can be captive-bred, and the even greater ease with which private individuals can conduct their own release experiments. This makes it difficult to distinguish between the results of genuine translocations as here defined, such as the mostly successful ones with the sand lizard on the heathlands of southern England, and such haphazard private enterprises as the very successful introduction of the marsh frog on Romney Marsh, Kent, in the 1930s. In view of these problems the British Herpetological Society has issued a policy on translocations of herpetofauna, which attempts to bring some order into what is at present a distinctly disorderly situation.

The Joint Committee for the Conservation of British Insects is working out a similar policy, as releases of butterflies and other insects by private individuals and even by public bodies are equally hard to control. Colonies of the silver-studded blue and brown argus butterflies have already been the subject of rescue operations in England. To save the silver-studded blue, some 5000 square yards of heather and grassland were lifted from a threatened site in Suffolk and laid down in other heathland sites. The distinctive subspecies *artaxerxes* of the brown argus is already thriving in magnesian limestone turves that were moved to a safe site in Co. Durham.

Plants are different again, in that it is much easier to collect seed from wild plants and sow it in suitable wild habitat, than to translocate an animal. On the other hand, it seems to be harder to transplant perennial plants successfully from one wild habitat to another. One of the earliest attempts, in the late 1940s, was the rescue of the brown bog-rush from what was then the only known British site, when Loch Tummel, Perthshire, was flooded by a hydroelectric scheme. Out of hundreds of plants that were removed, none survived near the loch and only one did so at all in the wild, a single plant taken a few miles away to Ben Vrackie. More recently, the progeny of another of the survivors, from the Cambridge Botanic Garden, have been more successfully returned to the wild in and by Loch Tummel. Ironically, in 1979 two more large natural populations, that could not possibly have originated from the previous transplantations, were found elsewhere in Scotland.

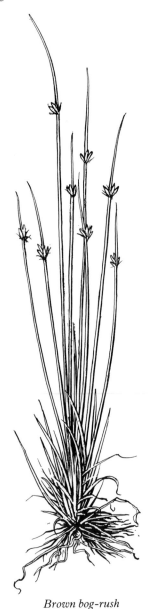

Brown bog-rush

6. Off-site Conservation

The more habitat is destroyed, the more those who seek to preserve endangered species are driven back to off-site methods: captive breeding and egg and semen banks for animals, and cultivation and seed banks for plants. Endangered plants were being grown in gardens as early as the 1720s, when the Governor of St Helena planted two inch-high specimens of the already endangered endemic redwood *Trochetiopsis erythroxylon* in his garden. Captive breeding of endangered animals began seriously 80 or 90 years ago with William Hornaday and the American bison, and the Duke of Bedford and Père David's deer; many of its successes are described in Chapter 11. It remains both the obvious thing to do, if an animal is endangered in the wild by uncontrollable habitat destruction or over-exploitation, and on the other hand a controversial and usually a more expensive solution, even if it is quite rapidly followed by reintroduction to the wild.

In recent years captive breeding of animals, mainly of vertebrates and in zoos, has been the subject of six international conferences: London 1964 and 1976; San Diego, California, 1966 and 1979; Jersey, Channel Islands, 1972; and Harderwijk, Netherlands, 1984. The third of these, held at Jersey Zoo, was the first of a series co-sponsored by the Fauna and Flora Preservation Society. It ended with a six-point declaration:

1. The breeding of endangered species and subspecies of animals in captivity is likely to be crucial to the survival of many forms. It must therefore be used as a method of preventing extinction, alongside the maintenance of the wild stocks in their natural habitat.
2. The techniques must be learned, improved, extended and published.
3. All who keep endangered species have a responsibility to carry out breeding programmes, and for this purpose to cooperate both with other zoos or collections and with conservationists in returning them to the wild.
4. Such programmes will reduce the demands being made currently on wild populations and may serve to reinforce them or, if they have disappeared in the wild, to re-establish them.
5. Even if reintroduction ultimately proves to be impossible, maintaining a captive population is obviously preferable to the irrevocable alternative of extinction.
6. Wherever possible breeding programmes should be encouraged and supported in habitats or regions natural to the endangered species. One important reason for this is the education of the indigenous human population, who otherwise may not completely understand the significance, the requirements or the future of the animals, upon which they themselves will depend.

Orang-utan

Broadly speaking, all these considerations are still valid, but subsequent conferences and practical experience have led to a fuller appreciation of the problems involved, particularly the genetic problems, which were largely side-stepped at Jersey. Point 1 is fully accepted today, although twenty years ago it was still being argued that to take animals from the wild in this way weakened the drive to maintain them in their natural habitat. Habitat destruction is now on such a scale as to completely outdate such a viewpoint. Point 2 has been actively pursued, and much more is now known about the techniques of breeding animals in captivity, thanks at least in part to stimulation by this series of conferences. Cooperation between those involved has also improved. When the World Herd of Arabian Oryx Trusteeship was wound up in 1979, San Diego and most of the other zoos which received the remaining oryx in the herd agreed to supply stock for future reintroductions. San Diego did in fact supply eight of the ten Arabian oryx (the other two were born in Oman) released into the desert in Oman in 1982, and in late 1983 two oryx born in East Germany were sent to London Zoo by East Berlin, under the agreement made when the World Herd was disbanded.

It is now almost universally accepted that the prime justification for breeding endangered species in captivity is to reintroduce them in the wild. Michael Brambell, Director of Chester Zoo, has described the problems involved in reintroduction, which he defined as the process of re-establishing a population of wild animals within the area of its original wild habitat. He stressed that such reintroductions should only be attempted where the original wild habitat can carry greater numbers than it is now doing, i.e. that pressures such as overgrazing, poaching or predation, which led to the original decline or local extinction of the animal in question are not continuing. In the Mauritius example cited on p. 151 these adverse factors, in the shape of rats, were in fact continuing. Brambell also outlined the many formidable technical obstacles to be overcome, such as the availability of a stock that contains as much as possible of the original gene pool. This problem of maintaining genetic variability lies at the root of the reservations that many conservationists still have about captive breeding as a conservation tool. While a captive stock is clearly better than no stock at all, one can still query the value of maintaining captive stocks for which no use in domestication is known, and which appear to have no prospect of being returned to the wild. Père David's deer is one such animal, though it is certainly both a scientific curiosity and of ornamental value, and like all other deer can in the last resort be eaten; in fact some surplus deer are already being sold for venison and there are plans to restore others to the wild in China. But suppose the animal to be kept indefinitely in captivity were a woodlouse (Isopoda), of no special aesthetic or present scientific value. The case for spending scarce conservation money on it then rests on the same basis as that for saving any little known species in the wild: may it not perhaps in future be shown to have some quite unsuspected value for human welfare?

Père David's deer

Janet Kear of the Wildfowl Trust has discussed the biological problems of maintaining stocks of captive animals, which are of course similar for both endangered and commoner animals, though stocks of commoner animals are more easily reinforced with fresh genes. Inbreeding, which often leads to infertility, is one of the main problems, and this is linked with the maintenance of genetic variability. Even if, as seems inherently unlikely, the captive stock starts with the full range of genes available in the whole gene pool of the species, it is bound, over the course of several generations, to change in many ways, some obvious, others subtle. As a result it will end up with a set of characters that may well prevent it from re-establishing itself in its original habitat, and the effect will be accentuated if, as usually happens, the captive stock represents only a small part of the total genetic variation of the species. To give only one example, a deer or antelope with a quick reaction to danger from predators will in the wild have a better chance of passing its genes on to the next generation than a slower, more placid animal. Yet that slower animal has a much better chance of breeding successfully in captivity, where an animal that is too quick off the mark at human approach is liable to break its neck against the walls of its enclosure.

Only with very small populations, such as fish species that live in a single desert spring, is there a real chance that the range of genes in the captive stock will be even roughly equivalent to that in the wild stock. Even then, to be sure of getting a full range, so many of the wild stock might have to be taken that its capacity to survive in the wild might be impaired. So the aim of taking a complete sample of any gene pool into captivity may be a chimaera. The SSC Captive Breeding Specialist Group has spent considerable time and effort in developing a computer programme that maximises the outbreeding of captive species. This will not stop inbreeding, but can minimise it.

Nevertheless each successive generation of a captive stock is still subject to selection pressures quite different from those in the wild, and at some point – Kear suggests when three-quarters of the individuals are separable from the original stock – captive breeding will produce a new subspecies. This, after all, as Darwin pointed out long ago, is how the innumerable breeds of pigeons, dogs and other domestic animals were produced and how broccoli, cauliflowers and Brussels sprouts were all derived from the wild cabbage *Brassica oleracea*.

On the other hand, nor are selection pressures in the wild static. The removal of top predators radically changes the pressures on all their potential prey, and the small red deer of the Scottish moors are classed as a separate subspecies because of this size adaptation to the largely man-made treelessness of their habitat. They were originally denizens of the extensive broad-leaved forests of western Europe, and those red deer which still inhabit such forests are appreciably larger, at least partly because they are better fed. Moreover, the fragmentation of wild populations, as currently with the African rhinos, not only reduces the diversity of the gene pool of each isolated stock, but may well skew the sex ratio and age structure so as to reduce the birth rate and hence the recovery potential. The maintenance of genetic variability is an admirable ideal, but it is just as likely that some genetic characters will be selected out in the wild as that others will in captivity. The process of evolution still maintains its own imperatives.

Two important tools have been developed over the years to facilitate the technical aspects of captive breeding: the studbooks and the ISIS information bank. A series of studbooks and world registers for endangered animal species in captivity was started in the 1950s by the International Union of Directors of Zoological Gardens, mainly for large mammals, such as Père David's deer, European bison and Przewalski's horse. In 1982 there were 57 officially endorsed studbooks, for 48 mammals, eight birds and the Chinese alligator. The launching of new studbooks is submitted for approval to the Species Survival Commission of IUCN. Their main purpose is to facilitate the planned breeding of the species in question, and to enable zoos and other owners to know the degree of inbreeding and outbreeding involved when they bring new stock into their collections.

This is also the prime aim of the much more ambitious ISIS scheme, which is a computerised record system for the management of wild animals in captivity. The acronym stands for International Species Inventory System, which is a programme of the American Association of Zoological Parks and Aquariums, aiming to develop a census and vital statistics inventory system for wild animals held in zoos. Virtually all the major and many smaller zoos in North America now participate in ISIS, but so far only a few in other parts of the world, mainly in Europe. In 1982 ISIS had catalogued more than 33,000 living mammals and birds (reptiles and amphibians will be added soon) at 175 zoos and primate centres, together with data (birth, death and breeding records) on another 40,000 ancestors of some of the animals on the main catalogue.

To rationalise captive-breeding management policies, the first major requirement is to determine the ability of the zoos or other collections to maintain adequate numbers of the animals to be bred. This means that

Wild cabbage

Douroucouli

Cheddar pink

most if not all zoos probably ought to reduce the number of species they exhibit, so as to make room for larger stocks of those they retain. A number of zoos, notably New York and San Diego, already specialise in breeding endangered species, and Jersey Zoo was the first zoo to be primarily devoted to this purpose. In Britain the Wildfowl Trust, which breeds ducks, geese, swans and flamingoes, was the pioneer of the specialised collections that have in recent years played an important part in breeding endangered species. Other such collections have specialised in otters, pheasants and birds of prey in Britain, lemurs in France and bustards in Dubai, United Arab Emirates. In the United States the International Crane Foundation in Wisconsin has bred cranes and the Cornell Laboratory, as mentioned on p. 192, has bred birds of prey, especially the peregrine. At Patuxent, Maryland, the US Government maintains an important research station devoted entirely to breeding endangered species, mainly birds. In Brazil, the Rio de Janeiro Primate Center concentrates on breeding endangered primates and the Argentine Primate Center in Corrientes Province is planning to breed the country's most endangered primate, the mirinquinha or douroucouli *Aotus trivirgatus*.

The second major requirement is to develop a model that, by randomising the breeding programme, will maintain the maximum genetic diversity of the available breeding stock, to avert the twin dangers of unintentional domestication and unconsciously breeding to a preferred type. ISIS collects systematic data to meet both requirements, concentrating on the history, pedigree and demography of those species in which zoos are currently most interested and for which studbooks and zoo records provide a core of serviceable information. Since ISIS is financed by zoos, their priorities rather than those of wildlife conservationists inevitably prevail at present. This is partly because captive stocks, that are numerous enough to benefit from the ISIS type of analysis, are not necessarily those of the endangered species that most need a captive breeding programme.

Botanic gardens do for plants what zoos do for animals, and the key part they can and should play in the preservation of rare and endangered plants was discussed at two conferences held at the Royal Botanic Gardens, Kew, in 1975 and 1978. The second meeting called for a world-wide network of regional botanic gardens, and for these both to act as gene banks themselves and to encourage the development of on-site conservation by supplying material for reintroducing species to reserves. The SSC Threatened Plants Committee undertook the task of finding out what endangered plants already existed in botanic gardens. In Europe, 481 out of 1878 rare or threatened vascular plants proved to be already in cultivation in botanic gardens, but 215 of these were grown in one garden only. The five species found in the largest number of gardens were the aberrant fern pillwort *Pilularia globulifera* (28), the aquatic clover fern *Marsilea quadrifolia* (25), the popular garden plant Cheddar pink *Dianthus gratianopolitanus* (21), lady's slipper orchid *Cypripedium calceolus* (20) and floating fern *Salvinia natans* (20); all of them are widespread, but severely threatened by drainage and other habitat destruction, and the lady's slipper also by uncontrolled picking and collecting. Since it is the attractive and horticulturally well known species, such as those of the bellflower, buttercup, lily, primrose and saxifrage families, that tend to be cultivated in gardens, efforts should also be made to cultivate as many less visually attractive species as possible.

Maintaining plants in cultivation differs in many ways from keeping animals in captivity. For animals, there is as yet no equivalent to taking cuttings or in other ways propagating from parts of a plant, and the long time-scale of the life history of trees also creates problems scarcely found in animals. However, this does mean that trees can be saved, albeit with maximum loss of genetic diversity, even if only one specimen survives, so long as it is not dioecious, i.e. has flowers of one sex only. Annuals present special problems, for unless they are to be kept only in a seed-bank, their seed must be collected each year and sown again if natural regeneration does not occur. Some perennials can be propagated by division, a technique available for only the lowliest animals.

How endangered plants can be saved by propagation is well illustrated by the project for St Helena put forward by S.Goodenough of Kew in 1983. He proposed four methods of propagation: cuttings, grafting, air layering and seed collection, together with the provision of a mist propagation bench and other equipment and materials. The highest priority would be given to propagating five endemic species reduced to fewer than five individuals: the composites *Commidendron rotundifolium*, *C.spurium* and *C.burchellii* (which is believed to have been rediscovered), the buckthorn relative *Nesiota elliptica*, the only species in its genus, and the bellflower *Wahlenbergia linifolia*. The St Helena ebony *Trochetiopsis melanoxylon*, once thought to be extinct, can be propagated by cuttings and may be used as a rootstock on which to graft the St Helena redwood *T.erythroxylon*, which does not now regenerate and so is reduced to only two substantial plants. Another great oceanic island rarity, the medusa tree *Medusagyne oppositifolia* of the Seychelles, an ancient relic which is the only member of the its family, has now been successfully grown from seed at the Berne Botanic Garden. As early as the 1840s seeds of another monospecific plant, the bellflower *Campanula (Azorina) vidalii*, were sent to Kew, so that twenty years later, according to Sir Joseph Hooker, there were a thousand times as many plants in English greenhouses as in its native Azores.

Golden barrel cactus

An important breakthrough for orchid conservation was achieved when Mark Clements, of the National Botanic Garden at Canberra, perfected a new propagation technique that brings together the seeds of orchids and the symbiotic fungus without which they cannot germinate. As a result, six endangered orchid species have been reintroduced to nature reserves in Australia. One was the purple double-tailed orchid *Diuris punctata*, whose last remaining wild population was 50 plants alongside a railway track in a Melbourne suburb.

The golden barrel cactus, mentioned on p. 95, illustrates another aspect of the problem. Since, like so many cacti, it can easily be propagated, it exists in many cactus collections around the world. Some rarity collectors lose interest in a plant once it is easy to obtain. So should it be propagated on a scale large enough to take the pressure off the remaining wild plants? There are, however, snags. It grows very slowly, so there is a premium on old mature specimens from the wild rather than young plants just out of the nursery. It has also been argued, as with the green turtle, that encouraging nurserymen to propagate large numbers may stimulate a new demand that will increase pressure on the wild stocks so long as these are easily obtained. This effect seems to be more prevalent in the United States than elsewhere, and is a difficult threat to assess.

Besides collections of endangered wild plants, there are many collections of the wild relatives of crop plants and also of cultivars, many of which have a potential value but are being rapidly eliminated by the bureaucratic zeal for standardisation. To combat this tendency, especially in the Third World, where Sri Lanka, for instance, grows more than 40 species of root crop compared with only a dozen in modern Britain, the Henry Doubleday Research Association has set up five vegetable sanctuaries so far, four in Britain and one in Sri Lanka.

Some cultivars, such as wheat, rice and other major cereals, must be preserved off-site, for even if farmers could be persuaded to set aside a few hectares for desirable old varieties, pollen from modern cultivars in nearby fields would all too often swamp them genetically. On the other hand, the seed of some crops, such as mango, does not store and so must be preserved on-site.

The ultimate off-site conservation technique, when species cannot be adequately maintained in natural reserves, is the gene bank. For plants, long-term collections preserve seeds, short-term ones, tubers or test-tube plantlets. Many botanic gardens and research institutions now keep seed banks, which are also extensively used to maintain important cultivars of many crop species. World-wide there are now two million accessions a year to active collections. There are 38 seed banks for rice and 53 for maize/corn, but only one collection, in North Carolina, has all 250 major corn races. Potato gene banks, both long- and short-term, contain some 44,000 accessions, of both species and varieties of *Solanum*. More than a quarter of these are stored at the International Potato Center at Lima, Peru, and other important banks are located at Leningrad, USSR, Braunschweig, West Germany, and Wisconsin, USA. Australia maintains a collection of *Glycine* as a potential source of disease resistance in soya beans. The problems associated with setting up the system of seed storage used at the Copenhagen Botanic Garden, Denmark, developing techniques that dated back to the 1780s, were discussed at the 1978 Kew Conference. One such problem may be how to maintain the seed parents intact. Attempts to conserve stands of rattans as seed orchards have run up against the difficulty that 'no rattan seems safe from rattan collectors'. An even more acute problem is who actually owns and controls these key genetic resources, a question that has entered the zone of conflict between developed and under-developed countries.

Animal gene banks can store either semen or eggs. Semen banks and artificial insemination are additional means of maximising the outbreeding of captive stocks. They are much used in animal husbandry, but their extension to endangered and other wild animals is only just beginning, under the watchful eye of the SSC Genome Specialist Group. This Group is concerned especially with the techniques of preserving, by means of deep-freezing and chemical fixation, the semen, eggs, gonads and somatic cells from both living and dead animals and plants.

Egg banks are also used in fish conservation. In Norway an Atlantic salmon egg-bank was established in 1977 with three aims: (i) to produce eggs from selected lines for fish farming; (ii) to preserve various salmon strains and produce eggs for rearing in hatcheries and later release; and (iii) to preserve salmon strains particularly threatened by environmental factors. A similar egg bank is being developed in Norway for the brown trout.

Atlantic salmon

7. Setting Priorities

All conservation action, indeed all action of any kind, involves setting priorities. This includes decisions, either deliberate or by default, to do nothing. So whatever IUCN, WWF and other conservationists do they are consciously or unconsciously setting priorities. Until quite recently the primary impulse to save any species has been the well-known 'fire brigade' syndrome. On hearing that a species is in danger, conservationists, from William Hornaday onwards, rush to save it. WWF was founded specifically to save species and their habitats, but not until it was well into its second decade was it able to escape from the fire-brigade syndrome, and start planning ahead to save species and habitats before they became acutely endangered. The first of its campaigns, Operation Tiger in 1973, was plainly a fire-brigade one, but since then there have been campaigns for tropical rainforests and wetlands and currently for plants. These do embody some thinking in advance, though both rainforests and wetlands were chosen because they were thought to be seriously threatened, so the fire-brigade element is still present – as it will be for the foreseeable future.

The fire brigade is indeed still much needed in species conservation because so many species are currently endangered and many of them acutely so. But how to decide whether to save the St Helena ebony or the San Benito evening primrose, the aye-aye or the kagu? Pressures are such that many species are still being lost every year, even though conservationists realise that they are becoming extinct. Some species perish because it is just too difficult politically to save them, as with the fourteen endemic invertebrates of Lake Pedder (p. 112); others because conservationists lack both time and/or money; and yet others because their plight is not yet known. So priorities are being unconsciously set all the time.

This has led some conservationists, notably Norman Myers, to recall the system used by World War I surgeons in the field, triage. Wounded men were divided into three groups: those able to walk back to the field station, those who might be saved by immediate treatment on the spot, and those with no hope of recovery. Clearly, unacknowledged triage is being practised all the time. What is now implicitly proposed is that these three groups should be deliberately identified among endangered species, and the limited time and effort available concentrated on those which are thought likely both to respond to the measures that are practicable, and to be of significant value to mankind. This of course raises immediate problems of how these criteria are to be determined, and opens up endless possibilities for argument among conservationists.

Aye-aye

In some ways triage is only common sense, and is already being used by, for instance, the Project Group of IUCN/WWF, even if the Group does not see it that way. One must also consider whether there is any advantage in publicising triage as a method of setting priorities, for it raises a serious public relations problem. It would not make a good image if it became known – and nowadays one must assume that everything will become known – that WWF considered the plight of some animals and plants as hopeless, and was giving up efforts to save them. What is more, any such decisions, even if they only trickle down through the grape-vine, merely stimulate those who are particularly interested in the abandoned species or group to go out and raise money to save it. This has already happened with land tortoises: when the SSC Tortoise Group found that its most urgent cases appeared not to fall within the priorities of WWF funding, it went out and collected grants itself. This is a good thing, insofar as it raises more funds for conservation. It is also a good thing if it means that the judgments of more than one group of conservationists can be applied to assessing priorities. But it probably means that any triage that is practised, while it is much better to be conscious than unconscious, is better not announced publicly, or as at present, only in the form of positive statements of what is to be saved. On the other hand, as just indicated, there is nothing like a feeling that the establishment is ignoring their species or group to stimulate enthusiasts to go out and raise funds for it. So on the whole it is better that triage remains a valuable philosophical concept rather than an actual working tool for conservationists. In any case the inconsistency and unpredictability of earmarked donations often circumvents the wishes of decision makers.

9 Sustainable Utilisation of the Resources

Sperm whale

It is Utopian to imagine that wildlife conservation can be carried out on a large scale without the use of wildlife for the benefit of mankind being a major consideration; and in this context benefit must mean largely material benefit. Sidney Holt has recently criticised what he calls the utilitarian approach of the World Conservation Strategy, and warned that it may backfire on conservationists. The dangers are all too evident, but they are nothing to the dangers that would result as conservationists were swept aside if they pressed for non-consumptive uses of wildlife only. Although habitat destruction and overexploitation, both legal and illegal, are a continuing grave threat to many wild species, in the present worsening economic climate politicians everywhere can very rarely be induced to act unless some material advantages to their electors can be demonstrated. Holt is perhaps unduly swayed by the recent success of the whale lobby in securing a whaling moratorium to start in 1986. This was only achieved because the great whales are an almost exhausted resource; the world conservation movement had made it a major objective; and the few remaining whaling countries continue to whale for political and social, rather than strictly economic reasons. Even so, at the time of writing, it is still by no means certain that the moratorium will actually stick. Moreover, the resources just do not exist to secure such a result with more than a handful of other threatened animals and plants. Nor can any migratory animal be managed or conserved without multi-national co-operation.

We need therefore to examine the problems of how to use species sustainably, remembering that often, as with timber trees or krill, it is impossible to draw a line between species and ecosystems. Philosophically, sustainable yield is a clearly understandable concept: that the take or harvest in any one year must not exceed the number of surviving young of the species or population, and so result in a lower take in the following year. Simple logic indicates that if you constantly impair the ability of an animal or plant population to reproduce itself, you will end up with no stock at all, or at least, as with the great whales, a stock too small to be worth exploiting. In effect you have destroyed the resource. Unfortunately natural population dynamics is more complex than that. To start with, wild populations are fluctuating all the time, depending on variations in their physical matrix: climate, nutrition and pressures from other species. We rarely know enough to be able to say whether any particular reduction in a breeding stock is primarily due to harvesting by man or to one of these natural factors.

Harvesting quotas therefore need to take natural population fluctuations into account, and since we know so little about these, a substantial safety margin needs to be built into the quotas. Such a safety margin, however, is rarely acceptable to the 'practical men' who are the actual exploiters. Hence the world-wide loss of so many once valuable wildlife stocks. Another difficulty in fixing quotas is that we hardly ever have the necessary scientific data – population size, number of females of breeding age, number of young recruited into the stock each year, and so on – in a sufficiently accurate form to be able to make a reliable assessment. This is one reason why the International Whaling Commission has failed to stop the continuous commercial overexploitation of the world's whale resource.

This lack of data also explains some of the problems of predator control. Bounty hunters often take credit for falls in population that are in fact natural fluctuations. Equally many predator control programmes have failed because the actual kill has been less than the sustainable yield. It is notorious too that bounty hunters like to leave an adequate breeding stock to provide their own next year's living. This is why wise administrators nowadays take the advice of their scientists not to indulge in these open-ended methods if others are available. This is something else that 'practical men' find it hard to accept.

Sustainable yield is hard enough to achieve, but in practice economic pressures have driven scientists concerned with the exploitation of wild species, especially fishes, to the more difficult concept of maximum sustainable yield (msy): the highest annual harvest which in theory can be sustained while maintaining the stability of the stock. The major weakness of msy is that it applies only to single species, and fails to recognise that the population fluctuations of a species cannot be separated from those of the rest of its ecosystem. Moreover, there is an implication that if any wild stock is not exploited up to the point of maximum sustainable yield – which works out at half the unexploited stock – then it is 'wasted'. In point of fact, since most species are more or less in balance with their ecosystem, any sustainable yield is what is available for exploitation by other species. To take even one individual out of an ecosystem minutely alters it, for at the very least when it died its nutrients would return to the soil for plant use. To take a large number out, and especially to take the maximum possible out, inevitably alters the ecosystem considerably. As Raymond Dasmann has pointed out, 'removing a high percentage of any species population can have immediate effects on the populations of predators dependent upon that species – along with scavengers, parasites and organisms of decay and recirculation which make use of the so-called harvestable surplus'. He adds that populations of existing or potential competing species may increase as a result, along with animals or plants upon which the species being cropped usually feeds.

A classic illustration of this effect was provided by the drastic die-off of rabbits that followed the myxomatosis epidemic in Britain in 1954-55. Some predators, such as buzzards, deprived of a large part of their food supply, just ceased to breed for two or three years; others, like the fox, turned to other foods, such as small rodents, possibly triggering off other population changes in these; and many plants that had been severely rabbit-grazed burst forth in a blaze of flowering. Similar results have been suspected as a result of the hunting to commercial extinction of the great whales of the southern oceans. Some biologists have attributed the buoyant stocks of the small minke whale and of certain seals and penguins to lack of competition from the larger whales for their main food, krill, and many other chain reactions must have been set off by this major change. If human krill harvesting develops on a large scale, some of these changes may be reversed.

Many fisheries scientists claim that politicians and administrators have

Fox chasing rabbits

misused the msy theory, or rather have failed to use it with any serious intent, so as to exhaust many valuable fishery and other resources, with the notable exception of the Pacific halibut fishery. Hence IUCN has proposed a more conservative approach, based on broader ecosystem considerations, and on continuing survey, monitoring, analysis and assessment of the likely results of any planned or ongoing utilisation scheme. This is reflected in the World Conservation Strategy (WCS), which has abandoned the msy in favour of sustainable utilisation. Moreover, the WCS makes it clear that ecosystems as well as species must be utilised sustainably so that in addition to overharvesting of timber trees and other species, overgrazing of grasslands must be avoided. The ultimate dilemma has been neatly stated by Dasmann: if we wish to preserve wild ecosystems in a state resembling their unexploited and unpolluted condition, we must be prepared to find that the sustainable yield from any species is much less than a resource-hungry world would like to admit. On the other hand, overexploitation leads remorselessly to the extinction of the resource. Both prongs of the dilemma are highly unwelcome. Few people really like to admit that they cannot have their cake and eat it.

1. Harvesting Marine Wild Animals

There are innumerable examples of wild stocks being harvested to actual or at least commercial extinction, as discussed in Chapter 5. Far fewer are the instances of successful harvesting of wild stocks to produce a sustainable yield. Most of the damage has been done in the past 300 years. The destruction of the North Atlantic right whale stocks in the Bay of Biscay in the late Middle Ages was exceptional. The world-wide loss of many fish and whale stocks during the present century is all too commonplace. At least 25 of the world's most valuable fisheries are seriously depleted, and by the mid-1970s the annual world marine catch was 15-20 million tonnes (20-24 per cent) below what it might have been if it had been exploited on a sustainable yield basis instead of using msy or just letting rip.

Twice in the twentieth century world wars have given the North Sea fish stocks a respite that enabled them to build up again, and each time the fishermen of the littoral nations fished them back down, especially the herrings, often in the genuine belief that their low catches were due to natural fluctuations. The third respite for the North Sea herring came in 1977 with a six-year total ban on herring fishing, and now that this has once more led to a recovery of the stocks, the nations bordering on the North Sea are once more arguing over the exiguous quotas which are all the scientists will allow them yet. Ironically, in Britain the ban led to a closure of most of the herring processing facilities, which has now resulted in a collapse of herring prices, and the use of the herring for animal feed or fertiliser instead of human food. In late 1983 the European Commission was driven to propose yet another ban, on mackerel fishing off south-west England. In western European waters there seems to be no half-way house between a total ban and a free-for-all. In *The Tragedy of the Commons*, Garrett Hardin pointed out that marine stocks were depleted because common property was nobody's business to safeguard. The North Sea shows just how difficult it is to make the effort to safeguard these stocks.

Similar if not worse stories can be told for other marine living resources, such as whales, seals and turtles. It is not that sailors are more undisciplined than landsmen, it is just that quotas, if any can be fixed, are much harder to enforce at sea. Moreover, the idea that marine species are not only common property but limitless as well, and so can legitimately be freely exploited without any danger of exhaustion, dies hard. As with the American hunters who killed off the bison, fishermen tend to think that if fish are not where they used to be, they have perversely gone off to some other part of the ocean. Finally, there is the fatal argument: if I don't, somebody else will.

One of the few hopeful signs in a gloomy outlook for the future is the Convention on the Conservation of Antarctic Marine Living Resources, the world's first ecosystem regime for any marine fisheries. So far only the most preliminary steps have been taken to bring it into effect, but despite the many difficulties, political, economic and technical, it could represent the beginning of rational exploitation of wildlife, especially fishes and krill. A recent BIOMASS report expresses concern about the potential overfishing off Kerguelen and the Scotia Sea, including South Georgia, the most heavily fished zones at present, of nine fish stocks, among them the Antarctic cod and ice-fish. IUCN has called for some areas to be closed to fishing to start with, and for a great deal more information to be amassed about the population dynamics of the various stocks before any quotas are fixed. A key decision will be the fixing of quotas for a krill fishery under this Convention. If this is mishandled, or proves to be unenforceable, the potential of all harvestable marine living resources in the Antarctic may be lost to mankind.

American bison

The history of the flawed attempt to regulate whaling through the International Whaling Commission is a salutary one. Not until the 1920s and 1930s did the overfishing of the Arctic whale stocks drive the, then mainly Norwegian, pelagic whalers with their factory ships to the Antarctic. Even then prophecies were made, and duly fulfilled, that the Antarctic whale stocks would follow the Arctic ones to commercial oblivion or, as it was put in 1931, would decline and die through overfishing like all previous whaling industries. By the late 1930s the evidence that the Antarctic whales were indeed following both the Arctic whales and the Antarctic fur seals to commercial extinction was too strong for even politicians and administrators to evade it. A conference held in London in 1938 eventually bore fruit (with the war intervening) in the International Whaling Convention of 1946. The resultant International Whaling Commission has ever since supervised the commercial extinction, one after another, of the whale stocks it was set up specifically to conserve. The IWC acted as a feeble umpire for the convenience of the whaling industry, while its existence enabled politicians and administrators to evade their clear responsibility to conserve a valuable natural resource and to flout the presumed will of their own governments.

Krill

In its early years the IWC refused to seek scientific advice at all, and when FAO persuaded it to do so in the mid 1960s, it at first failed to act on most of the extremely sound advice it received. By this time the average catch of a ship in a day's fishing had already fallen to one-third of its level in the 1930s, when the whalers used to catch some 30,000 blue and fin whales each year. Indeed by 1964 there were probably only 2000 blue and 40,000 fin whales left in the whole southern ocean, compared with a joint total of between 300,000 and 400,000 when the fishery began. Even then, although it completely protected both the blue and the equally depleted humpback whale, the IWC continued to drag its feet on realistic quotas and so to overexploit the much depleted fin whale stocks until these too had to be totally protected. In the early 1980s the once great Antarctic whaling industry, having successively overfished the blue, humpback and fin whales, lost also the sei whale and even Captain Ahab's quarry, the great sperm whale. By 1984 the pelagic Antarctic whaling industry – the shore stations had all long gone – which once knew nearly a dozen nations sending their fleets down south, was reduced to two countries, Japan and the USSR, with these two allowed to take only the relatively tiny minke whale, once despised by the whalers as being too small to be worth stopping to catch.

Uncontrolled individual human folly is one thing; institutionalised folly under an international aegis is quite another. The folly has been compounded by the continuing reluctance of Japanese and Russian scientists to agree on the validity of data accepted by almost all their colleagues on the IWC Scientific Committee. If the IWC were the best the international community could do to regulate the harvesting of wild stocks, one would be tempted to write the whole idea of international action off. Fortunately there are other precedents.

The Pribilof fur seal of the North Pacific provides the classic instance of successful sustainable utilisation of a living wild resource. The story of its overexploitation has already been told (p. 74). By 1911 stocks had fallen to some 200,000, or only 8 per cent of the original population. At that point Canada, Great Britain, Japan, Russia and the United States agreed to prohibit the pelagic sealing which had done the greatest damage, and the US and Russia became directly responsible for the management of the stocks in the Pribilofs and the Komandorskiye Ostrova (Commander Islands) respectively. Henceforth the US Fish and Wildlife Service controlled the seal hunting on a sustainable yield basis. The US and USSR share 15 per cent of their take with Canada and Japan.

Northern pribilof fur seal

After this the US stocks rapidly built up, reaching 2.25 million by the mid 1950s, with smaller numbers on the Russian side, totalling some 463,000 on the Commander Islands, Ostrov Tyuleniy (Robben Island) off Sakhalin and the Kurile chain between Kamchatka and Japan. However, in the mid 1950s Japanese fishermen complained that these seals were affecting their catches, and an excuse was made to kill female seals in the Pribilofs on a non-sustainable basis, ostensibly for the good of the 'overcrowded population'. When it was found that the yield did not increase as expected, this harvest of females was discontinued in 1968, but the stocks have not only not recovered from the lower level of 1.25 million which has prevailed ever since, but are now declining at a rate of 5-8 per cent a year. This is believed to be due to entanglement of the seals in fishing nets, the equivalent of the pelagic sealing at the beginning of the century. However, until the recent fall in the demand for seal skins, the Pribilof fur seal fishery was a thriving and profitable enterprise with an annual take of more than 20,000 seals, that has been a model of how to run a sustainable-yield fishery. In 1984 and 1985, the harvesting was contracted out to native Aleuts, but in 1985 the renewal of the international convention and indeed the whole seal harvest became the subject of a keen political battle in the US, especially since the clubbing of the seals, as in eastern Canada, is being condemned as inhumane.

The very large seal stocks of the Antarctic – the 30 million crabeater seals alone account for nearly half the world's seal total – are covered by the 1972 Convention on Antarctic Seals, which would enable crabeater, Weddell and leopard seals to be exploited sustainably with quotas if any country wished to do so. The three other Antarctic seals are at present completely protected.

Weddell seal

The annual hunt for the harp and hooded seals off the east coast of Canada is still, unfortunately, far from providing a model of enlightened exploitation. Stocks of both species are falling, certainly by at least two-thirds since the early 1960s, yet statistical argument as to their actual level is as fierce as with the great whales. The situation is complicated both by allegations that the methods of harvesting are cruel and by the severity of the Canadian Government's measures to stop protesters from interfering with the hunt. These have raised the emotional temperature so high that rational argument between the main contenders has almost ceased. In the light of the World Conservation Strategy, IUCN/WWF do not oppose the hunt, but have urged that it should continue only on three conditions: (i) if the best population data available indicate that the total allowable catch does not exceed the herd's potential for natural increase, i.e. that the yield is sustainable; (ii) if the entire seal is used as completely and non-wastefully as possible; and (iii) if the killing methods used are humane. Believing that the less numerous hooded seal has been more seriously overexploited than the harp seal, IUCN/WWF have also called for significantly lower quotas or even a temporary cessation of the hunt for this species, to allow numbers to rebuild. This did in fact almost happen in 1983, when fewer than 200 hooded seals were actually taken.

2. Harvesting Wild Land Animals

The success story of the saiga antelope is described elsewhere, and there are a good many other instances of the successful sustainable utilisation of rebuilt stocks of wild land animals. Among them is the vicuña, but it is still too soon to be quite sure that the excellent rebuilding of stocks at Pampa Galeras in Peru will be followed by continued sustainable utilisation. Provided the issue can be removed from politics, there is a good chance that Peru will not only have provided another classic example of repairing the folly of former overexploitation, but will have acquired a resource that can be sensibly exploited indefinitely. It is certainly vital that the local people, who have given up some of their grazing rights for the sake of the vicuñas, should benefit for their far-sightedness.

Vicuña

Many ranchers in Zimbabwe and South Africa have been exploiting the wild antelopes and other ungulates on their ranches both sustainably and profitably for twenty years or more, and this tradition is continuing with the Operation Windfall scheme of the Zimbabwe Government. In the 1960s the Galana River Game Management Scheme in Kenya and the hippo culling scheme in Queen Elizabeth National Park in Uganda were bold pioneer efforts that taught conservationists valuable lessons. The hippo scheme came to an end mainly because of problems in marketing the meat, inherent in such schemes remote from main population centres. The relative failure of the Galana River scheme, however, was due to more complex causes. It was, as Ian Parker points out in *Ivory Crisis*, the first positive attempt in Kenya, and probably in Africa, to integrate a hunting people's interests with modern conservation. The hunting people were the Waliangulu, traditional elephant hunters, and their failure to adapt to what was needed to make the scheme succeed was matched by a similar failure of the civil servants. To them, as Parker colourfully puts it, 'ivory was the sacred stuff of government', so all kinds of bureaucratic objections were raised, compounded by the Game Department's feeling that they were concerned with the welfare of animals, not of people. All in all, pages 20–23 of Parker's book made salutary reading for conservationists – and administrators.

Recently a proposal has been made to set up an Ivory Council to develop a coherent ivory trade policy. This body would consist primarily of ivory trade associations in consumer countries, together with conservation interests, perhaps through IUCN, and producer interests, perhaps through the CITES secretariat. Among its functions would be to prepare the statistical data needed to exploit elephant populations sustainably, and to consider how to protect any threatened populations.

African buffalo

Moustached tamarin

A recent very successful wildlife exploitation scheme in Mozambique was described to the 59th meeting of the SSC in Zimbabwe in April 1983, by Jose Lobao Tello of the Wildlife Department at Maputo. The Zambezi Wildlife Utilisation Area consists of 20,000 square kilometres on the south side of the Zambezi delta. It contains large and varied ungulate populations, the most numerous being 45,000 buffalo and 40,000 waterbuck, which were being heavily hunted or poached before hunting was forbidden in 1974, and cropping began two years later. Altogether more than 13,000 buffalo and 2000 waterbuck have now been harvested, and the meat supplied to villagers, to the military and even to refugees from Zimbabwe before its independence. All products and by-products have also been saved and sold. The result has not only been an economic benefit, but has not harmed the stocks and has led to a dramatic fall in poaching, especially of the smaller antelopes. The fact that the military were obtaining meat from the scheme enabled them vigorously to suppress poaching by their members, who formerly had the excuse that they were feeding themselves. This Mozambique scheme is a model of what can and should be done in many other Third World countries. It has already converted Mozambique politicians to the need to conserve their wildlife resources, and all the provincial governments are now demanding similar wildlife utilisation areas.

Two more excellent examples of the World Conservation Strategy in action, which combine sustainable utilisation of wild stocks with captive breeding, are provided by IUCN's recent 'Policy Statement on the Use of Primates for Biomedical Research' and by the Burma Elephant Project. The Policy Statement was put forward by the SSC Primate Specialist Group and agreed in 1982 by the Ecosystem Group and the World Health Organisation. It urges that endangered, vulnerable and rare primates should only be used in biomedical research if they come from existing self-sustaining captive-breeding colonies, and that species of indeterminate or unknown status should only be used when it is certain that they are not endangered, vulnerable or rare. Further, any wild-caught primates should be used primarily for the establishment of self-sustaining colonies in captivity, with the ultimate aim of using in research only animals from such colonies. In addition, apparently common monkeys should be trapped only when the stocks are continually monitored to prevent exploitation, or where they are agricultural pests or their habitat is being destroyed. It has, for instance, been shown that the moustached tamarin can be cropped every three years in Amazonian Peru without affecting its numbers.

In Burma some 2600 elephants are currently used in the forest industry, but although most are bred in captivity, their low breeding rate suggests that they are being overworked. Consequently, up to 200 elephants are still being taken from the wild. The Burma Elephant Project of IUCN/WWF seeks both improved management of the captive stocks, and measures to ensure that the wild stocks are not overexploited to augment the captive ones.

Australia's kangaroo industry is believed to be the world's largest commercial wildlife operation, and arouses passions as intense as those stirred up by the Canadian seal hunt. The species mainly involved are the two largest kangaroos, the red and the grey, and there can be no doubt that these marsupial equivalents of the ungulates still number many millions. Just how many millions, somewhere between 10 and 36, is strongly contested between the Federal Government and its opponents. The SSC Australian Marsupials Specialist Group, which is independent of both sides in the controversy, accepts what it describes as a conservative estimate of 19 million in 1981. Equally contentious is whether the National

Kangaroo Management Plan of 1980 is an effective management plan and if so whether it is effectively implemented. The SSC Group considers (i) that none of the currently harvested species is endangered, (ii) that these species are often agricultural pests and so would be killed even if commercial harvesting were to stop, and (iii) that commercial harvesting is the most humane and conservative method of control. The whole imbroglio illustrates how acute are the problems once the exploitation of a wild animal becomes a political football, the battleground between powerful economic and humanitarian interests. In these circumstances it is often little use appealing to scientific impartiality because the scientists consulted by each side tend to become polarised too. One can only say in this instance that a wildlife industry that kills and processes between 1.5 million and 2.5 million animals a year deserves to be treated rationally and, like the Canadian seal hunt, is not at present being treated rationally by either side.

Kangaroo

The American alligator has also recovered its numbers in many parts of the south-eastern United States, and is being exploited again in most states where it occurs, notably Florida, Louisiana and Texas. Again, it is too soon to know whether the authorities can control poaching sufficiently to make sustainable harvesting possible in the long term. Unfortunately, poaching is always easier when there is a legal sale than when all sales are prohibited.

Some 12 million wild waterfowl are harvested by sport hunters in North America every year, very largely on a sustainable basis. A successful small-scale example of such harvesting by sportsmen is the white-crowned pigeon, the most important game bird in the Bahamas. Before attempting to exploit pigeon-hunting as a tourist attraction, the Bahamian Government consulted the National Audubon Society. After research, the Society advised that the pigeon population could not withstand a major influx of American hunters. Accordingly a 99-day residence qualification for a hunting licence was imposed and the hunting season deferred till after the end of the breeding season. This has preserved the resource for the enjoyment of local hunters.

American alligator

It is clear that provisions for sustainable utilisation should be built into all future international agreements on the exploitation of wild living resources, similar to those in the two Antarctic conventions. Because of the problems associated with common property, the difficulty will always be in enforcing such international rules. There is a better chance that, as in Mozambique, national regulations can be enforced.

3. Farming and Ranching

It has often been suggested that wild ungulates or kangaroos are more efficient exploiters of savanna-type grasslands than domestic cattle, sheep or goats. So another way of using the genetic resources represented by wild animals is by farming or ranching them. Farming is strictly the rearing and exploitation of closely confined, or at least fenced-in animals, especially domestic animals, with no input from the wild. Wild animals, such as deer and crocodiles, can be farmed, but self-sustaining operations, not replenished by wild stock, are hard to establish, as the difficulty often experienced by zoos in maintaining breeding populations for more than a few years shows.

Ranching began as open-range cattle-rearing in the United States, but the term has now been extended to cover the exploitation of vertebrates which are allowed to range more or less freely over a natural habitat, which may or may not be fenced. Blackface sheep wandering freely over the hills and moors of Scotland could in one sense be said to be ranched. So could the ponies of the New Forest in Hampshire, which are all owned but feed at large in the Forest, as well as domestic pigeons when they are free to come and go, and honeybees, which may well go off and occupy some other hive or hole if not caught at the right moment. Capybaras are ranched in Venezuela and other large rodents are farmed in West Africa. Some twenty species of deer, especially red, fallow and sika deer, are farmed in at least 29 countries. The symbiotic relationship between the Lapps and their reindeer, in which they follow the deer during their normal migrations, can also be regarded as a form of ranching. Likewise an enterprise which puts Atlantic salmon or Pacific humpback salmon fry or smolts into a river or the sea, reckoning to harvest them when they return. To help control international trade, CITES has defined ranching very closely, depending on whether or not individuals, eggs or seeds continue to be taken from the wild, and taking into account the number of generations that have been reared in captivity.

Wildebeest

Game ranching in southern Africa also indicates how hard it is to draw a line between exploiting farmed and ranched wild animals. On an organised basis it has been operating for some twenty years, especially in the Transvaal and Zimbabwe, and the distinction would appear to depend on whether the ranches are actually fenced off from each other. Economic pressures tend towards fencing and thus may, as in Botswana for different reasons, interfere with migrations. The natural way to exploit migrant ungulates, such as the wildebeest of the Botswana savannas, would be to follow them as the lions and other predators do on the Serengeti Plains in Tanzania, or as the Lapps do their reindeer. This, however, is unlikely to be economic, except for people with a self-sustaining economy like the Lapps. Such species could also be harvested with drift fences that herd small groups into corrals. Unfortunately, would-be exploiters prefer to shoot them instead, which is both expensive and scatters the carcases, making it more expensive to get them to the abattoir.

Attempts have been made from time to time to domesticate new ungulates, notably the eland, a large antelope, which is one of the most promising. Eland have been at least semi-domesticated at Askaniya Nova in the Crimea for many years and have also been the subject of an interesting recent experiment in Kenya. Musk-oxen are currently being domesticated in Alaska for their wool. Repeated attempts have also been made in Russia and Scandinavia to domesticate the elk or moose, and in the past elk were ridden both by the Yakuts of eastern Siberia and by medieval and early modern Swedes. However, more recent efforts in the Urals have revealed that because elk are browsers and need to forage over an extensive area of forest, their value in domestication is limited. Moreover, most attempts at domesticating new animals meet with the indifference or even active hostility of existing stock-rearers. The veterinary profession too seems to take the view that it does not want any more problems than it already has with cattle, sheep and horses. These problems, however, should not affect the current experiments in Nigeria to domesticate two large rodents which are much hunted for bushmeat, the African giant rat and the grass-cutter or cane rat, whose meat sells at three times the price of mutton.

Musk ox

Crocodile ranching is one of the more successful enterprises for exploiting wild animals commercially. In 1984 there were existing or proposed crocodile ranches or farms in at least 38 countries, and 21 species are bred. In Zimbabwe it is strictly speaking farming, for understandably ranches are only licensed if they can guarantee the absolute containment of their stock. At first the Zimbabwe ranches depended on collecting wild eggs (they were not allowed to collect young crocodiles), but this soon became expensive enough to encourage ranchers to start breeding their stock in captivity. In 1982 five ranches held 11,344 rearing stock, 116 breeding females and 9194 hatchlings, mainly from collected eggs. The major source of income is from skins, but ranches near such tourist honeypots as Victoria Falls can get significant incomes from both gate takings and the sale of curios.

Similar ranching enterprises have been very successful for crocodiles in Papua New Guinea and Thailand and for alligators in Florida and Louisiana. In PNG the two native species, the saltwater and New Guinea crocodiles, are used in a scheme funded by FAO and UNDP, whereby hatchlings are taken from the wild, reared in village pens or larger commercial establishments, and killed for their skins when about three years old. The collection of hatchlings is said to be on a sustainable yield basis. The Samutprakan Crocodile Farm in Thailand dates back to 1950 and now has 30,000 crocodiles, mainly saltwater and Siamese. Animals are slaughtered for their skins, also at three years old ; at this point the cost of keeping and feeding them begins to outweigh the higher price fetched by larger skins. The Government of China has set up several farms for the Chinese alligator, but these are experiencing problems in becoming viable. There are also some 30 commercial crocodile farms in Taiwan, apparently mainly rearing *Caiman crocodylus* from South America.

The success of crocodile farming has led to repeated attempts to start similar enterprises for marine turtles, especially the green turtle, whose eggs and shells taken from the wild are currently being exploited world-wide. The most controversial of these enterprises has been in the Cayman Islands in the Caribbean. In its first ten years up to 1978 the Cayman Turtle Farm imported nearly half a million eggs and several hundred adults from the wild, especially from Suriname, many of them the so-called 'doomed eggs' that would otherwise have been destroyed by high tides. The Farm has always striven to achieve a self-sustaining captive breeding stock whose products could enter trade under CITES and so be sold in the United States, but although some farm- reared turtles have bred, it is still far from being able to produce genuine second-generation offspring. A similar project in Suriname, using the same 'doomed eggs' was discussed at the 1983 CITES meeting in Botswana, but no decision was made as to whether its products could be exported. A turtle ranch on Réunion depends on hatchlings from Tromelin and Europa islands, said to be taken from daylight emergences liable to heavy predation and to that extent also 'doomed'. The products of this ranch can legally be sold in France, but these again have not yet been accepted by CITES. Many conservationists oppose trade of any kind in marine turtle products, fearing that it will stimulate a demand that could not be satisfied by the farms and so lead to a substantial increase in poaching. A similar argument was adduced against allowing the recovered American alligator to re-enter trade, but so far we cannot tell whether it is well founded.

Fish hatcheries are a long-established method of making use of fish genetic resources. In Sweden they began in the 1860s with Atlantic salmon and in Norway about 1870 with salmon, sea trout and hybrids between sea trout and Arctic char. By 1884 a first consignment of eggs of North American rainbow trout arrived in Britain. Most of the early progeny were used to restock rivers and lakes, and only comparatively recently has the idea of rearing fish for commercial sale taken hold. Norwegian experience suggested that wild stocks were of very varying value for fish farming, and more suitable strains of both Atlantic salmon and rainbow trout are now being bred. Total production in Norway in 1979 amounted to some 6600 tons from 45 fish farms. In Scotland more than a score of farms are rearing salmon and rainbow trout either in cages in the sea or in shore-based tanks. In the United States aquaculture, as it is now called, is big business; in 1981

Green turtle

some 70 million humpback salmon fry were released at Prince William
Sound, Alaska, with a projected harvest of 5-6 million; and more than $14
million has been invested in the past eight years in the largest salmon-
rearing enterprise in the US, on the McKenzie River in Oregon. In
Newfoundland giant bluefin tuna are held in net pens and fattened for sale
to Japan.

But perhaps the oldest ranching enterprises of all, apart from the
honeybee, deal with another invertebrate, the oyster *Ostrea edulis*, which
was despatched from the Essex estuaries to gourmets in Imperial Rome. If
at first these were just harvested from the wild, by the late Middle Ages
Thames and Essex oyster beds were already being tended so as to provide
greater areas of settling surface for the spat. As early as the fourth century AD
oysters were brought from Brindisi to be fattened in the Lucrine Lake
north of Naples, which communicates with the sea by a narrow channel.
Today the lake is used for cultivating common mussels. Oyster culture
meanwhile has developed into a worldwide industry in temperate saline
waters, using different species: the Portuguese *Crassostrea angulata* in
South-west France and the Iberian Peninsula, *C.gigas* and *C.rivularis* in
Japan, the American *C.virginica* along the Atlantic coast of North America
and in the Caribbean, and many more. More than 40,000 acres of good
underwater oyster grounds lie along the coasts of Connecticut and Long
Island alone, and 1500 acres near New Haven are estimated to yield $10
million worth of oysters each year. In Japan pearl oysters *Pinctada* are also
farmed, and efforts are being made to ranch pink conchs *Strombus gigas* in
the Turks and Caicos Islands.

Lobsters, mussels and other shellfish also contribute worldwide to this
increasingly important method of exploiting marine genetic resources, and
are, incidentally, at greater and greater risk from the increasing pollution of
the sea and its inshore waters. Toads in Chile, giant snails *Achatina* in
Nigeria and earthworms in the Philippines are also being farmed, the first
two for food, the worms for their waste to be used as fertiliser, while an
extensive butterfly farming operation has been built up in Papua New
Guinea, to supply both collectors and the tourist trade.

The IUCN/SSC Ethnobotany Specialist Group has a list of some 70
wild Amazonian plants which, to judge from their use in tribal societies, are
potential new crop plants, sources of food, oils, gums, resins and waxes.

4. Forestry

Forestry is the most important form of utilising wild plants, but unfortunately by far the greater proportion of timber is felled on a purely
exploitative basis. Comparatively few forests are managed, like those in
Switzerland, entirely sustainably. The recommendations to this end of the
UN Conference on Tropical Timber in 1983 were mentioned on p. 135
IUCN had specifically recommended to this conference that timber should
only be harvested sustainably and only on lands capable of sustaining
timber production, though this constructive suggestion was not adopted.

One of the few instances of wild non-woody plants being harvested
sustainably comes from the United States, where some states now insist
that harvesters of ginseng scatter the seeds of any mature plants they pick.

5. Non-consumptive Uses

Sustainable utilisation of wildlife is, of course, much easier to achieve when
the uses are the non-consumptive ones which were discussed on p. 37
However, it cannot be taken for granted. As already indicated, great care

has to be taken that tourists do not, by getting too close, harm the animals they go to see, or trample down young plants in their eagerness to see mature ones. During the past 30 years there has been a great development in the provision and use of hides or blinds to enable people to watch wildlife without disturbing it, and of board-walks over swamps, forest floor and tundra to prevent damage to vegetation and compaction of the soil. The Mountain Gorilla Project in Rwanda is a good example of successful non-consumptive use of wildlife. It has habituated several family groups of the mountain gorilla to the near presence of tourists. This enables tourists to have a superb wildlife experience and to take photographs they never imagined would be possible. At the same time their fees increase the income of the national park, which now for the first time breaks even. In the Galapagos Islands too the park authorities have managed to keep tourists so well under control that they have not so far done any detectable harm to the wildlife. Indeed, at Punta Cormorante flamingoes returned to nest in 1978 for the first time for fourteen years, despite the big increase in tourism at the site.

African elephant

10 People and Conservation

In the long run wildlife conservation, the maintenance of stocks of wild animals and plants, the sustainable utilisation of genetic resources, call it what you will, depends on the goodwill of people. People do not normally give their goodwill to anybody or anything until their basic social and economic needs are satisfied. Advice from however august a body of foreigners cuts no ice with peasants whose crops are being damaged by elephants, housewives who have to walk miles each day to collect fuelwood, or people who are just plain hungry. As the Canadian conservationist Maurice Strong put it in the third World Conservation Lecture: 'People faced with the struggle for day-to-day survival cannot be expected to give priority to preserving resources for tomorrow when they have to make a choice today.' On the other hand, as the Indian ecologist Madhav Gadgil has pointed out, current economic arrangements leave virtually no section of his country's population with any personl stake left in preserving forests. Indeed in some areas, such as Khao Yai National Park in Thailand, disgruntled villagers prevent park guards from even patrolling their parks.

Conservationists therefore have to put themselves in the position of the people who live in the habitats and alongside the wildlife they seek to preserve, and must address the problem of inducing them to want to conserve both habitat and wildlife as much as the conservationists themselves do. This can only be achieved if the local people see it in their own immediate, as well as long-term, interest to conserve it, and not just for the sake of some vague body of outsiders, or 'the heritage of mankind' or any other high-sounding phrase.

Some progress, but far too little, has been made towards this desirable aim. And far too few politicians, administrators and scientists see it this way. Politicians and administrators tend to believe people are more important than their environment, which they treat as a kind of luxury extra. Biologists and conservationists, on the other hand, tend to think the reverse. Not nearly enough members of either group accept that the two interests are indissolubly linked. People will never reach their full potential without a satisfactory environment, and the environment will never be satisfactory unless people are persuaded to help in conserving it, at the same time understanding why this is necessary.

The long and tangled story of Amboseli National Park in Kenya admirably illustrates many of the problems. Founded in 1948 as a national reserve for the sake of the many antelopes and other wild animals that concentrated round the Ol Tukai swamps, it went wrong right at the start by not including within its bounds the areas to which the animals dispersed

during the wet season. Quite soon too it came into conflict with the local
Maasai, whose herds also relied on these swamps in the dry season. As
tourism built up and periodic droughts ravaged the Maasai cattle, mutual
resentments built up. The Maasai naturally felt their cattle, basic to their
way of life, should have precedence over zebras and wildebeest. Conservationists and tour operators, on the other hand, accused the Maasai of
ruining the habitat for wildlife with their cattle. As Amboseli grew more
and more profitable as a tourist honeypot and the Maasai way of life was
increasingly threatened by recurrent droughts and changes in the water-
table, efforts to safeguard the habitat by making it a national park constantly
foundered on Maasai resistance. It did not help that the contribution of
their cattle to the Kenyan economy was only a small fraction of the yield
from tourism.

Zebra

Not until 1977 was an agreement on the only possible basis worked out:
Amboseli became a national park and the Maasai herds were excluded, but
the Maasai were allotted not only a small part of the swamp area originally
within the park, but also a much larger area to the north that was irrigated
by a pipeline; moreover, they now benefit from the park's tourism
revenues. This Kaijado Wildlife Management Project, in which the
Government, the Kaijado County Council, the World Bank and the New
York Zoological Society all took part, is a model for Third World areas
where there is a similar conflict of interest.

Action has already been taken to prevent similar problems arising in the
new Kakadu National Park in northern Australia. This park actually
belongs to the Aboriginals, who manage it jointly with the Director of Parks
and Wildlife. Aboriginals continue to live in the park, and are being trained
in management techniques, while among the Parks Director's commit-
ments is to promote among non-Aboriginals a knowledge and understanding of Aboriginal culture, traditions and languages.

The Mozambique delta cropping scheme referred to on p. 166 is another
instance where the local inhabitants have been enabled to benefit from
wildlife conservation, and so is the vicuña management scheme at Pampa
Galeras in Peru. Although the sale of vicuña wool is not yet possible, the
local community already benefits from the sale of meat; a community centre
has been built out of the proceeds. Similar benefits accrued from the game
management schemes in Kenya and Uganda mentioned in the last chapter.
Indeed schemes whereby villagers benefit from the controlled exploitation
of wildlife are now quite widespread, although they are liable to run into
administrative problems, including opportunities for corruption.

Larger mammals and reptiles frequently come into direct conflict with
farmers and peasants. The Indonesian Environment Minister, Emil Salim,
has cited two such situations. The habitat of the last five Javanese tigers in
eastern Java lies in a densely populated region, where land hunger is severe.
The Indonesian Government has to ask itself why it should conserve these
tigers if this means relocating the human population. This, of course, is just
what has happened under Project Tiger in India, at Kanha National Park,
and also at the Royal Chitwan National Park in Nepal. At each of these
parks villagers within the park boundary have been relocated to better land
elsewhere, and have been satisfied once established in their new homes. In
more densely populated Java this would be more difficult.

Tiger

Salim's other example of conflict was of elephants whose territories had
been opened for human settlement in Kalimantan, Sumatra, Sulawesi and
other parts of Indonesia. Naturally they would continue to forage where
they always had done, but now it would be on crops. There are comparable
situations in Rwanda and Sri Lanka, with the additional complication that
the Ceylon elephant is an endangered race.

In Zimbabwe the Chirisa Wildlife Area in the Gokwe District also had an elephant problem, so the Government set up a scheme, named Operation Windfall, to crop surplus elephants and channel the resultant revenue back to the community. With the first cheque the district council planned to build a clinic waiting room and a store for elephant hides and to buy two lorries, with a bore-hole and the villagers' first supply of clean drinking water to follow. Since a large elephant contains at least 1000 kg of good meat, villagers now welcome the news that a crop marauder has been killed, for it means a free meat meal for every villager, while a compensation scheme looks after the damaged crops. Formerly the villagers had to poach the marauding elephant, sell its ivory to smugglers, waste the meat and get no formal compensation.

Similarly, as part of its project for the conservation of the Mediterranean monk seal, which had been persecuted by Greek fishermen in the Aegean, the Fauna and Flora Preservation Society raised enough money to build a cold store for the benefit of the entire fishing community on Alonissos in the Northern Sporades. A report to the European Parliament in 1984 stressed that the seal would be effectively protected 'only if the local population, which of course includes fishermen, makes itself responsible' for it.

The World Conservation Strategy maintains, and it is a main thesis of this book, that the conservation and sustainable utilisation of living resources is vital for the future welfare of mankind. Unfortunately many local cultural factors prevent this perception reaching both national and local communities all over the world. What seems the plainest common sense to internationally minded conservationists is seen by many people worldwide as outside interference that flouts their deep-rooted cultural beliefs. We shall clearly not be able to achieve our ends without taking these cultural factors much more closely into account.

Two classic instances can be quoted from the whaling sphere. One reason why Japan has so strongly resisted the whaling moratorium is that Japanese politicians, administrators and scientists have all seen it, not as a commonsense means of conserving a scarce resource, but as a kind of western plot to deny Japan its legitimate cultural heritage, which includes the eating of whale-meat. Aggressive tactics by western conservation activists merely arouse nationalistic resistance in Japan. Similarly, catching bowhead whales is an integral part of Alaskan Inuit culture, and the Inuit see the imposition of a quota – on which the IWC Scientific Committee has been agreed for years – as insensitive interference with their cultural identity. These are situations in which reason and logic fall by the wayside. Yet neither Japanese nor Inuit whalers can go on overfishing their stock indefinitely. Continued overexploitation is ineluctably followed by extinction, and that is the end of the cultural tradition anyway. Conservationists must learn to take these feelings into account and approach such traditions in a spirit of compromise, as they eventually did with the Maasai in Amboseli.

Bowhead whale

In addition to persuading people by giving them direct economic benefits from wildlife, a favourable public opinion can often be created by using modern communication techniques. These have been used, for instance, by the consortium of societies which run the campaign to preserve the mountain gorilla in Rwanda. A van equipped with visual aids travels round schools all over Rwanda. This has led to nine schools starting wildlife clubs, and some of their students have been taken to see degraded forest nearby. During the school holidays the van is used for similar presentations in towns and villages around the Parc des Volcans, where the gorillas live, and in the first year 35,000 people are believed to have been reached in this way. The people around the park have also benefited because the increased fees from showing the gorillas to tourists were used to increase the salaries of guards and guides.

A similar mobile education unit, funded by WWF-US, is visiting 50 towns and villages in the Brazilian state of Minas Gerais, to publicise the importance of wildlife and especially the highly endangered muriqui or woolly spider monkey and other primates. In the Philippines the campaign to save the perhaps even more endangered Philippine or monkey-eating eagle, includes films, posters and pamphlets directed at all employees of the logging companies and people living within the timber concessions. In the Caribbean area the Sea Turtle Rescue Fund has prepared a bilingual education packet which is being used with great success in schools in the Bahamas, the Dominican Republic and St Lucia. FAO has prepared educational material for use in the Central African Republic that includes outlines of the footprints of the principal large mammals.

In China more than 70,000 people come out by bus each year from the city of Qiqihar to the Zhalong reserve, where they watch the red-crowned cranes that are reared there flying around and being fed, and are told how important it is that wetlands should be preserved. This is just one instance of how, all over the world, captive and semi-captive animals in zoos and wildlife collections and plants in botanic gardens are powerful educators, and wild animals and plants in reserves even more so.

Sometimes the impulse to save wildlife and its habitat arises spontaneously from the people themselves, especially if commercial exploitation flouts long-held cultural beliefs. For instance, in the Garwhal district of the Indian Himalayas the Chipko 'tree-hugging' movement suddenly started one day in April 1973 when contractors arrived to cut ash trees for a sports equipment firm. The village women went to the grove and flung their arms around the trees to stop them being felled. This followed a 260-year-old tradition which began when people hugging trees that were sacred to their tribe are said to have been killed by axemen on the orders of the landowner. One of the Chipko leaders, Sunderlal Bahaguna, later marched for 4000 km along the Himalayas to persuade villagers to stop tree-felling. The movement has recently spread to Karnataka in the south, where a group of young people forced the state's foresters to stop felling trees in the North Kanara district. A similar spontaneous demonstration stopped foresters cutting down one of the last areas of sub-tropical rainforest in New South Wales, at Terania Creek.

The next logical step is to encourage tree-planting. Volunteers are now planting trees near their villages in many parts of Asia and Africa, for instance around Delhi, Bombay and Baroda in India, as well as in China, Sumatra, South Korea, Kenya and Tanzania. In China the ruling party has called for all its members, students, workers and soldiers to plant trees once a year. In Madhya Pradesh, India, a 13-year-old boy looks after a thousand tree seedlings in one school nursery. Two districts in Tanzania have also established tree nurseries. In Niger the success of a US-funded tree-planting scheme has encouraged villagers to plant their own woodlots, and in Madhya Pradesh the local Forestry Society plans to plant 100 million trees on 63,000 hectares of barren land by 1987, to provide a quarter of the firewood needs of 5000 villages. As an interesting variation, farmers in Karnataka have invaded a government forest nursery, pulled out alien eucalyptus seedlings and substituted tamarinds. However, an example from Haiti shows how important it is that peasants or tribesmen should themselves be motivated to preserve the forest. Here the peasants were paid to plant trees, but later some of them allowed the saplings to die so that they would be paid to plant more.

Woolly spider monkey

In Panama the Kuni Indians have a cultural tradition that the rainforest is inhabited by spirits that will rise up and destroy nearby villages if they are disturbed. Consequently the Kuni, who are themselves fishermen and coconut farmers, strive to preserve their tribal domain, a narrow coastal strip of rainforest, from illegal encroachment by cattlemen and cultivators. They have not only set up a 6000-hectare wildlife reserve and forest park, but they manage it themselves. This is the first example in Latin America of a tribe developing a scientific plan for their forest resources. IUCN and WWF have worked out a similar plan with the Cayapas Indians in Ecuador to manage the Cotachi-Cayapas Ecological Reserve.

An encouraging feature is the increasing development of voluntary conservation bodies in developing countries, to parallel the numerous such bodies elsewhere. China, for instance, has recently founded its first such body, the China Wildlife Conservation Association, and in Indonesia some 400 vigorous and active citizens' organisations co-operate closely with the Government in this field. Farmers and rural development officers throughout Zambia are becoming concerned for soil and water conservation. Of course there are also many existing conservation societies in the Third World, both long-established, such as the Sri Lanka Wild Life Preservation Society and the Bombay Natural History Society, and more recent ones, such as the East African Wildlife Society and its counterpart in Sierra Leone. One of the great successes in this field, the Wildlife Clubs of Kenya, have now introduced a great many Kenyan boys and girls to the wildlife of their country, with their mobile film unit and library, and hostels in the national parks. Founded around 1968, the 1050 clubs now have 70,000 members, are thought to reach nearly one-third of Kenya's high-school students, and have stimulated similar clubs in Uganda and Tanzania.

Often there is spontaneous local action to save endangered species, as in the Aligarh district of Uttar Pradesh, where a teacher and two elderly guards rigorously protect a colony of rhesus macaques in the schoolyard, and on Floreana in the Galapagos, where the settlers have declared their island's chief dark-rumped petrel nesting colony, Cerro Pajas, a protected area. Individual initiatives, such as the bird hospitals in various parts of Britain, are also important and to be encouraged. A striking example comes from Gujarat, north-west India, where the Shukla family of Bhavnagar operates a private snake-rescue service to remove unwanted snakes, which otherwise would be killed, and release them elsewhere. The Irula Snake Catchers' Industrial Cooperative Society of Tamil Nadu, southern India, both saves species and makes an income for its members from the sustainable use of wildlife. These members of the Irula tribe catch snakes, extract their venom and let them go again.

Hawaiian petrel

Citizen action that helps to conserve species and their habitats is very welcome, but ultimately governments must step in and take the strain. It is governments which represent the collective will, and there are always some actions which require the force of law to make them effective. The most effective actions of all are those where a government and its citizens are working in unison, so that law has the support of custom. This is why it is of the utmost importance that the World Conservation Strategy should be paralleled by national conservation strategies, approved and implemented by governments, with, wherever possible, the active support of voluntary bodies. At present at least 31 countries are in various stages of preparing such national strategies, some of them, as in the Philippines, Malaysia and the United Kingdom, by the voluntary bodies alone, but most of them, more effectively, by or with the active support of the government itself. The future of genetic resource conservation will not be secure until all governments have adopted national strategies based on the World Conservation Strategy.

Saving endangered species is a comparatively small part of species conservation, for clearly it is more important for human welfare to conserve genetic resources that are being actively and beneficially utilised. This is not to belittle the great efforts that many governments, non-governmental bodies, notably the IUCN Species Survival Commission and the World Wildlife Fund, and individuals are putting into saving endangered species, but to suggest that in many ways these are more in the nature of an insurance policy than a policy for immediate human welfare. Among the most effective measures to save endangered species are the recovery plans in the Endangered Species Program of the US Fish and Wildlife Service. Substantial resources and manpower have been devoted to these plans since they were first instituted under the Endangered Species Act making use of all the various methods of species conservation discussed in the preceding chapters. At the beginning of 1985 recovery plans were in hand for 21 mammals, 53 birds, 15 reptiles, 6 amphibians, 36 fishes, 7 snails, 14 clams, one crustacean (the socorro isopod *Thermosphaeroma thermophilus*), 9 insects and 33 vascular plants. Only one of these plans has so far actually failed: the blue pike *Stizostedion vitreum glaucum* was officially declared extinct in September 1983.

11 Depleted and Endangered Stocks Rebuilt: Some Success Stories

As we have seen, some wild stocks have already recovered, sometimes from a very small base, to be of productive value to mankind again. Even more have been rescued from the brink of extinction and put on the way to recovery. Some of the most spectacular recoveries date from long before the present concern for endangered species. Hornaday, for instance, began to rescue the American bison before the turn of the century. The pronghorn and saiga antelopes, Père David's deer and the koala were all saved before World War II.

There are two ways of grouping these recoveries from severe depletion. They can be arranged, as is done here, by the methods used: (i) controlling exploitation, (ii) protecting habitat, (iii) removing predators or competitors, and (iv) captive breeding followed by return to the wild. Or they can be classified by the degree of success in restoring them as viable wild populations. There are four of these success-based groups too, which unfortunately so far include very few plants.

1. Species restored to such numbers in the wild that they can once more be hunted or otherwise utilised sustainably: Pribilof fur seal, southern elephant seal, pronghorn antelope, saiga antelope, capercaillie (in Scotland), American alligator.

2. Species whose numbers in the wild are increasing well, though not yet to the stage of controlled exploitation, if that should be thought desirable: koala, northern sea otter, Kerguelen fur seal, Cape mountain zebra, American and European bison, Palestine mountain gazelle, Arabian oryx, California gray whale, whooping crane, nene or Hawaiian goose.

3. Species whose numbers while still small are nevertheless outgrowing the sanctuary areas available for them: southern white rhino, perhaps Javan rhino, tule elk.

4. Species of which there are adequate stocks in captivity or semi-captivity, but which have not yet been re-established in the wild: Père David's deer, Przewalski's horse, bontebok, black wildebeest.

There are also a number of species which are more numerous as introduced feral populations in regions far from their natural range, than as natives within that range. These include the blackbuck and nilgai or blue bull, both now more numerous in Texas than in the Indian sub-continent; the goat-like Himalayan tahr, probably more numerous in New Zealand than in the Himalayas; the Chinese muntjac and mandarin duck, both more numerous as ferals in England than in their native China; and the white-throated or parma wallaby, more numerous as a feral stock on the island of Kawau off the North Island of New Zealand than in its native New South Wales.

A plant example is the Monterey cypress, now almost confined to a single headland in California, Point Lobas, although in many parts of the world it is one of the most numerous cultivated trees. Nearby too grows another species endangered in the wild, the Monterey pine *Pinus radiata*, which is extensively planted in the southern hemisphere.

1. Recovery by Controlling Exploitation

The simplest way of preventing a species from being depleted by overexploitation is to stop exploiting it altogether. This has led to a number of quite striking recoveries; in one of the first the Soviet Union led the way. The saiga antelope, noted for its curious swollen nose, once inhabited almost the whole of the Palaearctic, from Britain eastwards across Siberia and even to the western tip of Alaska. Within historic times, however, it has been largely confined to the steppes of Central Asia, where the Tartars, Kazakhs and other then nomadic tribes hunted it for its meat and hides and also for its horns, valued in Chinese medicine. By the beginning of the present century they had so overhunted it that barely a thousand were thought to survive, in nine widely scattered localities. So one of the first acts of the new Soviet government was to pass, in 1919, a law forbidding the hunting of the saiga. This almost miraculous event, for Russia was in its post-revolutionary turmoil, with armies of all kinds laying waste the countryside, saved the remaining stock. It took ten years or so for the saiga to start increasing again, but once it took off, it did so with remarkable speed. Within 30 years it had again become the most numerous wild ungulate in the USSR, so that hunting was allowed again by 1951 in European Russia and in 1954 also in Kazakhstan. Today, with a total population of around three million, the saiga is once more an important natural resource, exploited sustainably to supply every year hundreds of thousands of hides, 6000 tons of meat, industrial fats and various pharmaceutical products.

Saiga antelope

The American counterpart of the saiga is the pronghorn antelope, the only antelope in the New World. When Europeans first arrived, as many as 30–50 million pronghorns may have been ranging the prairies from southern Canada to northern Mexico. As cultivation and livestock grazing consumed the prairies, the pronghorns steadily fell back, until by 1915 fewer than 15,000 survived. At this point conservation measures began, and within ten years numbers had doubled. By 1985 the population had risen to 800,000 in what has reasonably been claimed as 'the wildlife success of the century' in the western hemisphere. The pronghorn is now well protected in reserves and refuges throughout its former range, except in Mexico, where two subspecies, in Baja California and the Sonora Desert, still have very low numbers and are constantly threatened by domestic stock overgrazing their range. In the US the pronghorn is an excellent example of a wild animal that is being managed as an economic asset without interfering with other land uses.

Pronghorn antelope

Another antelope saved in this way is the subspecies of the mountain gazelle *Gazella gazella*, which inhabits Syria and Palestine. Hunting bans removed the immediate danger in Israel and Jordan, but most of the Jordanian desert is quite close to Saudi Arabia, which has a tradition of somewhat intemperate hunting.

In South America the vicuña provides another success story. This relative of the camels and llama inhabits the puna, the treeless plains of the high Andes, and originally extended from 7°S in Peru to south of 30° in both

Chile and Argentina. Valued even in pre-Conquistador times for its extremely fine wool, it has over the years been increasingly overexploited for this now-luxury product. Unfortunately, though the Incas used to round the animals up for an annual shearing, their successors have disregarded the wise advice of Simon Bolivar to do the same, preferring to follow the easier, but non-sustainable practice of killing them for their fleeces. By 1957 only 400,000 were left, and over the next eight years gross overexploitation reduced them to a mere 6000 throughout their range. In 1967, however, Peru began the process of recovery by establishing the Pampa Galeras reserve, and two years later an agreement signed by four Andean countries in La Paz, Bolivia, banned both hunting and trade in vicuña products. More recently the CITES Convention has put more teeth in the laws controlling its export from South America by banning imports into most of the developed world. By 1982 the world population of wild vicuña had risen again to 101,215 in 21 national parks or reserves, of which 70 per cent were in Peru, mainly in Pampa Galeras.

Only in Pampa Galeras, however, was it possible to contemplate starting to exploit vicuña once more, and so redeem the Peruvian Government's pledge to the local people, whose grazing lands the vicuña use, that they should benefit from any future legal trade in vicuña products, which include meat and hides as well as wool. Unhappily the public relations side of the resumption of exploitation was badly handled. Some conservation bodies challenged the stock estimates on which it was based, and alleged the culling methods were inhumane. However, the validity of the Peruvian annual counts has now been vindicated by a scientific mission from IUCN/WWF, whose recommendations, if carried out, should ensure that this most successful Peruvian essay in the sustainable conservation of a natural resource should in future not only maintain the gene pool, but also benefit both the local inhabitants and the national exchequer. It is of the utmost importance for the future of genetic resource conservation world-wide that this particular enterprise should not only be successful, but be widely seen and acknowledged to be successful. Implicit in this, of course, is the proviso that all harvesting should be done humanely.

The koala is a marsupial that is sometimes called the native bear of Australia. Of course it is no such thing, but it certainly looks even more attractive than the teddy bears of toyshops. Once abundant throughout the eucalyptus forests of eastern Australia, such was the level of commercial exploitation for its fur that by 1939 the koala was extinct in South Australia and reduced to 200 in New South Wales and about 1000 in Victoria. Only in Queensland did it survive in any numbers, and there only 10,000 were left, where a century before there may have been as many millions. An added hazard was that so-called sportsmen derived a perverted pleasure from picking off stationary koalas in the trees above them, even in national parks, often with such indifferent marksmanship that the animals were left to die after several inaccurate shots. Not until the early 1920s had the authorities been prevailed upon to do anything at all to stem this wanton destruction. Even then Queensland relapsed, and allowed an open season in 1927, when 600,000 skins were exported. However, since World War II the various state wildlife departments have made amends, and there are now more than 40,000 koalas in Victoria alone. Indeed this animal, which featured strongly in Harper's *Extinct and Vanishing Animals of the Old World* in 1945, did not qualify at all for the first edition of the IUCN Mammal Red Data Book only 21 years later.

Marine mammals provide several good examples of how an over-exploited stock can quite quickly recover, if exploitation ceases and the habitat remains unimpaired, as the sea otter, until the late twentieth

Koala

century, has done. The recoveries of the sea otter and Kerguelen fur seal were described earlier.) Protection has also enabled both the Galapagos fur seal and the Cape fur seal to rebuild their stocks. Populations of king penguins, which were almost exterminated on Heard Island and the McDonald Islands off Tasmania, are also recovering.

Northern pribilof fur seal

The recovery of the northern or Pribilof fur seal is even more instructive. In 1786, when the Russian navigator Gerassim Pribilof discovered the two islands in the far North Pacific that now bear his name, 2.5 million of these seals may have been breeding there. The sealers of Russia, Canada and the US quickly cashed in on this cornucopia, and within twenty years had almost succeeded in exterminating the resource. In 1805 Russia imposed the first of a series of stop-go bans that lasted through the nineteenth century. By allowing only males to be killed the Russians, and the Americans after they bought the islands in 1867, managed to preserve some stocks until the 1880s, when British and Canadian sealers took to sealing on the high seas. This nearly finished the seals off once more, until an international treaty forbade pelagic sealing. Japanese and Canadian sealers were bought off with small quotas of seal-skins, and the US Government established a management regime based on sustainable yield. Stocks have now been built right back to more than 1.5 million, and the controlled harvest produces sums well in excess of $1 million a year for Alaska's state budget. However, numbers are now falling again, for reasons not yet fully understood, but perhaps connected with the ghost nets discussed elsewhere.

In the southern hemisphere, when the Kerguelen fur seal became commercially extinct for the first time, in the 1820s, the sealers turned to the southern elephant seal and within 70-80 years came near to exterminating that too. Elephant seals are named from their strikingly inflatable proboscis, fully developed only in adult bulls. By 1910 numbers had recovered to permit sealing to restart on the strictly controlled lines that were proving so successful with the northern fur seals. Only bulls more than three metres long may be taken, and each seal yields an average of some 400 litres of oil. The world population of southern elephant seals is now estimated at upwards of 700,000, of which around half are on South Georgia, where sealing is forbidden, about 100,000 each on Kerguelen and Macquarie, and the rest scattered around the Antarctic and Sub-antarctic, including the Falklands and Gough Island. A similar story can be told about the northern elephant seal on the Pacific coasts of the US and Mexico. Down to barely a hundred a century ago, it now numbers more than 90,000. Likewise Hooker's sealion in the sub-antarctic Auckland Islands, which has recovered from near extinction 90 years ago to 6000-7000 today.

Southern elephant seal

The prescription of ceasing to hunt has, however, succeeded with only one whale stock so far, the eastern or California stock of the gray whale. Although the North Atlantic right whale has been protected for nearly 50 years, it still shows no sign of recovery, so it is probably too soon to expect any significant results from the protection of the blue whale and the humpback, which dates back only some twenty years. Indeed, once a whale stock falls below a certain level, the chance of a male and female meeting at the right time of year to mate must be very small.

The gray whale breeds in the waters off Baja California, Mexico, travelling north to summer in the plankton-rich waters of the Arctic. It escaped serious whaling until the 1840s, after which the usual bonanza reduced it to near extinction by the 1920s. When the whalers were no longer interested, the customary procedure of shutting the stable door too late was invoked. Protection in both Mexican and US waters has built the number of gray whales wintering off California up again to 6000. Indeed they have

Humpback whale

become such a tourist attraction in both US and Mexican California that
restrictions have had to be placed on the boatloads of tourists who were
disturbing the calving whales in Scammons Lagoon and elsewhere along
the Baja coast. At San Diego thousands of people are able to watch the
migrating whales as they come close inshore. The western stock of the gray
whale, which breeds off Korea, has taken longer to recover, doubtless
because protection was less efficient. However, Russian biologists claim it
is now increasing slowly, and Kamchatka fishermen are allowed to take fifty
a year.

   The classic instance of a bird saved in this way is the whooping crane.
Thanks to overshooting and marsh drainage, this magnificent large white

Whooping crane

bird had by 1941 plummeted to the extraordinarily low level of only 15
birds known in the wild, all at the traditional winter quarters at Aransas on
the Texas coast. Even in the mid-nineteenth century there may only have
been some 1300 birds, including a sedentary breeding stock in Louisiana,
but trigger-happiness disposed of this stock by 1918. As Kai Curry-

Lindahl says, probably no government agencies or conservation societies in the world have ever made such tremendous efforts to save a species as have the United States and Canada to save the whooping crane. Massive education campaigns have aimed to prevent hunting losses, and Aransas has been set aside as an official wildlife refuge. When the Texas stock was shown to be breeding in Wood Buffalo National Park in northern Canada, special measures were taken here too. Numbers at Aransas have now built up to more than 70, and captive breeding has begun to augment the wild flocks.

American alligator

At least two reptile stocks have been brought back from the verge of extinction by hunting bans, the American alligator in the south-eastern United States and the green turtle on Aldabra. Originally numbering millions, the alligator ranged west beyond the Mississippi and north into Virginia. Drainage of marshes and hide-hunting, as well as the killing of what were often believed to be animals too dangerous to be allowed near human settlements, reduced their numbers, on a scale matching the fall of the passenger pigeon, from over 10 million to a mere 600,000 in 1969, mostly between Florida and Louisiana. In that year the US banned international trade in alligator hides and products; interstate trade was also forbidden and some states prohibited internal trade too. The result was a spectacular increase back to several million by 1979. The authorities were therefore able to start exploitation again on a sustainable basis, although this has also regrettably led to a resurgence of poaching. When alligators were completely protected, special steps had to be taken to deal with those which were a physical danger to human life and welfare; thus in 1978 Florida set up an Alligator Control Program, whose products could be traded.

In the Seychelles the green turtle has been overexploited for many years, especially on Assumption and Aldabra. The total ban on green turtle capture imposed in 1968 was, as Jeanne A. Mortimer of the SSC Marine Turtle Group says, 'unenforceable, unpopular, and ignored virtually everywhere but at Aldabra'. As a result the green turtle stocks of Aldabra have recovered significantly, more than doubling from the fewer than 1000 nesting females a year estimated in the early 1970s.

Green turtle

However, the halting of exploitation does not always lead to recovery. The California sardine fishery collapsed from overfishing – as Michener recorded in *Cannery Row* – but despite 40 years of almost no fishing, the California stock of this widespread Pacific fish has not recovered. Other fishes appear to have increased as the sardine decreased, and by maintaining their new dominance have pre-empted the sardine's revival.

2. Recovery by Protecting the Habitat

Saving a species from extinction is rarely achieved by one method only. For a species to survive, it must both have habitat and not be overexploited. However, at least as many animals have been saved primarily by preserving their habitat as by checking their overexploitation. The most striking instance is provided by the tiger in India. The third quarter of the present century saw unprecedented destruction of both wildlife and its habitat in newly independent India. The tiger, being top of the food chain, was one of the chief sufferers, and by 1969 may have been reduced from some 40,000 at the turn of the century to no more than 2500 in the whole of India. The first alarm was sounded at the New Delhi meeting of IUCN in 1969, but at first many people were reluctant to believe that so numerous an animal could actually be in danger of extinction. They had, however, failed to take adequate account of the twin effects of widespread destruction of the jungle for timber, firewood and cattle grazing, and direct killing both by hunters in search of skins and trophies and by villagers who poisoned animals that, thanks to a shortage of natural prey, had become a threat to their livestock. And of course there were always the few man-eaters to give the tiger a bad name, especially in the mangrove forests of the Sundarbans in Bengal. Here a whole population of man-eaters, extending into Bangladesh, regularly preyed on woodcutters and other peasants seeking their livelihood in these wet jungles. In 1972 a more scientific estimate of 1827 tigers for the whole of India provided the final stimulus to enable WWF to persuade the Government of India to launch Project Tiger.

This has been one of the most successful single conservation exercises of the past 20-30 years, and represents a remarkable co-operative effort between the Indian Government and two international non-governmental bodies, WWF and IUCN. In India eleven areas, most of them already national parks or wildlife sanctuaries, were designated as special tiger reserves, each with a central core area free from all human use and a buffer area in which only conservation-oriented use is allowed. Four more were added later, and the core areas of these fifteen reserves totalled 8608 square kilometres with a further 23,437 square kilometres in their buffer zones. They included such well known sites as Corbett National Park, Uttar Pradesh; Bandipur, Karnataka; Kanha, Madhya Pradesh; and Sundarbans, West Bengal.

The net result of spending much more money on these fifteen areas was the effective protection of more than 30,000 square kilometres of habitat both from poaching and from encroachment by logging and grazing. Sometimes it involved the resettlement of whole villages on more fertile land. The response of the habitat has been swift. Streams are flowing for a longer period of the year, and carry much less silt during monsoons. Fire protection has increased both the food available for wild ungulates and the amount of humus forming on forest floors. Consequently the animal populations have also increased and along with their prey the number of tigers; the estimate for all India had risen by 60 per cent to 3012 by 1979. In the actual tiger reserves the number of tigers rose even more sharply, from 268 in nine reserves in 1972 to 757 in eleven reserves in 1981.

Project Tiger is the answer to those who maintain that species conservation is unimportant, so long as habitat is conserved. The essential extra expenditure on the tiger reserves could never have been achieved without using the tiger's name. No Indian central or state government would have been allowed to spend an extra 150 million rupees ($16 million) on 30,000 square kilometres of habitat for its own sake; only association with the tiger made this possible. Indonesia and Thailand have also launched major tiger conservation programmes under the aegis of WWF's Operation Tiger.

A similar story on a smaller scale can be told for the Indian lion. In former times the lion, not the tiger, was the symbol of strength in India, whence at a long remove the British lion symbol. Today the only remaining lions in Asia are in the Gir Forest in Gujarat, where they survived solely because the Nawab of Junagadh protected them in his private domains. The same factors that affected the tiger told still more against the lion; even its last stronghold was so overgrazed by cattle that there was less and less grazing for the lions' natural prey, such as wild pig and sambur deer. By 1968 the annual census figure was down to 177. Soon afterwards the Gujarat state authorities began to treat the Gir in the same way as the tiger reserves. The central area was declared a national park, with stock grazing forbidden, and sealed off by a 220-kilometre rubble wall. The villagers

Tiger

Asiatic lion

whose cattle had been grazing in the forest were resettled elsewhere, and this in turn has led to a recovery both of the habitat and of the lions' natural prey. In May 1985, 239 lions were counted in the Gir Forest.

Two species of rhinoceros have been saved, and their stocks rebuilt, by a combination of banning hunting and preserving habitat: the white or square-lipped, and the Javan. The southern race of the white rhino, the largest land mammal after the elephants, was once widespread and locally abundant in southern Africa, but by the end of the last century Boer and British farmers and sportsmen had almost exterminated it. When a tiny remnant was discovered in 1894, near the junction of the Black and White Umfolozi Rivers in Zululand, sportsmen hastened to shoot six more of them in that year. Although the Umfolozi game reserve was created to protect them in 1897, as late as 1929 only twenty southern white rhinos survived in the world, all in Umfolozi, and three had been poached in 1928. A year later it was actually proposed to abolish the reserve, but an outcry secured the reversal of that decision, and at long last the Natal Government began to combat poaching effectively. Within five years the rhinos began to spread into the nearby Hluhluwe reserve, and by 1945 the joint population of the two reserves totalled 250-300. The situation having thus been saved, the pendulum soon swung to the other extreme, and by 1960, with 800 rhinos, they were beginning to overgraze their habitat. Since the reserves could not be enlarged, the Natal Parks Board began the enlightened policy of translocation.

White rhino

The saving of the Javan rhino was one of the great achievements of the IUCN Survival Service Commission (as it then was) under Sir Peter Scott's chairmanship. This smaller relative of the great Indian rhino was once widespread throughout south-eastern Asia, but today, despite reports of its presence on the borders of Laos and Cambodia, the only certainly known population is in the Udjung Kulon reserve at the western tip of Java. By 1964 no more than about two dozen were believed to remain, and the SSC made great efforts to secure proper management of this reserve, including the provision of a motor-boat for communication both with and within it, which was the first project financed by the Revolving Fund of the Fauna Preservation Society and WWF. The need for a continuing scientific presence was recognised and the reserve has ever since been in the capable hands of the Swiss zoologists Rudolf and Lotte Schenkel. The latest census shows between 40 and 60 rhinos, or an approximate doubling in fifteen years. Constant effort is still needed to maintain Udjung Kulon in a condition suitable for the rhinos, as their preferred diet of saplings and small trees seems to be diminishing, driving them to eat vines and even mangroves. It may well be that the rhino capacity of this reserve too has reached its ceiling.

There are a good many examples of birds being saved by the protection of their habitat. Thus when the takahe, a large gallinule believed extinct for 50 years, was rediscovered in 1948 in the Murchison Mountains in the extreme south of New Zealand, a reserve of 400,000 acres was immediately set aside for it, to safeguard the future of the 250 takahes against all but natural forces. Control of the introduced red deer, which had been overgrazing the habitat, led to an improvement of the critically important forest understory and tussock lands. Unfortunately natural forces are at the moment adverse and severe winters are taking toll of young takahes; if the adults were not long-lived, the prospects would be bleak.

A similar effort to preserve the much less extensive habitat of the giant Atitlan grebe in Guatemala, where it is confined to the 130-square-kilometre lake of that name, rebuilt the population from 80 birds in 1964 to about 100 pairs – the lake is believed to be able to hold a maximum of 280

Giant Atitlan grebe

birds. However, development threats of all kinds still hang over the lake and its rarity, whose future is far from clear. In 1968 ICBP bought Cousin Island in the Seychelles, sole home of the Seychelles brush warbler, and set about restoring its habitat, which had been partly replaced with coconut palms. Numbers have now increased from 85 to well over 300.

The peregrine in Britain is an excellent example of a species restored by ceasing to pollute its habitat. As mentioned, voluntary restriction on the use of certain pesticides in agriculture allowed the peregrine population of Britain, which by 1963 had fallen to only 16 per cent of its pre-war total of 825 pairs, to rise again to 92 per cent of that figure by 1981. Similarly, the brown pelican recovered from a severe pesticide-induced crash in the south-eastern United States in the late 1960s and early 1970s to the point where by 1985 it was no longer officially regarded as endangered or threatened.

One of the main methods used to rebuild the populations of the Galapagos giant tortoise has been to restore the habitat by removing the many goats that had grazed the vegetation in so much of the islands down to the ground, e.g. on Española (Hood). On Aldabra the habitat is pristine, but the very large population of Aldabra giant tortoises would undoubtedly have been severely reduced if the Anglo-American plan to develop the atoll as a military airfield had not been scotched in the 1960s. Mention was made previously of the Devil's hole pupfish and how its tiny habitat in California has been preserved.

A plant which has recovered as a result of the clearance of goats which were overgrazing its range is the cabbage tree *Cordyline kaspar*, confined to Three Kings Islands off the northernmost point of New Zealand. When the goats were removed from the largest of these islands in 1946, the tree began to regenerate well from seed. There are eleven other endemic plants on these islands, one of which, *Tecomanthe speciosa* (Bignoniaceae), reduced to a single tree, does not seem to be regenerating, perhaps because of the total loss of its forest habitat.

Cahow

3. Recovery by Removing Predators or Competing Species

Several examples have already been given of the danger to small populations of introduced predators, or of native predators which have increased, so adding to the threats to many already endangered species. It is not so easy to cite instances where the removal of such predators has been a primary factor in the recovery of an endangered species. Perhaps the best known example is the Bermudian cahow, a petrel that was so numerous in the sixteenth century that the early colonists relied on it for food. Even by 1616 it had been overexploited, and none were seen after the 1660s, until in 1951 a small stock was located on an offshore islet. David Wingate and others, struggling to preserve the small group of no more than eighteen pairs, have constantly been obliged both to clear the nesting islets of rats and to deal with competition from the larger and more aggressive white-tailed tropicbird for the relatively few suitable nest sites. The struggle has succeeded, but so far the number of cahow pairs has never risen above 26. Artificial nesting burrows, to which the cahows are now accustomed, have been made, and wooden baffles have been fitted to the entrances of occupied burrows; both devices keep the tropicbirds out but let the cahows in.

There are many more instances where the control of predators or competitors makes an important contribution to a recovery. Kirtland's warbler, confined to lower northern Michigan, was threatened by the spread of the parasitic brown-headed cowbird, against which it had evolved no defences. The cowbirds were trapped and removed, and this particular threat seems to have receded, although the warbler's habitat requirements, stands of jack pine *Pinus banksiana* that are 8-22 years old, are not yet secure. Attacks by the pearly-eyed thrasher, a recent immigrant, on the nest sites, eggs and young of the critically endangered Puerto Rico parrot, now down to fewer than twenty birds, seem to have been stemmed by manipulation of their nest cavities.

Destruction of rats and feral dogs, which preyed on their eggs and young, has been another important weapon in rebuilding the stocks of the giant tortoise, the land iguana and the dark-rumped petrel in the Galapagos.

Galapagos land iguana

4. Recovery by Captive Breeding and Release

More and more species, especially mammals, are being saved and their wild stocks restored by taking a few (occasionally all) of the survivors into captivity, usually in a zoo or botanic garden, breeding them up and then releasing them back into the wild. The first to benefit in this way was the American bison, of which Professor W. A. Fuller of the University of Alberta has said: 'As an example of the profligate waste of an abundant natural resource, the story of the near extermination of the bison probably stands unsurpassed in recorded history'. When Europeans first invaded North America, buffalo, as they were often called, roamed the prairies in many millions, from Canada down to Texas. They were the staple of the life of the plains Indians, and it was partly to deprive them of their livelihood that the US Government deliberately encouraged the boundless slaughter of a resource one might have supposed they would regard themselves as fortunate to possess. By 1883 only a single genuinely wild herd remained outside Yellowstone National Park, which was founded nine years before and was by no means secure from poachers. This herd of about 10,000 was in North Dakota; by November hunters had killed them all. It may be some small consolation that many other hunters bankrupted themselves by setting out that year to seek the non-existent huge herds which they firmly believed had perversely migrated northwards. In 1889 only 541 plains bison were known to remain in all North America (there were still some wood bison in northern Canada), all of them either in Yellowstone or in captivity.

American bison

Three years earlier William Hornaday, Superintendent of the National Zoological Park in Washington DC, had led a Smithsonian expedition that secured 25 of the last wild specimens for the national museum. A few years later he went again and found none. Then at last he saw the light and became the first penitent butcher, to use the nickname applied to members of the Society for the Preservation of the Wild Fauna of the Empire in London twenty years later. In 1894 Congress passed the first law protecting the bison. Eight years later it appropriated $15,000 to buy animals to build up the small herd surviving in Yellowstone. In 1905 the American Bison Society was founded at the Bronx Zoo in New York to breed bison in captivity for later release, and the New York Zoological Society gave fifteen animals to help establish a free-ranging herd in the newly established Wichita Mountains reserve in Oklahoma. In all these moves the hand of the penitent Hornaday was not far away. Today, with well over 30,000 plains bison in national parks and wildlife refuges in the US, still including Yellowstone, and 10,000 more in Canada, the American bison has definitely been saved.

When the plains bison was under increasing pressure in the wild at the end of the last century, so was the woodland race, whose original range extended northwards from the open aspen woodland of Saskatchewan and

Alberta to the coniferous forests of the North-west Territories, and southwards along the wooded parts of the Rockies to Colorado. In 1891 the wood bison was down to a remnant south of the Great Slave Lake, where the Canadian Government protected it. By 1922, when Wood Buffalo National Park was created in northern Alberta, the wood bison had built back to some 1500-2000. Then came an uncovenanted disaster. In the mid-1920s more than 6000 plains bison from the Wainwright Park in southern Alberta were removed to Wood Buffalo Park and proceeded to hybridise the wood bison out of existence. Not until 1957 was a small pure-bred herd of the original wood bison stock found on the upper Nyarling River, some 75 miles across swampy country from the main hybrid herds. In 1965 this pure-bred stock was estimated at less than 100, but two dozen have been moved to another isolated site close to the Great Slave Lake, and 45 more have been taken to Elk Island Park in the aspen zone of central Alberta. So the future of this race too seems to be assured.

European bison

The European bison or wisent has also been saved by captive breeding. Once found in the forests of the greater part of Europe and western Siberia, by 1900 the only surviving herds were in the Bialowieza Forest in eastern Poland and in the foothills of the Caucasus, the latter being a distinct race. In both places World War I and its turbulent aftermath led to the extinction of the wisent in the wild, apparently in the early 1920s in Poland and about 1925 in the Caucasus. The Caucasian race became totally extinct, but luckily enough of the Polish stock remained in captivity to enable the International Society for the Protection of the European Bison, founded in 1923, to restore it. In 1931 the Society published its first pedigree book, with records of 30 pure-bred beasts. World War II was less disastrous, and 98 animals survived to be listed in the first post-war pedigree book, all in various European zoos. Today there are well over 1000 wisent in the world, and they have been re-established in the Bialowieza Forest and in at least eleven reserves in various parts of the Soviet Union, including Prioksko Terrasny south of Moscow and the Caucasus National Park. The wisent can therefore be counted as one of the great successes of captive breeding, and Poland and the Soviet Union deserve full credit for the persistence with which they have pursued this aim, often in very difficult circumstances.

One step further back in the process of restoration to the wild is Przewalski's horse, which, ever since it was discovered in the mid-nineteenth century by the Pole whose name it bears, seems to have been confined to the mountainous country along the Chinese-Mongolian border. The acquisition of firearms by the nomads of this region, coupled with the steady spread of their domestic livestock across the the wild horses' plains habitat, has made these increasingly scarce, until they now appear to be extinct in Mongolia, at least since the 1960s, and also probably in China. Even before World War I they were being bred in captivity at the two famous collections at Askaniya Nova in the Ukraine and Woburn Abbey in Britain. Both these stocks, however, died out, and the present world population of 219 animals derives entirely from two small herds, each about a dozen strong, which survived at the Prague and Munich zoos in 1950. We have now reached the point where reintroduction into the wild can be contemplated, and plans are going ahead to release some into what are termed 'semi-reserves', at first in the Netherlands, and later in the horses' original Asian range in Mongolia.

Przewalski's horse

The mi-lu or Père David's deer is unique in several ways. It grows two sets of antlers a year and has a long donkey-like tail. It is also the only large animal, not changed by domestication, whose natural habitat we do not know, although it is believed to have been marshy because of the mi-lu's broad feet. This zoological oddity was made known to western science in

1865, when the French explorer-priest Armand David became the first foreigner to see what lay inside the 45-mile wall of the Imperial Hunting Park of Nan-Hai-Tsoe just south of Beijing (Peking). He realised at once that these strange deer were something new and bribed the guards to let him have a specimen for the Musée d'Histoire Naturelle in Paris. The mi-lu, which has since been found in subfossil deposits, may have been extinct in the wild for some 3000 years, and we shall probably never know just how it came to be preserved in the park. It was fortunate that British and French diplomats later also managed to smuggle some live specimens out, for in 1895 a flood breached the park wall and all but a handful of the deer escaped and were either drowned or poached. Five years later the foreign troops quelling the Boxer rebellion killed off most of the remainder, and within a few years the mi-lu became extinct in China. However, at this juncture the eleventh Duke of Bedford stepped in and persuaded the zoos of Europe to let him collect together all the available animals, to a total of eighteen, in his large park at Woburn Abbey and build the stock up again. Despite many vicissitudes during the two world wars, there are now 1188 mi-lus in captivity throughout the world, including 385 still at Woburn, and they are soon to be restored to the wild in a reserve in China.

Père David's deer

Three South African ungulates, the bontebok, the black wildebeest and the Cape mountain zebra, have been saved by being taken into near captivity. The ancestors of both Afrikaner and British communities bear total responsibility for the decline of these three and of the white rhino to near extinction, as well as for the actual extinction of two zebras, two antelopes and the local race of the lion. The Dutch arrived at the Cape of Good Hope in 1652 and only four years later the Cape mountain zebra, which was apparently never numerous, was in need of protection. When the British took over in 1806 they relaxed the hunting laws and the usual hunters' free-for-all took place, with the following trophies being chalked up on the board:

Blaauwbok *Hippotragus leucophaeus*: extinct 1800
Cape lion *Panthera leo melanochaitus*: extinct c1865
Quagga *Equus burchelli quagga*: extinct c1878
Bontekwagga *E.b.burchelli*: extinct before 1909
Red hartebeest *Alcelaphus buselaphus caama*: extinct in South Africa by 1945

The bontebok was always rather restricted in its range, in south-western Cape Province, and but for a few Afrikaner families, who preserved it on their farms in the 1860s, it would certainly have become extinct. By 1931 it was down to only seventeen individuals, but now, thanks to careful restoration policies, there are nearly 1000, a few in the wild state in the Swellendam district, but most either in reserves, notably the Bontebok National Park near Cape Town with more than 250, or on private farms or ranches.

The history of the black wildebeest, the original gnu, is very similar. It once extended as far north as the Transvaal, but since it is an inquisitive animal that stands and stares at any strange object, including a man with a gun, Boer farmers were able to shoot huge numbers in the 1870s to feed their labourers, and numbers eventually fell to a few hundred. However, once they were protected, they thrived so well in Mountain Zebra National Park that they now total well over 2000 and the species appears to be out of danger. The situation of the red hartebeest is somewhat different, in that the original South African stock was exterminated, but it has been successfully reintroduced from Namibia to various reserves in Cape Province, Orange Free State and Transvaal.

Like the bontebok, the Cape mountain zebra was saved by a few Boer farmers who preserved it on their farms, where breeding proved only patchily successful, so its future was not assured until the Mountain Zebra National Park was set up in north-eastern Cape Province in 1937. Even then the first attempt failed and it took two large infusions of fresh breeding stock and a substantial extension of the park boundaries to bring about the present encouraging position, with 171 of the surviving world stock of about 215 in the park.

Arabian oryx

The most recent example of successful restoration of a captive-bred large animal to the wild is the white or Arabian oryx, in an operation which took twenty years to bring to fruition. By the early 1960s the white oryx, which once inhabited the whole Arabian peninsula, was down to 100-200 animals in the extreme south of the great Rub al Khali desert, the Empty Quarter, on the borders of what are now Oman and South Yemen. They were being hunted each year, mainly by motorised parties of Arab princes, whose increased mobility, coupled with the efficiency of modern firearms, were clearly going to eliminate the oryx within a very few years. In 1962 the Fauna Preservation Society, largely financed by the new-born World Wildlife Fund, sent an expedition to the Empty Quarter to secure a stock for captive breeding and eventual return to the wild. Only three oryx were actually caught by Operation Oryx, but with a few more added from the London, Kuwait and Riyadh Zoos, a breeding herd was soon established at Phoenix Zoo, Arizona, chosen because of its desert climate. This was the World Herd of Arabian Oryx, run by four societies as informal trustees.

Meanwhile in 1972 another raiding party, apparently from Abu Dhabi, succeeded in actually exterminating the white oryx in the wild, just inside Oman. This is one of the few instances where we know the actual moment of extinction of a mammal in the wild. No reliable reports have been received of any wild white oryx since that date. However, the white oryx fortunately breeds well in captivity. The World Herd flourished at Phoenix and later also at San Diego and Brownsville Zoos; an independent herd did well at Los Angeles Zoo; and the Arab raids of the 1950s and 1960s led to numerous small breeding herds on sheikhs' private estates up and down the Gulf, with one substantial herd of 30-40 at Qatar. Then white oryx began to be returned from America, first from the World Herd at San Diego to Jordan, later from Los Angeles to Israel, for Avraham Joffe's Hai-Bar Reserve in the Negev Desert. In 1983 the Jordanian herd of 31 was released into the large, fenced 22 km² enclosure at Shaumari near Azraq.

Finally, in 1980, four years after Oman had decreed the total protection of the white oryx, San Diego began to send the nucleus of a breeding herd back there. Two years later the far-sighted plans of Sultan Qaboos bin Said bore fruit and, after an integrated herd with a stable social hierarchy had been built up in the pens, the first oryx were released back into the open Jiddat al Harassis desert in 1982. Here they are guarded by the Harassis, a tribe which holds the white oryx in especial esteem. By 1984 a second herd could be released and the white oryx was re-established as part of the desert ecosystem, the first instance of an animal extinct in the wild being successfully reintroduced.

The Parque de Rescate de la Fauna Sahariana, at Almeria, Spain, specialises in the captive-breeding of endangered North African gazelles. It is likely to supply stock for two reintroduction experiments: of the dama gazelle to the Langue de Barbarie National Park in Senegal, for which stock is also available at two zoos, Bronx and Pretoria; and of three gazelle species in Morocco. The Moroccan Government plans to reintroduce dorcas, dama and Cuvier's gazelles and is currently searching for a suitable national park, and also preparing to set up a captive breeding centre for the dama gazelle. Similarly captive stocks of Speke's gazelle, apparently now extinct in the wild, are being built up in five American zoos against the time when they can be restored to their former range on the borders of Ethiopia and Somalia, one of the more war-torn corners of the modern world.

The tule elk, a small pale race of the red deer or American elk, was also successfully restored to the wild from semi-captive stock. The tule elk is endemic to California, where it originally inhabited the marshy and perennial bunchgrass plains of the valley bottoms, including those dominated by tule (cattails). At first it numbered hundreds of thousands, but after gross overexploitation during the Gold Rush, which began in 1849, it was believed extinct by the late 1860s. In 1874, however, a tiny remnant, possibly only a single pair, was found in the tule marshes north of Buena Vista Lake in the southern San Joaquin Valley, and careful protection built numbers up again, though no longer on this site. Complaints from neighbouring farmers led to repeated attempts to establish herds elsewhere, the first to succeed being at Cache Creek in the coastal range north of Sacramento in 1922, where there are now 120 deer. In 1933-34 a herd was established in the Owens Valley, on land belonging to the city of Los Angeles and actually outside the elk's original range. This proved embarrassingly successful, and when the elk began to break out into neighbouring farms, a political battle ensued between farmers and sportsmen on the one hand and conservationists and animal welfare societies on the other. Eventually the federal authorities were brought in and the carrying capacity of the valley fixed at 490 animals. The surplus deer are now being relocated within their original range instead of all being shot, and by 1982 thirteen areas had been stocked with a total of 872 elk, including 487 in Owens Valley. The management plan for this subspecies, no longer considered in danger of extinction, wisely includes an eventual controlled harvest.

In 1972 several hundred northern sea otters from Alaska were translocated to more southern parts of the coast, where the species had become extinct: 412 to south-eastern Alaska, 89 to Vancouver Island, and 152 to Washington and Oregon. Of these the Alaskan release seems to have proved the most successful.

A rodent once found throughout the Bahamas, the Bahamian hutia, was by 1970 confined probably mainly by introduced predators, to a single islet, East Plana Cay. Thanks to translocations in 1973 and 1981, however, it is now breeding on three islands and is considered well on the way to recovery.

Replenishment of depleted wild stocks of gamebirds and waterfowl with captive-bred specimens is a widespread practice of long standing, referred to on p. 82. Game farms for rearing pheasants, partridged and ducks are a thriving industry in North America and western Europe, but virtually all their output is 'consumed' by hunters. Overall there is probably just as much replenishment of native stocks, such as grey or Hungarian partridge in Europe or of long-established alien stocks, as with the pheasant in western Europe and North America.

There have been fewer successful reintroductions of endangered birds than of mammals. The most notable recent effort has still not proved itself in the wild, although it has succeeded very well in building up the captive stocks. The nene or Hawaiian goose is confined to the Hawaiian archipelago, where 80 years ago some 25,000 inhabited the flanks of three volcanoes on the 'Big Island' of Hawaii, with perhaps another stock on Maui. Habitat destruction by introduced feral goats and pigs and predation by introduced cats, dogs, rats and mongooses reduced this total to no more than about 30 in the wild by the early 1950s. Luckily there were also thirteen in captivity, so that a captive-breeding rescue operation could be

Ture elk

Sea otter

Nene or Hawaiian goose

launched in Hawaii in 1949; the supply of a few birds resulting from this to Sir Peter Scott's infant Wildfowl Trust was the fuse of a veritable explosion, which has led to a world captive stock of well over 1250 today. By 1960 some could be returned to the wild, and nearly 2000 captive-bred birds, many of them from the Wildfowl Trust, have now been released, both on the Big Island and on the Halekala crater on Maui. It is not clear, however, whether the wild stock will be able to maintain itself without further reinforcements. On Maui the nene is clearly not maintaining itself, probably because of attacks by mongooses and other introduced predators on both eggs and goslings.

More successful is the peregrine recovery effort based at the Cornell Laboratory of Ornithology at Ithaca, New York, in the east and the World Center for Birds of Prey at Boise, Idaho, in the west. The peregrine falcon or duck hawk was one of the main victims of the great pesticide splurge of the 1950s and 1960s, which provoked Rachel Carson's *Silent Spring*. By 1965 the whole peregrine stock of eastern North America appeared to have been wiped out, with similar but less complete crashes elsewhere on the continent. In 1970 Tom Cade began his pioneer breeding programme at Cornell, and within three years three captive pairs produced twenty young in one season. Other breeders had similar successes, so that by 1985 the Peregrine Fund was able to produce 260 young birds at its western captive breeding centres. After some anxious discussion about the genetic consequences of mixing blood lines, releases began. In eleven years from 1971 the US and Canadian breeding programmes between them released more than a thousand birds. By 1985, 38-40 pairs originating from Cornell were nesting along the East Coast, of which two dozen produced eggs and at least sixteen hatched young. In the west, where the bird never actually died out, peregrines are now seen more often in the mountain and western states, thanks to the efforts of the Peregrine Fund.

A similar programme is now being planned for both the osprey and the bald eagle in North America, and one is already under way for the Mississippi sandhill crane in a specially created reserve on the Gulf coast. Eggs of the still highly endangered whooping crane from Wood Buffalo National Park in Canada were put under foster sandhill cranes in Grays Lake wildlife refuge, Idaho, and this has established a second wild flock. Eggs of the even more endangered California condor have recently been hatched in San Diego Zoo for rearing and captive breeding with a view to ultimate release. In the Philippines an attempt is being made to breed Philippine eagles in captivity, also for eventual release, but it faces formidable difficulties. The plan to save the Mauritius pink pigeon has achieved around 100 birds in captivity, and the first pair has recently been released into the wild in Mauritius.

The New Zealand Wildlife Department has pioneered 'marooning', the translocation of stocks of endangered species to safer habitats, usually offshore islands, and has also engaged in more orthodox captive-breeding operations. The principal success has been with the saddleback, a starling-like bird threatened by rats on several islands, and now after several maroonings considered safer than at any time this century. Brown teal raised at the Mount Bruce Native Bird Reserve have been successfully released on Kapiti Island and several other places.

The most hazardous operation so far has been with the Chatham Island black robin, always very scarce and occurring on only four islands of the Chatham group, some 1000 miles east of New Zealand. It had vanished from two of them by 1871 and from a third when cats were introduced later in the century. By 1976 there were thought to be only seven birds left in the world, all on Little Mangere Island, where their five remaining hectares of

Chatham Island black robin

scrub habitat was being denuded by petrel burrows and damage from the helicopters of poachers harvesting the muttonbirds. So it was decided to remove the entire population to nearby Mangere Island, a former habitat with better scrub. As a trial beforehand, small numbers of South Island robins were removed to three islands in the Marlborough Sounds and became established on two of them. As a further precaution some of the robins' eggs were cross-fostered in the nests of Chatham Island warblers. When this proved unsatisfactory more eggs were cross-fostered with the closely related tomtit on nearby South East Island. By 1984, after vicissitudes including the fall of total numbers to five, the joint population of robins on the two islands had risen to twenty and it was possible to be cautiously optimistic for the success of what had seemed rather a desperate step.

In Bermuda two birds have been successfully reintroduced. A colony of yellow-crowned night herons was re-established on Nonsuch Island, to help control the overabundant land crabs. The restoration of the native forest of *Juniperus bermudiana* on the same island has also made it possible to reintroduce the endemic race of the white-eyed vireo. Its density on Nonsuch is now more than twice that on the mainland, due mainly to the absence of introduced predators.

Giant tortoise

There are also an increasing number of captive-breeding and release programmes for reptiles. The pressures that have brought the Galapagos giant tortoise to extinction, near-extinction or severe depletion, on several of the islands (which incidentally all have both a Spanish and an English name) were discussed earlier. The captive breeding programme at the Charles Darwin Research Station has so far led to the return of more than 500 well grown young tortoises of five races: 139 to San Cristobal (Chatham), where they are threatened by feral donkeys trampling their nests and feral dogs killing their young; 115 to San Salvador (James), where feral pigs destroy both nests and young; 114 to Cerro Azul in eastern Isabela (Albemarle), where predation by feral dogs, cats and pigs is almost total; 182 to Pinzon (Duncan), where the problem is black rats and 79 to Española (Hood), where overgrazing by goats had reduced numbers to two males and fourteen females that were so widely separated that apparently no opportunities for mating ever occurred. It takes so long for giant tortoises to mature sexually that it will be well into the twenty-first century before these returned hatchlings are themselves able to breed.

A similar breeding programme for the Galapagos land iguana has been more successful for the critically endangered Isabela population than for an even more endangered one on Santa Cruz, and these are now beginning to be released into the wild.

At its meeting at Kuala Lumpur, West Malaysia, in 1982 the IUCN Species Survival Commission was shown the Tapah hatchery for the river terrapin *Batagur baska*, and witnessed the release of some hatchlings. The Game Department has several other breeding facilities for this terrapin, which is potentially a valuable natural resource.

The gharial, the most endangered crocodilian of the Indian subcontinent, was on the verge of extinction in the mid-1970s with only 141 surviving in India, 65-70 in Nepal and even fewer in Bangladesh and Pakistan. Captive breeding programmes were started, by India in 1975 and by Nepal in the Royal Chitwan National Park in 1978. From the several Indian breeding stations, including the first two at Tikerpada, Orissa, and Kukrail near Lucknow, a total of 324 young were released into the wild up to March 1980. A year later the first batch of 50 were released in Nepal. It is, of course, too soon to judge the success of these operations in rebuilding the wild stocks. A similar programme for the mugger, the other Indian

Gharial

freshwater crocodile, has returned to the wild more than 400 hatchlings, some contributed by the Madras Crocodile Bank, a voluntary enterprise funded by WWF India.

The restocking of depleted freshwater fish stocks is, like that of gamebirds, a considerable industry in many developed countries. Most of the restocking probably does little more than provide anglers with fish to catch, rather than re-establish self-sustaining populations. There is, however, currently a serious attempt to restock the Thames, once an important salmon river. Some thousands of Atlantic salmon fry have been released in the upper reaches of some Thames tributaries, and numerous adult salmon have returned to the river, so looks as if the Thames has almost recovered from its 150-year-long pollution. A captive stock of the viviparous fish *Gambusia gaigei* is maintained for reintroduction into Big Bend National Park, Texas, where it is threatened by introduced mosquito fish *G.affinis*. So far it has had to be reintroduced three times, on one occasion due to warm spring water failing to reach their pool, so that the whole wild stock died of cold.

One of the best known instances of successful reintroduction of an

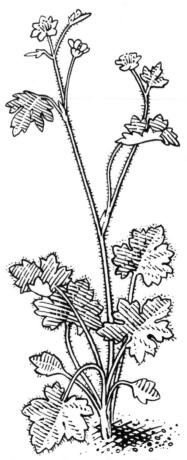

Buttercup Ranunculus pauciflorus

invertebrate is the large copper butterfly at Woodwalton Fen in eastern England. The original British stock became extinct about 1848 due to the drainage of the Fens combined with overcollecting, and 50 years later the European race *rutilus* was unsuccessfully introduced not far away at Wicken Fen. In 1927, however, a further attempt at Woodwalton with the subspecies *batavus*, only discovered in 1915 in Friesland in the Netherlands, succeeded and has persisted to the 1980s. Two more attempts with *rutilus*, in Co.Tipperary, Ireland, lasted from 1913 to 1936 and from 1942 to 1955. Two other successful butterfly introductions were the heath fritillary from Kent into a wood in Essex, where its food-plant cow-wheat was plentiful; and the adonis blue at Old Winchester Hill, Hampshire, the sward of this national nature reserve having been carefully managed by sheep grazing to produce the conditions that favour it.

Large copper butterfly

A good instance of a plant reintroduction is the endemic buttercup *Ranunculus pauciflorus*, which has only one known site, 760m up in the South Island of New Zealand. It is a plant adapted only to dry cold areas on limestone and produces very little seed. In 1948, due to trampling by livestock and grazing by sheep and hares, only 32 plants could be found. So six years later the landowner set up a reserve and seeds were sown. Today there are some 400 plants, and the delegates to the IUCN General Assembly at Christchurch in 1981 were taken to see some more being planted out. This itself was a minor triumph, for it took some time to find out the conditions in which the seeds will germinate freely.

In Europe specimens of the endangered milk-vetch *Astragalus physocalyx*, grown in the Sofia Botanic Garden, have been planted out in its original locality at Plovdiv, Bulgaria, and the feathergrass *Stipa bavarica*, grown in cultivation from wild-collected seed, has been planted out to augment the few remaining wild tufts in its only known locality, a rocky platform above the Danube at Neuburg, Bavaria, which is much visited for its fine view. Two more examples come from North Wales: Cwm Idwal in Snowdonia has been restocked with some 50 plants of tufted saxifrage *Saxifraga cespitosa*, here in its only British locality south of Scotland, that were grown from seed gathered from the only two surviving wild plants; and a similar operation with cuttings and seedlings has doubled the number of plants of wild cotoneaster *Cotoneaster integerrimus* at its only British site, on the headland of the Great Orme.

12 Coda

We already know how to save animals and plants from depletion and extinction. Basically, all we need to do is to maintain their habitat and not to overexploit them. What we do not yet know is how to achieve these two very simple aims in a world where pressure of human population on resources of all kinds is increasing exponentially. The scientific knowledge we already have would suffice if only we could overcome the economic, political and social obstacles to making use of it.

We come back again and again to the responsibility of the public figures of the world, politicians, economists, administrators and churchmen, to ensure the future welfare of those they have been elected or appointed to care for. Most of them, of course, think they are doing their best already. But as we have seen their best is woefully short of what is needed. The genetic resources contained in the animal and plant populations that make up the world's ecosystems are being steadily eroded. Within the lifetime of the majority of people living today an immense potential for their future welfare will be lost if present trends are not sharply reversed.

The last resort is the ecologists and conservationists. It is only they who fully realise what is in store. It is their responsibility to make sure that everybody else, and especially those in authority, understands this too.

APPENDIX
A Glossary of
International Institutions

Nothing is more forbidding to the reader than a text lumbered with information about institutions, whether governmental or non-governmental, and how they work. Wildlife conservation is particularly rich in such institutions, mostly with long names and their almost equally off-putting acronyms. Since the work of many of these bodies is nevertheless vital to species conservation, this information, which has been excluded from the main text in the interest of readability, is given here, in alphabetical order. A list of acronyms is given at the end.

Animal Research and Conservation Center: see New York Zoological Society

Antarctic Convention: the Convention on the Conservation of Antarctic Marine Living Resources, which came into force in April 1981.

Berne Convention: the Convention on the Conservation of European Wildlife and Natural Habitats, an example of regional conventions designed to protect the wildlife of continents or parts of continents; launched in 1979 by the Council of Europe and in force since June 1982. Annexes contain lists of endangered animals and plants that are to be strictly protected.

Biological Investigations of Marine Antarctic Ecosystems and Stocks (BIOMASS): an international research programme of SCAR

Bonn Convention: the Convention on the Conservation of Migratory Species of Wild Animals, originating from a Conference at Bonn, FRG, in 1979, protects scheduled endangered migratory vertebrates and insects and their habitats.

CITES Convention: the Convention on International Trade in Endangered Species of Wild Fauna and Flora, sometimes known as the Washington Convention; ratified by 91 countries by 1986. Five biennial meetings of the Parties had been held by 1985.

Conservation for Development Centre : see IUCN

Conservation Monitoring Centre: see IUCN

Convention on Long-range Transboundary Air Pollution: signed within the framework of the UN Economic Commission for Europe in 1979 and came into force in

March 1983; 35 countries have signed and 24 of these have ratified.

Earthwatch: see UNEP

Ecosystem Conservation Group (ECG): periodic meetings of official representatives of FAO, IUCN, UNEP and Unesco, to consider matters of mutual interest and co-ordinate their programmes in the sphere of ecosystem conservation.

Fauna and Flora Preservation Society (FFPS): the first voluntary body in any country to have a primary interest in species conservation overseas; founded in London in 1903 as the Society for the Preservation of the Wild Fauna of the Empire, soon dropping the 'Wild' and in 1950 converting to Fauna Preservation Society. It assumed the present name in 1980. Best known for its journal ORYX, one of the very few journals primarily concerned with species conservation worldwide. It maintains a worldwide network of correspondents, and has been noted for a number of major projects: Operation Noah, to save the wildlife threatened by the filling of Lake Kariba on the Zambesi River in Central Africa; Operation Oryx, to capture a breeding stock of the Arabian oryx; a project to save the remaining mountain gorillas of the Parc des Volcans, Rwanda; and a project to gain the goodwill of fishermen in the Greek islands who might be affected by the small colony of Mediterranean monk seals remaining there.

Fauna Preservation Society: the former name of the Fauna and Flora Preservation Society.

Food and Agriculture Organisation of the United Nations (FAO): an executive agency of the UN concerned with renewable resources, especially those that form the basis of agriculture, forestry and fisheries. It is the main agent for disbursing funds provided by UNDP for agriculture, forestry and fisheries, and has been concerned with supporting national parks, protected areas and game departments as well as research into the conservation of crop species of both animals and plants.

Frankfurt Zoological Society : the Zoologische Gesellschaft von 1858, located at Frankfurt-am-Main, Federal Republic of Germany, has for many years provided financial and technical assistance for both species and ecosystem conservation throughout the world, especially in conjunction with national parks and reserves.

Global Environmental Monitoring Service (GEMS): see UNEP

Infoterra; see UNEP

Institute for World Conservation and Development (IWCD) : founded by the IGF in 1983 and dedicated to the conservation of wildlife and harmonious development of the human environment for the best long-term benefit of mankind.

International Board for Plant Genetic Resources (IBPGR): created in 1974 to act as a focus for the conservation of valuable varieties of plants.

International Council for Bird Preservation (ICBP): the oldest of the international wildlife conservation organisations, founded in 1922. It has 66 national sections and three continental sections, for Asia, Europe and the Americas; between them they have more than 270 national member organisations. It seeks the conservation, management and wise utilisation of birds and their habitats. Its headquarters are at Cambridge, England, and it holds quadrennial conferences, linked with the International Ornithological Congresses. Like the Species Survival Commission of IUCN, it operates through specialist groups of experts on various groups of birds. At present there are 13 such groups, which also collaborate with the SSC on the same basis as its own groups.

International Council of Scientific Unions (ICSU): an international non-governmental scientific organisation, which aims to encourage international scientific activities for the benefit of mankind, such as initiating, designing and co-ordinating international scientific research projects. It also acts as a focus for the exchange of ideas. Its members consist of 18 international scientific unions, including IUBS, 65 national members and 17 scientific and four national associates. Three of its many committees are SCAR, SCOR and SCOPE.

International Crane Foundation : located in Wisconsin, USA, the Foundation concerns itself with the conservation of the world's fifteen species of crane (Gruidae), at least half of which are endangered. It has five aims: research, restocking areas where cranes have become extinct, habitat preservation, captive propagation and public education. It already holds captive stocks of fourteen species.

International Foundation for the Conservation of Game (IGF): a Paris-based foundation that is especially concerned with activities that will help to conserve game species, using the term 'game' in the broadest sense.

International Institute for Environment and Development (IIED): works in the area between the UN and other international institutions, national governments and non-governmental organisations; currently especially concerned with the resources and environment of Antarctic and the Southern Oceans and with the environmental consequences and sustainability of development aid.

International Maritime Conservation Organisation (IMCO) is concerned with persuading countries to adhere to and enforce the various international conventions for preventing oil pollution of the sea.

International Society for the Protection of the European Bison: founded in 1923 and with headquarters at present at Frankfurt-am-Main, FRG, the Society has been largely responsible for the rescue of the wisent or European bison and for its reintroduction into the wild. Its studbook enabled zoos and collections with surviving specimens to make the best use of their resources.

International Species Inventory System (ISIS). See index for reference.

International Tropical Timber Agreement/Organisation (ITTA/ITTO): an agreement reached at Geneva in 1983 to set up an international organisation to promote the production, sustainable utilisation and conservation of tropical timber.

International Union of Biological Sciences (IUBS): aims to promote international co-operation in biology, and has 49 member countries.

International Union for Conservation of Nature and Natural Resources (IUCN): an independent international conservation organisation, unique in having both governmental and non-governmental members, which aims to promote scientifically based action for conservation of the environment and its associated wildlife, including the sustainable use of living natural resources. It was founded (as the International Union for the Protection of Nature) at Fontainebleau, France, in 1948, and at present has 176 governmental members (including 56 state members) and 322 non-governmental members spread over 114 countries. IUCN's major functions are monitoring, planning and promoting conservation action, and providing assistance and advice. It has a network of several thousand voluntary scientific associates, organised through its six commissions: Ecology; Education; Environmental Planning; Environmental Policy, Law and Administration; National Parks and Protected Areas; and Species Survival. The commission most concerned with species conservation is the Species Survival Commission (SSC), which has a network of more than 1000 voluntary members organised in 76 specialist groups, dealing with specific groups of animals and plants. These groups cover the whole range of IUCN's functions. Two important elements of IUCN are the Conservation Monitoring Centre (CMC) and the Conservation for Development Centre (CDC). CMC consists of four units. The Species Conservation Monitoring Unit (SCMU) is responsible for preparing the Red Data Books and otherwise monitoring the status of threatened and endangered animal species. The Wildlife Trade Monitoring Unit (WTMU) gathers information on all kinds of wildlife in international trade, but especially those species covered by the CITES Convention. Both these are located at Cambridge, England, as is the

Protected Areas Data Unit (PADU), which collects information on national parks and other protected areas. The Threatened Plants Unit (TPU), the counterpart of the SCMU for plants, is located at the Royal Botanic Gardens, Kew, England. CDC was set up to obtain tangible sustainable benefits for mankind, and especially for the poorest communities, by integrating conservation principles with economic development. It is located at IUCN headquarters. These are at Gland, near Geneva, Switzerland, where IUCN shares the World Conservation Centre with the World Wildlife Fund. The two organisations work very closely together, and frequently issue joint statements. IUCN and WWF were jointly responsible, with UNEP, for the World Conservation Strategy.

International Union of Directors of Zoological Gardens (IUDZG): a union to which only directors of zoological gardens as individuals can belong, and the directors of the world's principal zoos are in fact members. IUDZG's main concern is with species conservation and with its captive-breeding aspects.

International Union for the Protection of Nature (IUPN): the former name of IUCN.

International Waterfowl (formerly *Wildfowl*) *Research Bureau* (IWRB): the Bureau, located at Slimbridge, England, has (21) member countries and acts as a centre of information and communication between countries, seeking to stimulate research into wildfowl (ducks, geese, swans – Anatidae) and waders (shore birds – Charadrii). It has been particularly associated with the Ramsar Convention on Wetlands.

International Whaling Commission (IWC): founded in 1946 under the International Whaling Convention, to promote the conservation, development and optimum utilisation of whale resources. Originally consisting entirely of whaling nations, by 1984 only a small minority of the 40 member countries were still engaged in whaling. The Commission meets annually in July to fix quotas for the ensuing whaling season, and operates through two main committees, technical and scientific. Quotas when fixed can be, and sometimes have been, rejected by any member country, under the so-called 90-day rule. The IWC covers only large pelagic whales, not dolphins and porpoises.

International Wildfowl Research Bureau: see International Waterfowl Research Bureau

Man and the Biosphere Programme (MAB): see Unesco.

New York Zoological Society (NYZS): in addition to running the Bronx Zoo, the NYZS has for many years been a major force in species conservation. As long ago as 1905 it gave fifteen American bison to help establish a free-ranging herd in Oklahoma. In recent years its Wildlife Conservation International Division, formerly the Animal Research and Conservation Center, has been its main instrument for promoting research in species and habitat conservation. Its current programme includes work in Asia on the giant panda in China and the Nilgiri tahr in India; in Africa on the mountain gorilla in Rwanda and the giant sable antelope in Angola; and in South America on the Humboldt penguin in Peru and two species of macaw in Bolivia. The Society also still concerns itself with studying the gene pool of the Wichita Mountains herd of bison which it helped to found in Oklahoma.

Protected Areas Data Unit (PADU): see IUCN.

Ramsar Convention: the Convention on Wetlands of International Importance, especially as Waterfowl Habitat, ratified by 38 countries by 1985, has resulted in the designation of 292 sites, covering more than 20m ha.

Scientific Committee for Antarctic Research (SCAR): appointed by ICSU to promote international co-operation in scientific research in Antarctica.

Scientific Committee for Oceanic Research (SCOR): appointed by ICSU to further international scientific activities in all branches of oceanic research.

Scientific Committee on Problems of the Environment (SCOPE): appointed by ICSU to investigate and promote environmental research.

Species Survival Commission (formerly Survival Service Commission) (SSC): see IUCN.

Threatened Plants Unit (TPU): see IUCN.

TRAFFIC (Trade Records of Fauna and Flora in Commerce): the SSC Group which became WTMU.

United Nations Development Programme (UNDP): the main vehicle by which United Nations members fund development aid projects, including species and other environmental conservation projects, as distinct from the primarily promotional and co-ordinating function of UNEP. Funds are disbursed through other bodies, such as FAO and Unesco, on the basis of requests submitted by recipient countries.

United Nations Educational, Scientific and Cultural Organisation (Unesco): the executive agency of the United Nations that is most closely concerned with wildlife conservation education and pure, as distinct from applied research. Its Man and the Biosphere Programme (MAB) seeks to develop the scientific basis for the rational use and conservation of the biosphere and for the improvement of the global relationship between man and his environment. By the end of 1980 nearly 2000 biosphere reserves had been designated in 46 countries under this scheme, whose two main aims are (i) to conserve representative ecosystems, with their full array of component species, as a strategy for maintaining genetic diversity, and (ii) to provide sites for long-term research on the structure, functioning and dynamics of ecosystems.

United Nations Environment Programme (UNEP): founded by the UN General Assembly in 1972, following the UN Conference on the Human Environment in Stockholm, Sweden, in June 1972. It has four components, charged with carrying out the plan of action developed at Stockholm: a Governing Council for Environmental Programmes; a small secretariat, to act as the focus for environmental action and co-ordination within the UN system; a voluntary Environment Fund, to finance the programmes; and an Environmental Co-ordination Board, consisting of members of all relevant UN bodies. These latter include FAO, the World Meteorological Organisation (WMO), UNDP, Unesco, and the World Health Organisation (WHO). UNEP aims to co-ordinate the work of, promote policy initiatives with, and provide environmental information to these other members of the UN family. The area of most direct relevance to species conservation lies within UNEP's environmental assessment programme, Earthwatch, and in particular with the Global Environmental Monitoring System (GEMS), located, like UNEP itself, at Nairobi, Kenya. Within GEMS the renewable resources monitoring programme has obvious links with IUCN's Conservation Monitoring Centre. UNEP's international referral system, Infoterra, now has a network of 119 partner countries.

Washington Convention: (1) CITES (q v); (2) the Convention on Nature Protection and Wildlife Preservation in the Western Hemisphere, signed at Washington, DC, October 1940.

Wildfowl Trust: founded in 1948 as the Severn Wildfowl Trust, this was the first major conservation centre for a single group of animals, setting an example which has been followed, for instance, in the United Kingdom for pheasants and otters, in the US for cranes, and in France for lemurs. Besides maintaining, at Slimbridge and four other locations, a unique and almost complete reference collection of living ducks, geese and swans of the world, the Trust has engaged in several important captive breeding and release projects. These include the nene or Hawaiian goose, perhaps the best known, the white-winged wood duck of southern Asia and the Laysan teal of the westernmost part of the Hawaiian chain.

Wildlife Conservation International: see New York Zoological Society.

Wildlife Trade Monitoring Unit (WTMU): see IUCN

World Charter for Nature: adopted by the UN General Assembly in 1982, on the initiative of President Mobutu of Zaire, lays down universal principles of wildlife conservation and outlines the functions and responsibilities of states, corporate bodies and individuals that are needed to implement these. It was drafted with the advice of IUCN.

World Conservation Centre: see IUCN, WWF.

World Heritage Convention: the International Convention for the Protection of the World Cultural and Natural Heritage came into force in 1975 and has been ratified by 69 countries. It provides an international framework for safeguarding the cultural and natural heritage of mankind, including areas of outstanding natural beauty or scientific interest, and grant-aids projects in countries whose resources are, for the time being, insufficient. Among the areas so far included in the Convention that are of special importance for species conservation are the Galapagos Islands, Ecuador, the Serengeti National Park and Ngorongoro Conservation Area, Tanzania, and the Bialowieza National Park, Poland.

World Wildlife Fund (WWF): an international foundation launched in 1961 to raise funds to conserve wildlife, interpreted as comprising fauna, flora, landscape, soil and water. WWF has national affiliates in 24 countries, and shares the World Conservation Centre at Gland, Vaud, Switzerland, with IUCN. The two organisations work closely together. WWF also aims to create awareness of threats to the environment and to generate on a world-wide basis the strongest possible support for safeguarding the living world. Although some of its early programmes, such as Operation Tiger, directed public attention to single species, WWF seeks species conservation primarily through habitat conservation, and has had important campaigns based on wetlands and tropical rainforests. Its current (1984) campaign is based on plants. WWF also attaches great significance to educational activities and the provision of information, and many of its national affiliates have important programmes of their own in all these fields.

A List of Acronyms

ARC : Animal Research and Conservation Center (NYZS)

BIOMASS : Biological Investigations of Marine Antarctic Systems and Stocks (SCAR)

CDC : Conservation for Development Centre (IUCN)

CEPLA : Commission on Environmental Policy, Law and Administration (IUCN)

CITES : Convention on International Trade in Endangered Species of Wild Fauna and Flora

CMC : Conservation Monitoring Centre (IUCN)

CNPPA : Commission on National Parks and Protected Areas (IUCN)

ECG : Ecosystem Conservation Group (FAO, IUCN, UNEP, Unesco, WWF)

FAO : Food and Agriculture Organisation (U N)

FFPS : Fauna and Flora Preservation Society

GEMS : Global Environmental Monitoring System (UNEP)

ICBP : International Council for Bird Preservation

ICSU : International Council of Scientific Unions

IIED : International Institute for Environment and Development

IGF : International Foundation for the Conservation of Game

ITTA : International Tropical Timber Agreement

ITTO : International Tropical Timber Organisation

IUBS : International Union of Biological Sciences

IUCN : International Union for Conservation of Nature and Natural Resources

IUDZG : International Union of Directors of Zoological Gardens

IUPN : International Union for the Protection of Nature (IUCN)

IWC : International Whaling Commission

IWCD : Institute for World Conservation and Development (IGF)

IWRB : International Waterfowl Research Bureau

MAB : Man and the Biosphere Programme (Unesco)

NGO : Non-governmental organisation

NYZS : New York Zoological Society

PADU : Protected Areas Data Unit (CMC)

RDB : Red Data Book (CMC)

SCAR : Scientific Committee for Antarctic Research (ICSU)

SCMU: Species Conservation Monitoring Unit (CMC)

SCOR : Scientific Committee for Oceanic Research (ICSU)

SSC : Species Survival Commission (IUCN)

TPU : Threatened Plants Unit (CMC)

Traffic : Trade Records Analysis of Fauna and Flora in Commerce (CMC)

UN : United Nations

UNDP : United Nations Development Programme

UNEP : United Nations Environmental Programme

Unesco : United Nations Educational, Scientific and Cultural Organisation

WCI : Wildlife Conservation International (NYZS)

WHO : World Health Organisation (U N)

WMO : World Meteorological Organisation (U N)

WTMU : Wildlife Trade Monitoring Unit (CMC)

WTO : World Tourist Organisation

WWF : World Wildlife Fund

Select Bibliography

General

Ayensu, E S, Heywood, V H, Lucas, G L & DeFilipps, R A 1984. Our Green and Living World. Cambridge, UK

Council on Environmental Quality and Department of State 1980. The Global 2000 Report to the President: entering the twenty-first century. Washington, DC

Darwin, Charles 1859. The Origin of Species. London

Darwin, Charles 1868. Variation of Animals and Plants under Domestication. London

Fitter, R S R 1959. The Ark in our Midst. London

Fitter, R & M Eds. In press. The Road to Extinction: Symposium on the problems of categorising the status of taxa threatened with extinction

Fitter, R & Scott, Sir P 1978. The Penitent Butchers. London

Frankel, O H & Soule, M E 1981. Conservation and Evolution. Cambridge, UK

Hall, A V 1983. Interpreting the Environment. Cape Town, SA

Hekstra, G P 1981. The Green Revolution Confronted with the World Conservation Strategy. Ecoscripten no 14

Hellouin, M 1982. Wildlife a basis for development. IGF Bulletin, nos 12-14: 2-8

Huxley, A 1984. Green Inheritance. London

International Union for Conservation of Nature and Natural Resources (IUCN) 1980. World Conservation Strategy. Gland, Switzerland

Lyster, S 1985. International Wildlife Law. London

Mayr, E 1963. Animal Species and Evolution. Cambridge, Mass

Meinertzhagen, R 1959. Pirates and Predators. London

Myers, N 1983. A Wealth of Wild Species. Boulder, Colo

Prescott-Allen, R & C 1982. What's Wildlife Worth? London

Ratcliffe, J 1983. (Animals crossing roads). Wildlife, 25: 304-07

Salim, E 1982. Conservation and Development. 2nd World Conservation Lecture. London

Schultes, R E 1984. Address at Presentation of WWF Gold Medal

Siegfried, W R & Davies, B R 1982. Conservation of Ecosystems: theory and practice. Pretoria

Strong, M 1984. 3rd World Conservation Lecture. London

Worthington, E B 1958. Earth, air, fire and water: the 'elements' of conservation. Proc XVth International Congress of Zoology, Sect 1, 61-2

Regional

Babington, C C 1860. Flora of Cambridgeshire. London

Bahaguna, S 1982. (Chipko movement, India) WWF Monthly Report, 1982, 327-29

Benavides, F 1983. From the Incas to CITES. Paper to 3rd World Wilderness Congress

Blower, J 1982. Conservation in Burma. WWF Monthly Report, December 1982, 349-51

Diamond, J M 1972. Avifauna of the Eastern Highlands of New Guinea. Publication no 12, Nuttall Ornithological Club, Cambridge, Mass

Gaston, A J et al. Eds 1981. The Wildlife of Himachal Pradesh, Western Himalayas: Report of the Himachal Wildlife Project, 1981. Orono, Me

Hall, A V 1981. Fynbos futures: facts and figures

Hall, A V et al. 1980. Threatened Plants of Southern Africa. Pretoria, SA

Hiltbrunner, U 1983. Report from Madagascar. IUCN Bulletin, 14: 6, 14

Malpas, R 1980. Wildlife in Uganda: report to IUCN/WWF

Marshall, J 1966. The Great Extermination: a guide to Anglo-Australian cupidity, wickedness and waste. London

Obara, H & Yasuma, S 1984. Conservation of the Nansei Shoto, Part 1. Tokyo

Roberts, B B 1966. Wildlife Conservation in the Antarctic. Oryx, 8: 237-43

Rodgers, W A and Homewood, K M 1982. Species richness and endemism in the Usambara mountain forests, Tanzania. Biol J Linn Soc, 18: 197-242

Scott, D A and Brooke, M de L 1982. Forest birds of southeastern Brazil. WWF Monthly Report, November 1982, pp 307-13

South Pacific Commission 1982. South Pacific Regional Environmental Plan. Noumea, New Caledonia

Strahm, W 1983. Rodrigues: can its flora be saved? Oryx, 17: 122-25

Tindle, R W 1983. Galapagos conservation and tourism – 11 years on. Oryx, 17: 126-29

Verschuren, J 1982. Hope for Liberia. Oryx, 16: 421-27

White, A T & Wells, S M 1982. Coral reefs in the Philippines. Oryx, 16: 445-51

Sustainable Utilisation

Curry-Lindahl, K 1982. A tale of mismanagement at sea. Oryx, 16: 415-20

Dasmann, R F 1976. Thoughts on MSY. IUCN Bulletin, 7: 15, 17

F A O 1976. Review of the state of exploitation of the world fish resources; quoted World Conservation Strategy, 4

Graham, Michael 1943. The Fish Gate. London

Loudon, A & Fletcher, D 1983. (Deer farming). New Scientist, 14.7.83, 88-92

Luxmoore, R 1985. The environmental effects of fish farming. Ecos, 5(2): 24-28

Luxmoore, R 1985. Game farming in South Africa as a force in conservation. Oryx, 19: 225-231

Parker, I 1983. Ivory Crisis. London

Prescott-Allen, R & A 1982. Wildplants and Crop Improvement. London

Talbot, L M 1966. Wild Animals as a Source of Food. Bureau of Sport Fisheries & Wildlife Special Scientific Report no 98. Washington, DC

Watson, A & Lance, A N 1984. Ecological aspects of game shooting and upland conservation. Ecos, 5(3) 2-7

Endangered Habitats, including Pollution

Brown, M H 1984. (Lake Ontario) Audubon, 84(6): 88-95

Cramer, L H 1983. The undesirability of *Pinus* plantations in the catchments (Sri Lanka). *Loris*, 16: 167-71

Ehrlich, P R *et al.* 1983. Long-term biological consequences of nuclear war. *Science*, 222(4630)

Gorski, W *et al.* 1976. (Pollution, Baltic Sea). Przeglad Zool., 20: 81-87

International Waterfowl Research Bureau. n.d. Wetland Management Manual

Last, F 1983. Acid rain. *Scottish Wildlife*, 19: 12-14

Mailer, S 1982. A marine park in Jamaica. WWF Monthly Report, 1982, 319-25

Mendelssohn, H & Paz, U 1977. (Pesticides, Israel). Biol Cons, 11: 163-70

Poore, D 1983. Deforestation and the population factor. IUCN Bulletin, 14: 25-6

Reed, T M 1983. Agent of change in the uplands. *Ecos*, 4(3): 13-18

Saenger, P *et al.* 1983. Global Status of Mangroves. IUCN Ecology Commission Paper No 3

Salvat, B 1980. Death to the coral reefs. *Oryx*, 15: 341-44

Scriabine, R 1983. (Acid rain, PCBs, Sweden) IUCN Bulletin, 14: 60-63

Stowe, T & Underwood, L 1983. (Oil spills, UK). *Birds*, 9(5): 51-53

Turco, R P *et al.* 1983. Nuclear winter: global consequences of multiple nuclear explosions. *Science*, 222(4630)

White, A T & Wells, S M 1982. Coral reefs in the Philippines. *Oryx*, 16; 445-51

Endangered Species: General

Brambell, M 1977. Reintroduction. International Zoo Yearbook, 17: 112-116

Brambell, M R & Mathews, S M (Eds) 1977. Breeding endangered species in captivity. International Zoo Yearbook, 17: 1-122

Davy, A J & Jefferies, R L 1981. Approaches to the monitoring of rare plant populations: in Synge 1981, 219-32

de la Mare, W in press. On the definition of threats to the survival of species: in Fitter & Fitter, in press

Engbring, J 1984. Birds of Guam face extinction. ICBP Newsletter, 6(4): 6

Fitter, R 1974. 25 years on: a look at endangered species. *Oryx*, 12: 341-46

Fitter, R & Fitter, M Eds. in press. The Road to Extinction: SSC Symposium on Problems of Categorising the Status of Taxa Threatened with Extinction.

Harper, J L 1981. The meanings of rarity: in Synge 1981, 189-203

Hills, L D 1983. The conservation of vegetables. Threatened Plants Newsletter, 11: 10-12

Kear, J 1977. The problems of breeding endangered species in captivity. International Zoo Yearbook, 17: 5-20

Lovejoy, T 1975. Accelerating rates of extinction. 11th Annual Report, Jersey Wildlife Preservation Trust, 11-12

Luoma, J 1982. Prison or Ark? *Audubon*, 84(6): 102-09

Martin, R D Ed 1975. Breeding Endangered Species in Captivity (Proceedings of 1972 Jersey Conference). London

Myers, N 1979. The Sinking Ark. Elmsford, NY

Myers, N 1984. (Triage). IUCN Bulletin, 15: 16-17

Olsen, O & Arnklit, F 1979. Setting up a practical small seed bank: in Synge & Townsend 1979, 185-88

Rabinowitz, D 1981. Seven forms of rarity: in Synge 1981, 205-17

Seal, U *et al.* 1977. ISIS. International Zoo Yearbook, 17: 68-70

Synge, H, Ed. 1981. The Biological Aspects of Rare Plant Conservation. Chichester, Sussex

Synge, H and Townsend, H (Eds) 1979. Survival or Extinction: the practical role of botanic gardens in the conservation of rare and threatened plants. Kew, UK.

Talbot, L M 1960. A look at threatened species. *Oryx*, 5: 153-293

US Fish & Wildlife Service 1985. List of approved recovery plans. *Endangered Species Technical Bulletin*, 10(1): 3-6

Veprintsev, B N & Rott, N N 1980. Genome Conservation. Puschino, USSR

Wahlberg, S 1979. (Project Linnaeus): in Synge & Townsend 1979, 25-30

Walters, S M 1979. The Eastern England Rare Plant Project . . .: in Synge & Townsend 1979, 37-46

Williams, G R 1977. Marooning – a technique for saving threatened species from extinction (New Zealand). International Zoo Yearbook, 17: 102-06

Williamson, M 1984. Sir William Hooker's lecture on insular floras. *Biol J Linn Soc*, 22: 55-77

Yates, S 1984. (Hawaiian endemic birds). *Audubon*, 86(4): 62-85

Red Data Books:

N.B. The Red Data Books are the main source for data on endangered species in this book.

Red Data Book, Vol 4: Pisces, Freshwater Fishes. Revised volume compiled by R R Miller. IUCN, Morges, Switzerland, 1977.

Amphibia-Reptilia R D B, Part I, Testudines, Crocodylia, Rhynchocephalia, compiled by B Groombridge, assisted by L Wright. IUCN, Gland, Switzerland, 1982.

Endangered Birds of the World, compiled by W B King. ICBP, Washington, DC, 1981

Threatened Birds of Africa and Related Islands, by N J Collar and S N Stuart. Part 1 of the 3rd edition of the ICBP/IUCN RDB for Birds. ICBP & IUCN, Cambridge, UK

Invertebrate RDB, compiled by S M Wells, R M Pyle and N M Collins. IUCN, Gland, Switzerland, 1983

Mammal RDB, Part 1 (America, Australasia), compiled by J Thornback and M Jenkins. IUCN, Gland, Switzerland, 1982

Red Data Book, Vol 1: Mammalia, compiled by H A Goodwin & C W Holloway. IUCN, Morges, Switzerland, 1978

Plant RDB, compiled by G Lucas and H Synge. IUCN, Morges, Switzerland, 1978

Borodin, A M *et al.* 1978. Red Data Book of the USSR. Moscow

Perring, F H & Farrell, L 1983. British Red Data Book 1: Vascular Plants. 2nd ed. Lincoln

Williams, G R & Given, D H 1981. The Red Data Book of New Zealand. Wellington, NZ

Species: Mammals

Allen, G M 1942. Extinct and Vanishing Mammals of the Western Hemisphere. New York

Goodwin, H A & J M and Fisher, J 1973. List of Mammals which have become Extinct or are possibly Extinct since 1600. IUCN Occasional Paper no 8. Morges, Switzerland

Fitter, R 1968. Vanishing Wild Animals of the World. London

Harper, F 1945. Extinct and Vanishing Mammals of the Old World. New York

IUCN Red Data Book: see above

PRIMATES: Aveling, C & R 1981. Mountain Gorilla Project: Progress Report 4. *Oryx*, 16: 135-37

Caldecott, J & Kavanagh, M 1983. Can translocation help wild primates? *Oryx*, 17: 135-39

Johns, A D 1983. Tropical forest primates and logging. *Oryx*, 17: 114-18

Mallinson, J 1984. Lion tamarins' survival hangs in the balance. *Oryx*, 18: 72-78

CETACEANS: Global Conference on the Non-Consumptive Utilisation of Cetacean Resources 1983. Whales Alive Wethersfield, Conn

Holt, S 1983. Who really threatens whales and seals? *Oryx*, 17: 68-77

Mackintosh, N A 1965. The Stocks of Whales. London

CANIDS: IUCN Position Statement on Wolf Conservation. SSC Newsletter, 2: 18

BEARS: McNamee, T 1982. (Grizzly bears) *Audubon*, 84(6): 68-83

OTTERS: Howe, J R 1983. The sea otter puzzle. *Audubon*, 85(1): 34-39

SEALS: Laycock, G 1986. (Pribilof fur seal). *Audubon*, 88(1): 94-103

Proceedings of the 2nd International Conference on the Mediterranean Monk Seal

Torres, D 1983. (Juan Fernandez fur seal. WWF Monthly Report, October 1983, 641-44

ELEPHANTS: Hatton, J *et al*. 1982. Elephant poaching and vegetation changes in Uganda. *Oryx*, 16: 404-5

Parker, I 1983. Ivory Crisis. London

Parker, I S C & Martin, E B 1982. How many elephants are killed for the ivory trade? *Oryx*, 16: 235-39

Ruggiero, R 1982. (Central African Republic) WWF Monthly Report, 1982, 331-35, 337-40

EQUIDS: Williams, T 1985. (Feral asses, USA) *Audubon*, 87(5): 20-23

RHINOS: Western, D. & Vigne, L 1984. The status of rhinos in Africa. *Pachyderm*, 4: 5-6

DEER: Bergman, C A 1982. (caribou, Idaho) *Audubon*, 84(5): 10-14

Fraser Darling, F 1937. A Herd of Red Deer. London

IUCN/SSC Deer Specialist Group 1978. Threatened Deer. Morges, Switzerland

Povlitis, A 1983. The huemul in Chile. *Oryx*, 17: 34-40

PIGS: Laycock, G 1984. (Introduced wild boars, USA). *Audubon*, 86: 32-35

ANTELOPES: Fitter, R 1982. Arabian oryx returns to the wild. *Oryx*, 16: 406-10; also 18: 136-7

Henderson, D S 1974. Were they the last Arabian oryx? *Oryx*, 12: 347-50

Newby, J 1983. Heat and tourists harass the addax. WWF Monthly Report, 1983, 623-4

Schuster, R 1980. Will the Kafue lechwe survive the Kafue dams? *Oryx*, 15: 476-89; and SSC Newsletter, 2: 6; 1983

WILD CATTLE: Egerton, P J M 1964. The bison in Canada. *Oryx*, 7: 305-14

Heck, H 1950. The breeding-back of the aurochs. *Oryx*, 1: 117-22

Species: Birds

Fisher, J & Orenstein, R I 1985. Extinct birds: in Campbell, B & Lack, E 1985. A Dictionary of Birds. Calton

Greenway, J C 1958. Extinct and Vanishing Birds of the World. New York

ICBP/IUCN Red Data Book: see above

HERONS, STORKS: Graham, F 1984. (Yellow-crowned night heron, Bermuda). *Audubon*, 86(3): 38-41

Ogden, J C 1983. (Wood stork) *Audubon*, 85(1): 90-101.

FLAMINGOES: Graham, F 1983. (Bahamas). *Audubon*, 85(1): 50-65

WILDFOWL: Birkhead, T R 1982. Causes of mortality of the mute swan *Cygnus olor* on the River Thames. *J. Zool. Lond.*, 198: 15-25

Forshaw, W D 1983. Pink-footed geese in Lancashire. *Wildfowl*, 34: 64-76

BIRDS OF PREY: Gohier, F 1983. (Griffon vulture). *Wildlife*, 25: 286-91
Harwood, M 1982. Peregrine redux. *Audubon*, 84(5): 8-11
GAMEBIRDS: Williams, T 1984. Resurrection of the wild turkey. *Audubon*, 86(1): 71-75
BUSTARDS: Goriup, P 1985. (Houbara bustard). *Birds*, 10(5): 29-31.
PASSERINES: Bullock, I D *et al*. 1983. (Chough). *British Birds*, 76: 377-401
Lack, David 1947. Darwin's Finches. Cambridge
van der Zon, A P M 1980. (Rothschild's starling) *Oryx*, 15: 345-49

Species: Reptiles and Amphibians

British Herpetological Society, Conservation Committee 1983. Herpeto-fauna translocations in Britain – a policy. Brit.J.Herp., 6: 314-16
IUCN Red Data Book: see above
TURTLES, TORTOISES: Balasz, G H 1982. Driftnets catch leatherback turtles. *Oryx*, 16: 428-30
Bjorndal, K (ed.) 1982. Biology and Conservation of Sea Turtles. Washington, DC
Curl, D 1986. (Geochelone yniphora). *Oryx*, 20: 35-39
Mittermeier, R A 1978. South America's River Turtles: saving them by use. *Oryx*, 14: 222-30.
Stubbs, D *et al*. 1981. (*Testudo hermanni*, Greece) *Oryx*, 16: 176-78
CROCODILES: IUCN/SSC Crocodile Specialist Group 1971. Proceedings of First Working Meeting, New York, 15-17 March 1971. IUCN Supp Paper no 32. Morges, Switzerland
Suvanakorn, P & Youngprapakorn, C 1983. The Breeding of Crocodiles in Captivity at Samutprakan. Bangkok, Thailand
Watanabe, M E 1983. The Chinese alligator: is farming the last hope? *Oryx*, 17: 176-81
LIZARDS: Bloxam, Q 1983. (Reintroduction of *Leioleipisma telfairii*) *Dodo*, 19: 37-41
Gibbons, J 1984. Iguanas of the South Pacific. *Oryx*, 18: 82-91
Milliken, T 1985. Frilled lizards in Japan. Traffic Bull, 6: 84.
SNAKES: IUCN/SSC Snake Group 1982. Proceedings of First Meeting: Madras, India, November 1982.

Species: Fishes

Ryman, N (Ed) 1981. Fish Gene Pools. Ecological Bulletin No. 34 Stockholm
Salmonids: Johansson, N 1981 (Salmon, Sweden): in Ryman 1981, 75-83
Mills, S 1982. Salmon: demise of the landlord's fish. *New Scientist*, 11.2.82, 364-67
Naevdal, G 1981 (Salmon, Norway): in Ryman 1981, 85-93
Quammen, D 1982. (Arctic grayling). *Audubon*, 84(3): 96-103.
SNAIL DARTER: Anon 1978. IUCN Bulletin, 9: 33-4.
TUNA: Reiger, G 1982. Bluefin tuna in dire strait. *Audubon*, 84(3): 112-16

Species: Invertebrates

IUCN Red Data Book: see above
CORALS: Wells, S M 1981. International Trade in Corals. IUCN Conservation Monitoring Centre, Cambridge, UK
MOLLUSCS: Laycock, G 1983. (Freshwater mussels). *Audubon*, 86(1): 26-28.
Madson, J 1985. Mississippi shell game. *Audubon*, 87(2): 46-68
Wells, S M 1981. International Trade in Shells. IUCN Conservation Monitoring Centre, Cambridge, UK
LEPIDOPTERA: Thomas, J 1980. Why did the large blue become extinct in Britain? *Oryx*, 15: 243-47

Species: Plants
Heywood, V H (Ed) 1978. Flowering Plants of the World. Oxford
IUCN Red Data Book: see above
BUTTERCUPS: Frost, L C 1981. The study of *Ranunculus ophioglossifolius* and its successful conservation at the Badgeworth Nature Reserve, Gloucestershire in Synge 1981, 481-90
McCaskill, L W 1983. The Castle Hill Buttercup *Ranunculus paucifolius*: a story of preservation. Christchurch, NZ
CACTI: Oldfield, S 1984. The Cactaceae: a family threatened by trade. *Oryx*, 18: 148-51
Steinhart, P 1982. Killing for cacti (USA). *Audubon*, 84(6): 6-9
GRASSES, SEDGES: Brookes, B S 1981. The discovery, extermination, translocation and eventual survival of *Schoenus ferrugineus* in Britain: in Synge 1981, 413-20
Jones, M 1983. Papyrus: a new fuel for the Third World. *New Scientist*, 11.8.83, 418-19
Ricciuti, E R 1984. Elegant builder of southern dunes (sea oat). *Audubon*, 86(5): 48-53
Simmons, J C 1986. (Bamboos). *Audubon*, 88(1): 58-69
LEGUMES: Bell, E A 1981. (Dogstooth pea *Lathyrus sativus*) *Food Chemistry*, 6: 213-22
LICHENS: Fenton, A F-G 1964. Atmospheric pollution of Belfast and its relation to the lichen flora. *Ir. Nat. J.*, 14: 237-45
MANGROVES: Saenger, P *et al.* 1983. Global Status of Mangroves. IUCN Ecology Commission Paper no 33
PALMS: Dransfield, J 1981. The biology of Asiatic rattans in relation to the rattan trade and conservation: in Synge 1981, 179-86
TREES: Borland, H 1983. (Pecan nuts). *Audubon*, 85(6): 61.
Knees, S G & Gardner, M F 1983. Mahoganies: candidates for the Red Data Book. *Oryx*, 17: 88-92.
Leon, C 1983. (*Abies nebrodensis*) Threatened Plants Newsletter, 12: 3-4

Periodicals
Audubon
Ambio
Endangered Species Technical Bulletin (US Fish & Wildlife Service)
International Wildlife
IUCN Bulletin
IUCN/SSC Specialist Group Newletters
Marine Turtle Newsletter
Nature Conservancy Council (UK), Annual Reports
New Scientist
Oryx
Species, formerly *SSC Newsletter*
Threatened Plants Newsletter
Traffic Bulletin (IUCN Conservation Monitoring Centre)
World Wildlife Fund Monthly Report
World Wildlife News
WWF News

General Index

Geographical Index

Countries, and some islands and regions, are separately indexed on p. 222.
Numbers in *italics* denote illustrations.

Abbreviations:
GR Game Reserve,
NP National Park,
NR Nature Reserve
Individual sites are also indexed alphabetically in the main index.

X